FAMILY
THERAPY
AND
TRANSACTIONAL
ANALYSIS

FAMILY
THERAPY
AND
TRANSACTIONAL
ANALYSIS

James S. Horewitz, M.D.

New York • Jason Aronson • London

ISBN: 0-87668-381-2

Library of Congress Catalog Number: 79-51923

Manufactured in the United States of America

Dedicated to the Memory of
My Father

Preface

Ever since Freud, psychotherapists and psychiatrists have been developing their various conceptions about how they engage in their occupation of "helping" people. The psychoanalytic tradition has emphasized the resolution of an individual's most basic and deeply hidden fears and conflicts through prolonged free association and interpretation, dream analysis, and so on. In my opinion, psychoanalysis is an effective technique which, if properly carried through, can make an individual highly "well" within himself or herself.

The question arises as to whether that is the kind of "help" people need most. I think of a couple (he was a therapist himself) who underwent long-term individual analysis. His analysis took eight years and was successful. Both of them worked out their own inner conflicts and discomforts to a T, and then came to like themselves very well. Unfortunately, they also agreed that they didn't like each other and concluded that a divorce was necessary. Before and during the analysis, their conflicts had been creating two sick children, who later needed treatment themselves.

I was trained in the psychoanalytic tradition—as was Eric Berne, the founder of transactional analysis (TA)—and once I would have accepted the history just outlined without too much thought. Like most analytically trained people then, I knew that it took people a long time to get better, that time was no object, and that it indeed took a lot of time just to get at those deeper anxieties and fears that were the cause of the individual's sickness. That was the kind of help we knew how to provide.

I've quite obviously done some reconsidering since. I became sympathetic with, and joined, the TA scoool of psychotherapy because I saw that TA offered patients the chance to participate in and speed up their own therapy. I participated in the evolution of TA and saw its concepts and theory deepen and became increasingly coherent. The charges of my analytic colleagues that TA was "oversimplified" seemed less and less justified.

I began to raise my own family and naturally began to look at people more in the context of family structures. I read about, and eventually took training in, a number of family treatment methods.

I now look back with quite a different perspective at the case of that couple, their prolonged analysis, and the problems of their two children. Now I know about a number of different dimensions of "help" that are feasible and, I argue, important for psychotherapists to give. Why couldn't that couple have had help, early on, with the dynamics of their everyday relationship, their interpersonal conflicts, and their interactions with their children? Would that kind of help have prevented the psychiatric disabilities of the children? Today, we know that that kind of help can be given, that it is a legitimate psychotherapeutic enterprise, and that it indeed can prevent later problems with the children involved.

Other therapists must make their own answers to questions like these, but I think I have found mine; and since this book is based on them, the reader deserves at least a simplified overview of my point of view at the outset. I put my answers in terms of the following four statements about "helping" individuals and their families via psychotherapy:

1. Speedy help is highly important to anyone in a therapeutic situation but is especially critical for those in a couple relationship and in a family. In a family, people are in the business not only of growing themselves but also of growing each other. People grow each other through an identifiable range and pattern of daily interactions, and if those interactions are not functional and positive, the growth of everyone concerned is going to be affected. I would say that in a case such as the therapist's family, it is highly negligent for any individual any one individual to focus primarily on fixing up his or her own psyche for himself or herself while failing to take responsibility for day-to-day interactions that are going to create disability in others. It is negligent for a therapist today to go along with that kind of choice.

2. Speedy modification of that pattern of interactions within the family or couple is achievable, particularly via the use of Transactional Analysis, but also via a number of other family systems approaches. This type of modification is what Eric Berne has referred to as the *social control* level of cure and is epitomized by his reply to people who would ask him what one did about a game once it had been identified, "Keep your mouth shut." Eric Berne was also fond of saying, "Get better first. Analyze it later."

3. Achieving a psychiatric cure of an individual in a family later on, after the immediate interactional patterns have been modified, is not made any more difficult by the earlier stage of the therapy and is usually a lot easier as an extension of family or couple therapy that it was as an individual project. I, of course, also favor Transactional Analysis as the basic approach to these later stages. But I've also found that for many people, the easing of the relation ship patterns in the family is enough. They are much more confortable with their immediate social surroundings; they can ask for support and nurturing from one another; and in short, they may not really want a deeper level cure and may not, except in the therpist's view, need such a cure.

If an extension of therapy is desired, it can be easier, faster and more fun with Transactional Analysis that with traditional psychoanalysis. This is no slight of Freud. Eric Berne (1970) has written that just as modern airplanes are faster and more confortable without this being considered a slur on the Wright brothers, so TA can be faster, simpler, and more comfortable without being considered a slur on Freud. I'd add that Orville Wright only had a machine that allowed him to fly solo, but we don't insist on traveling that way in airplanes today; and we may not have to travel alone psychotherapeutically, either, as much as everyone has always thought.

4. When a child is suffering obvious or not so obvious distress, it almost invariably means that there is pain in the relationship between the parents, and probably within both parents, distorting the growth environment. But the answer usually is not to try to heal the child separately or either of the parents individually. It is first to help all the people in that growing environment to gain social control of it and them later to get at the roots of the pain insofar as that is affordable and desired.

The four convictions I've just outlined aren't novel by any means; family systems therapists have stressed many aspects of them for some years now. But their implementation specifically through TA techniques has not received a lot of treatment in the literature. I'm certain that this is not because TA is not already being used by many people in conjunction with a family systems approach. An interweaving of concepts and techniques from these two schools is so logical as to be inevitable. But probably much of that tandem use of TA and family systems therapies is being undertaken by ministers, family counselors, and others who have not had extensive psychiatric training. One purpose of this book is to add to the material such paraprofessionals have available to guide their much needed efforts, as well as communicating to those with more extensive training.

Assembling some detailed TA family therapy techniques for those not highly trained in a particular therapeutic school is probably easier to accomplish than my other major objective in writing the book. The second purpose of this book is to persuade the specialist, those already highly trained and strongly identified with particular approaches, to seriously consider a synthesis of approaches and to esperiment with techniques that vary from those they have been developing and using for many years. Such a task is worth attempting because I am convinced that gains in therapeutic effectiveness would thereby be realized.

The book is addressed, in part, to my former colleagues in analytic psychiatry. I'd like to persuade them to try helping more people more quickly through a TA-based family systems extension of their practices, and I'd also like to convince them that there is a need for their experience in psychodynamics among family systems people and nonpsychiatrically trained TA people, as well as among nonspecialists. A principal weakness of both TA and family systems practices is that social control cures have an element of instability, particularly if a deeply repressed pain is the root cause of the family or couple problem. Psychiatrists from any of the analytic schools are better equipped to deal with such cases than are most other practitioners, and we can use their help in learning how to take family and couple "cures" further and to cure them more firmly. Such professionals probably ought to take on the more serious family cases directly or by early referral from a nonspecialist who knows he or she is out of his depth. Psychiatrists also ought to have enough experience with family work that they can serve as consultative support for others dealing with a particular family. On a very basic level, I would at least like to reassure my more traditional psychiatric colleagues about the imagined difficulties of seeing more than one patient at a time or of including children in therapy sessions.

I also hope that I can encourage more TA people (some of whom, of course, also have had psychiatric and analytic training) to engage in work with families. Family work, I hope to make clear, is a natural extension of their approach to therapy in general. One exciting thing for a TA practioner getting into family work is the opportunity to see script dynamics in action (Berne 1961). Many

TA practioners are already deeply involved in group work, and the transition to family groups is not difficult.

I would like to bring friends of various family therapy persuasions toward and ultimately into the use of TA in their work for a number of reasons. First, family systems people have long needed a precise sets of concepts for analyzing and labeling communications events and aspects of relationships, and TA's ego state and interactional maps are tailor-made for these purposes. Second, TA theory is an elegant undergirding for family systems practice, often both in helping the therapist understand in TA's accessible, simple terms why a particular pattern is resistant to change and in suggesting a way change might be achieved. Finally, since TA provides an easy way for the therapist to suggest and work for personality change beyond the resolution of the immediate family stress, it offers a convenient framework for the extension of family therapy toward more complete psychiatric cures.

I have reviewed some of the basic concepts of Transactional Analysis and of family systems theory in the course of developing the book's argument, but that review should not be regarded as adequate basis for applying more specific suggestions about technique. In other words, if the reader has not done other reading or training in Transactional Analysis and family work, he or she is urged to do so before taking these techniques into therapy sessions. A bibliography of what I consider to be the most useful and well-founded works in both fields is included, and chapter 8 describes where family training of various types is available. Chapter 9 provides an example of how I work. That chapter is a transcription of a tape made of a study group led by me with two to four psychiatric social workers.

This book itself can be used in several ways. Those already familiar with the concepts of TA and family systems therapy can skip the section of chapter 1 that reviews them for the general reader. Chapters 5 and 6 contain the bulk of the case-to-case, day-to-day techniques.

A NOTE ON SEMANTICS

Actual parents, children, and adults are referred to by the appropriate words with lower case "p," "c," and "a." Parent, Adult, and Child (with capital letters) refer to *ego states.*

Feel free throughout to substitute *client* for *patient.*

Acknowledgments

My indebtedness to many of the founders and developers of both family systems therapies and Transactional Analysis is profound. In particular, I'm grateful to D. Stuart MacRobbie, M.D., for his insights about the families I presented to him for consultation and to Ken Everts, M.D., who read the manuscript in its entirety and helped me amplify and clarify a number of points.

My editors, Peter and Margaret Cross, deserve a particular vote of thanks for substantial help in shaping the overall sequence of the presentation and for reflecting my ideas back to me so that I could fill in, connect, reargue, and explain. I don't know if the book would have made it through without them. My thanks to Carol Black and Karen Paskey for their steady, rapid, and responsible typing and diagraming. Also, I am grateful to all my teachers and all my patients during my learning process. I am especially grateful to Charles B. David, M.D., and Gordon Bermak, M.D., for their help in understanding psychodynamics.

Families and couples seeking therapy do so because they feel "Not OK"; they are in psychic pain. From this posture they also see their offsprings as "Not OK." They often label them the "Problem." The goal of therapeutic work with such families is to guide parents into a new position, a new view of life, in which they can say, "We're OK." It then follows that they can say of their children, "They're OK too."

Contents

Contents

CHAPTER 1

An Introduction
to the
Basic Concepts of TA

Two decades ago, Eric Berne introduced Transactional Analysis (TA) to the psychotherapeutic community when he read a paper entitled "Transactional Analysis: A New and Effective Method of Group Therapy" before the assembled members of the American Group Psychotherapy Association in Los Angeles. Following that meeting, Berne continued to work with and expand his concept of Transactional Analysis. He wrote about Transactional Analysis both in books intended for profesional therapists and the lay public. Among those most widely read are *Games People Play* (1964) and *What Do You Say After You Say Hello?* (1971).

Many people in the helping professions—psychotherapists, psychologists, pastors, family counselors, and others—attended seminars and lectures in which Berne discussed these new approaches to therapy. Many of them incorporated his ideas into their own work and further amplified the concepts. Other popular books were written, including *I'm OK, You're OK* (1967), by Thomas Harris, and *Born to Win* (1971), by Muriel James and Dorothy Jongeward.

In the twenty years since its inception, TA has spread from the therapist's office to the classroom, to management seminars, and to many other settings, It has grown from a strictly therapeutic method to a popular social movement. This broad popularity and usefulness is, I believe, directly sttributed to the accessibility of the vocabulary and the elegant simplicity of the basic ideas.

In my practice, I give most incoming patients a thirty-minute lecture outlining the fundamental concepts of TA. I find that by inviting people to become co-therapists with me on their own behalf and instructing them in this way, we can progress more rapidly toward their goals. For this lecture I choose those topics that are most appropriate to my patient's immediate needs. Any concepts not covered in this initial briefing can, of course, be introduced later as openings occur in our discussions. Along with my own lecture, I recommend that patients select one or two of the basic TA books from the Transactional Analysis Bibliography at the end of this book. This reading will offer more detailed information in each of the basic areas.

EVERYBODY HAS A SET OF EGO STATES

Most people are aware that anyone they know well and see on a variety of occasions behaves in more than one way. These same people may also have noticed that they themselves behave in different ways at different times. Eric Berne found that these ways of being could be grouped into three categories, which he decided to call ego *states.*

As I introduced the concept of three ego states to the patient, I sometimes simply give them the definitions for each ego state, but more often I dramatize these typical behaviors to show that each ego state involves a tone of voice, body posture, and choice of words. For example, I may shake my index finger at an imaginary individual, frown, and say in a stern voice, "You should know better that to do that!" Next, I might throw mu arms up, even jump out of my chair and shout gleefully, "Hurrah! They made it! Whoopee!" Finally, I compose my face into a matter-of-fact expression and ask in a cool analytical tone, "Do you think the boycott will affect our coffee prices?"

Then, I ask patients to tell me who they see acting in each of these ways. Generally, they recognize the first as a parent-type behavior, the second as associated with children, and the third as typical of mature grown-ups or adults.

All of us, including children, have the potential for acting in each of these ways. Thus, we can say that everyone has a *Parent Ego State*, a *Child Ego State*, and an *Adult Ego State*. In discussing what is going on with these three ego states, it is often useful to draw a diagram in which a circle represents each ego state (Berne 1961), as shown in Figure 1.

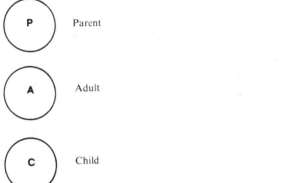

Figure 1

If each individual has a complete set of ego states, why is it that we are only aware of one ego state at a time? Berne theorized that within the individual there is a finite quantity of psychic energy, and this quantity is just enough to energize one ego state. Therefore, if the Parent ego state is energized and acting, the Adult and Child are quiescent. We can show this graphically by drwaing the circle of the acting ego state larger than the other two. In some cases one ego state is energized to the extent that it is said to "contaminate" (Berne 1961) or decommission another state, as shown in

Figure 2. The energy component of the ego states may also be described graphically in an *egogram* (Dusay 1972.) In the egogram, the three states appear as varied height bars on a graph (see Figure 3).

It's helpful to be able to recognize and identify the acting ego state when we are trying to understand and change behavior, but how do we know which ego state is energized, or in control? Four clues can guide us in understanding this process.

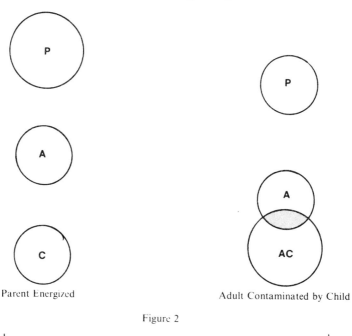

Parent Energized   Adult Contaminated by Child

Figure 2

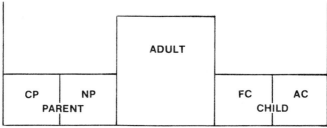

Energized Adult

Figure 3

Clue 1: *Who does this remind you of?* As an individual listens to the conversation inside his or her own head, do the *ideas* being discussed remind that person of a real mother or father? If so, then the Parent ego state is probably talking. On the other hand, if it is *feelings* that are most apparent as the person looks inward, the question to ask is, "Did you feel that way when you were a real child?" If the answer is "yes," that feeling is probably coming from the Child ego state. Other actions that don't seem to be either Parent or Child are probably Adult.

Clue 2: Listen for the tone of voice. Does the voice sound stern, commanding, or is it warm, conforting? Either one may indicate the use of the Parent ego state. A light, playful tone, weepiness, and angry bellow, all these are the voices of emotion and are associated with the Child ego state. The Adult usually speaks or questions in a calm, matter-of-fact manner.

Clue 3: Look for gestures, posture. As with voice, this clue is easiest to see in some one else. Does he or she wag an accusatory finger or proffer a pat on the back? These gestures probably come from the Parent. If he or she is jumping up and down, waving arms about,swinging fists, these and similar body movements showing emotion indicate the Child.

Clue 4: Notice the choice of words. Both in self and others it's easiest to spot choice of vocabulary. The selection of particular words is quite obvious either when considering internal voices or the conversations of others. Watch for these key phrases and other similar ones:

> The Parent begins strong statements with "you."
> The Parent uses "should, must, have to, ought to, are supposed to, mustn't ever."
> Parent ego states also say, "That's better, good, right, wrong, bad," and also, "You're doing fine."

The Child ego state begins statements or phrases with "I ought to, I have to, I'll try."

The Child sprinkles these adjectives around: "great, super, magnificent, horrible, wow."

The Adult ego state often uses questions, "What might happen if we...?"

When the Adult is turned on, the conversation includes phrases like these, "That's unfortunate (the Parent or Child might say it's awful). It seems like, Let's consider. That's desirable."

Think of the two major ways real parents act toward their children: They instruct and direct them, but they also encourage and reassure them. The encouraging, reassuring role of Parent we call the *Nurturing Parent*. In this role a father brings a cool glass of water to a sick child. The censuring, directing parent we've labeled *Critical Parent*. This Critical Parent leaps into action when a small child decides to drop his or her pants in the supermarket.

Did you notice that among those verbal clues there are two quite different ways of speaking attributed to the Parent ego state and again two different patterns associated with the Child? To help people further clarify the image of Parent and Child, these ego states are both divided into two parts (Berne 1961). The Parent is then either Critical Parent or Nurturing Parent and the Child is either *Natural* or *Adapted Child* (see Figure 4).

As counselors and therapists began working with TA and the concept of Critical Parent, they came to view the qualities of this ego state in slightly different ways. For the most part, people coming into therapy are people in distress, and this distress has often been fostered by the Critical Parent message that came from the real parent, during the patient's childhood. Those parents in the past issued harsh injunctions, "You've got to . . ." or meted out depreciatory criticism "You're no good . . ." on the emerging real child. Today the patient's Critical Parent may be repeating the same messages to the Adapted Child. It often seems, therefore, that the Critical Parent can do no good!

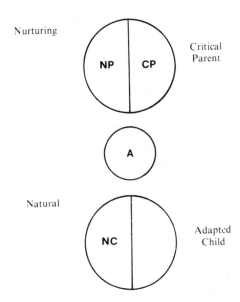

Nurturing

Critical
Parent

Natural

Adapted
Child

Figure 4

But Berne saw this negative, punitive aspect of the Critical Parent as only part of that ego state, and my own observations support his view. Critical Parent isn't always criticizing or commanding. Critical Parent may also be simply instructing or educating the novice in appropriate ways to manipulate things in order to achieve everyday goals. In this way, the Critical Parent acts as the agent for socializing the young child to heat a can of soup without burning his or her hands and/or messing up the kitchen. It is also the Critical Parent who says, "What's the magic word?" and smiles when the child responds with a "please" or "thank you." Critical Parent, then, has the potential for being very severe and damaging, but that ego state also can function as a very helpful informative force.

As mentioned, the Child ego state can be divided into two parts (Berne 1961) too. The part that giggles or bellows in rage is called the *Natural Child.* The Natural Child behaves and feels the way real children do when they are just being kids. This part of the Child is creative, spontaneous, intuitive, rebellious, and affectionate and is out for fun wherever it can be found. Usually, the people we meet in therapy are looking for ways to allow the Natural Child ego state to function. Very often the Natural Child of patients simply cannot come out and play.

The other Child ego state, which is usually much more in evidence in patients, is called the *Adapted Child*. As the Critical Parent can be harsh and negative, so the Adapted Child can be sad and frightened. We call this Adapted Child *Not OK*, and the Not OK is not an evaluation from without, but rather a feeling from within. The Adapted Child is really the response of all the directions from the real parents and others important to the child as he or she was growing up. Thus, it is the Adapted Child that says "please" and "thanks," that always brushes its teeth after meals, that makes its bed promptly after arising, and so forth. The countless little routines of the day that we do in much the same way our real parents or other important adults told us to do them are the activities of this ego state.

It is a basic assumption in TA that the infant enters this world with an internal feeling that he or she is OK. This quality of OK means that one is quite acceptable as is, and it is felt within the Child ego state. What happens to replace this OK feeling? At birth, the new baby is thrust into a world of people—people who will provide food, warmth, clean clothes, and the stimulation of human contact. Sometimes those people neglect one or more of these infant needs. Sometimes they attend to the physical needs, but for one reason or another find the baby a bother. As the baby grows, he or she absorbs some of this and somewhere deep within the Child ego state the original OK feeling changes to a Not OK feeling. With this, the little child feels inadequate, not all that he or she should be, not quite pleasing to those big people who surround him or her.

As the real child grows, all three ego states are also developing. If you listen to the talk of little children, you can hear Parent almost as soon as they are able to talk in complete sentences. For some, this will be as early as the age of three years and most will have quite vocal Parents by age four. This ego state is totally borrowed from others. All the notions within it come from the real parents or others important to the young child. Ideas may continue to be added to this ego state, probably until about the time of late adolescence.

The Adapted Child grows from within the individual fed by internal messages from the Parent and external messages from the real parents. Almost all feeling response originates in this ego state, and all redecisioning (Goulding 1972, Goulding and Goulding 1976) must occur there if there is to be any real change.

It seems to me, then, that the *self*—that is, the self-representation—is synonomous with Adapted Child. This view differs from Berne's notion that unless the person is psychotic the real self is the Adult (Berne 1961). I believe, as does Kernberg (1976), that the self-representation has feeling-tone dispositions to it (the Adapted Child) and that there are object images (the Nurturing and Critical Parent). This Not OK Adapted Child that sends an individual into therapy, then, I consider the core of being, the heart of things, the real self. A fear of the dissolution, diffusion, or destruction of that self is the profound anxiety of the Adapted Child. The Adapted Child must defend itself from all that is perceived as threatening, including any change toward OK-ness.

The Adult ego state also grows from within the organism; it is not borrowed from anyone else. Some people have very strong, functioning Adults capable of processing great quantities of information, making rational judgements, and recalling complex data as needed. Others may have less able Adult ego states, but in either case this part is mainly functional and almost devoid of feelings. It does seem likely to me that the Adult can feel interested in things that are worthwhile to it and also feels joy as, for example, in sports. The Adult is the part that can view objectively what's going on. In Freudian terms, it might be called an "observing ego." The Adult is a conflict-free ego sphere.

Everyone, then, has or has the potential for a complete set of these ego states. The ego states can carry on conversation with each other more or less all the time an individual is awake. However, these conversations with self are not sufficient to maintain mental health and balance; people must have contact with other human beings. Over the years people have observed people placed in voluntary solitary confinement and have concluded that such confinement is disastrous to the individual. Berne also observed that everyone needs a daily quota of human contact, or *strokes*. A stroke is a verbal and/or physical transaction that stimulates another person.

It is true that internal dialogues can produce some strokes. For example, the Nurturing Parent can say, "You did a great job, there," stroking the internal Adapted Child. However, people must also seek stroking from others in their world. Some strokes are pleasant, or *positive*: some are merely acknowledgment of one's existence, or *neutral,* and others are painful, or *negative.*

TRANSACTIONS—ACCESS TO THE STROKE PILE

When a person interacts with another person a number of complex events take place. Berne calls them *transactions*. The examination of those transactions forms the basis of Transactional Analysis. All transactions result in the giving and receiving of strokes, and by analyzing the transactions we can identity those strokes as positive, neutral, or negative.

The map of ego states can be used to analyze transactions by finding out precisely which ego state each person in the interaction is using. It's helpful at this stage to draw two sets of those Parent-Adult-Child (PAC) diagrams side by side. If the transaction is from Parent ego state to Parent, Adult to Adult or Child to Child, the transaction is called *parallel.* All positive, growth-oriented, fun outcomes have their roots in parallel transactions.

However, all parallel transactions don't necessarily have positive payoffs. Some may result in neutral or negative strokes and still be parallel. Parallel transactions may also occur between different ego states. The critical factor is simply, Does the response come from the ego state to which the initial remark was directed and is that response aimed at the ego state that opened the transaction? For instance, if the Adapted Child asks the Nurturing Parent for reassurance, is the Nurturing Parent responding with a comforting remark directed back to the Adapted Child? If so, the transaction is said to be parallel—or complementary, or straight, or something similar that carries that notion.

Transactions that carry an ulterior motive can be parallel. They originate with a remark from one person's ego state to that of another, but the response doesn't come from that ego state nor does it go to the first speaker's original ego state. When a transaction like this is drawn out using two PAC diagrams the lines that indicate the flow of the transaction aren't parallel, they are *crossed*. Therefore, this kind of transaction is usually called crooked, or *crossed*.

Positive strokes seldom come from crossed transactions. It works like this. One day a man called me on the phone and told me about a scene between himself and his wife that had taken place earlier that evening. Shirley, his wife, was a traditional, full-time housewife, whereas he commuted to the nearby city each day. He told me he had said, "Do you think it'll rain tonight?" Now this would be a question from his Adult to her Adult, a request for information or at least an opinion based on available data.

Shirley replied, "don't bother me....Look in the paper...." She was obviously annoyed, and it had nothing to do with the possibility of rain. Her response came from the Critical Parent and was directed toward his Adapted Child (see Figure 5). She had the option

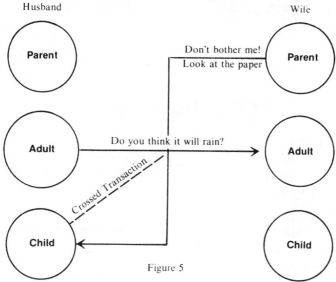

Figure 5

of simply grunting a "yeah." or "no," but instead she chose to re-spond in a way that invited further verbal conflict. The issue stopped relating to the weather and instead became his "bother-ing" her or his asking too much of her. It led into a verbal free-for-all that ended that night with Shirley marching into their bedroom, slamming the door and he striding out the front door, slamming it, and, when he found a phone booth, calling me.

Transactions can occur between any two ego states, they may be parallel or they may be crossed, and this can be positive stroke, a neutral or negative one. Now let's look at the ways people com-monly employ transactions in the business of daily life.

TIME TO FILL

The challenge of living is filling the time between birth and death. On a smaller scale that means that people need to fill each minute of each hour. In TA we have divided the various ways peo-ple fill their rime into six categories: withdrawal, rituals, pastimes, activities, games and rackets, and intimacy.

The first category of actions, *withdrawal,* describes a person who is very far away from others mentally or physically. *Intimacy,* the last category, includes all the ways people can be very close to each other. All the rest are spaced out on an imaginary continuum from very alone to very not alone.

Rituals are all the ordinary idiomatic greetings or exchanges that people commonly use to acknowledge that they are aware of anoth-er's presence. "Good Morning, How are you?" "Fine, and you?" is a classic ritual.

Pastimes include all those small-talk conversations at parties, in doctor's waiting rooms, and in other places where "talking about" something fills time but usually doesn't involve any action or closeness.

Activities are things people pour energy into doing like work, tennis, gardening and the like. Most people spend a lot of their time engaged in activities.

The important thing to remember about these rituals, pastimes and activities is that they are often used to select people for the more risky ways of structuring times—games and intimacy.

Games are a series of complementary ulterior transactions with a predictable outcome. The term *racket,* or *trading stamp,* may describe the bad-feeling payoff or racket received at the end of a game. A trading stamp means a feeling that can be used to produce a behavior. Players know which bad-feeling payoff they're after. Those payoff feelings can be called "stamps or racket feelings" (Berne 1966). Players collect these stamps in the same way shoppers collect trading stamps at a supermarket. Later, a number of stamps can be turned in for a really big bad feeling (racket) or behavior. A discussion of some of the games people in families often play follows later in this chapter.

Intimacy implies a total acceptance of another person mentally, physically, or both, during which truly candid conversations are possible and spontaneous actions are acceptable. It is a completely game-free state. Intimacy becomes possible when one feels fully OK and sees others as OK too.

GREASEPAINT AND FOOTLIGHTS

The choice of ways any individual may use to structure the time in any given day is limited somewhat by locale and opportunity, but the element that exerts the most profound influence over that choice is the individual's own *life script*. Berne has defined the *life script* as the collection of directions concerning *what to do* given to a person by the parent of the opposite sex and also the directions on *how to do it* given by the same sex parent. These stage directions are called *script injunctions.*

The Gouldings (1976) have listed a number of basic family commands or injunctions that are passed on in dysfunctional families by strong Child ego states. They are expressed in terms of "Don't be." Usually, there is also an implied, "because I don't want you." These messages from the real parent's Adapted Child are many times more potent than those of the real parent's Parent. Messages from the real parent's Parent, however, also contribute to the scripting process.

To arrive at the script injunctions for a particular patient, I ask, "What is the Parent in your head saying?" I find that most patients, even on the first visit, can deal with this question and their answers are usually on target. It is that phrase that an individual can't forget that is a script injunction. All case histories referred to as examples are provided in chapters 5 and 6.

In the case of Jack and Jenny, (chapter 6), Jack recalled that his mother said, "You always take everything for granted!" and he did. Jack's father provided the model for "how to take everything for granted" by never showing any appreciation to Jack's mother. Once Jack identified this script injunction, he could also see that his behavior mirrored his father's.

As we note these particular stage directions we may draw the *script matrix diagram* (Steiner 1972), in which the individual is represented by the PAC in the center and the messages from father and mother are noted on either side. The script matrix was described by Berne and Steiner in a seminar in 1969 (Steiner 1972).

In the case of an alcoholic, the script matrix might look like the one presented in Figure 6.

The life plan for a family, then, includes a life script from each partner. The more troubled the family, the more restrictive, less flexible, and ultimately more identifiable the plan is.

The script matrix shows quite clearly the script injunctions the individual received verbally from each parent (usually from the real parent's Parent) and nonverbally or indirectly from the real parent's Adapted Child. In the case of the patient who had been scripted to be an alcoholic, we might also conclude that his life script, as it related to the choice of mate and sexual activities, would fall into the category termed *never*.

Life scripts in the Never category prohibit sex or love or both. One of the features of the alcoholic life is that it makes sex physiologically difficult for a man, and it almost always interferes with love as well. This is not to suggest that all Never-scripted people are

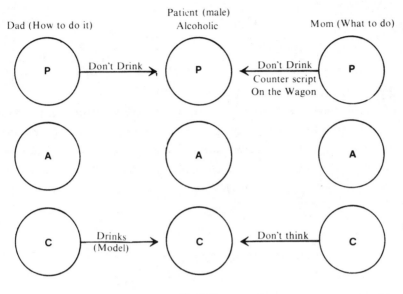

Figure 6

also alcoholics, but only that this sort of alcoholic script is probably part of the large never Life plan.

Since the life script embodies all the script injunctions a person may receive, it can be considered the master blueprint for the whole of life containing the specific directions for how time will be used until the moment of death. For those working with families, however, the segment of the life script that deals with how and why a mate is chosen or what kind of sexual expression is permitted is of primary importance. I have therefore presented the six major categories of scripts as they relate to sex life and choice of mate in Table 1. Berne first identified these categories as they relate to time structuring in general. A full discussion can be found in *Sex in Human Loving* (1970).

The original life plans, forerunners of the current version in use by today's distressed family, came about to meet a dangerous or life-threatening circumstance in the real world of an earlier time. It was a plan for survival and may have functioned to some extent to ameliorate a particular crisis. Several generations later it may still be in use. Now is has taken on the aura of a drama or farce that calls for people to live in a particular manner, encounter certain obstacles, respond to them in a prescribed way, and end up in a given situation. Of course, this senario may include badly outdated elements and may no longer be an appropriate vehicle for today's players on the contemporary stage of life.

Several books deal principally or wholly with scripts, and these may be found listed in the general bibliography in the back of this book. These studies are important reading for anyone working with families. *Games Alcoholics Play* (1971) by Steiner, as well as his *Scripts People Live* and *What Do You Say After You Say Hello?* (1971) by Berne focus on scripts.

FAMILY ALBUM OF FAVORITE GAMES

People who enter therapy whether as family members or spouses almost always have an enlarged and overactive Not OK Adapted Child ego state. According to the theory of Transactional Analysis, it is this overgrown ego state that generated unhappy, unsatisfying relationships, particularly within a home. It is also a fundamental TA concept that the Not OK Adapted Child, to maintain that negative feeling, must engage in frequent ulterior transactions or games. Technically, a *payoff* is a position—for example, people are ungrateful. Therefore, the therapist can expect to observe, identify, interact with, and, perhaps, abort a great deal of game play within the therapy sessions.

The first complete description of transactional games was published by Eric Berne in *Games People Play* (1964). Since then, many other competent TA professionals have recorded their observations about those and other games. Naturally, each of us sees any given game played out in a variety of ways, colored by the personalities of the players and their unique setting. The classic example noted in *Games People Play* may bear little resemblance to the scene in your office, although the structure and dynamics of both are the same.

Table 1
Scripts as Related to Sex Life

Six Primary Classes of Scripts	Injunction From Parent	Effect on Sex Life
Never	There are lots of tempting things out there but don't you try any of them!	Either sex or love may be forbidden, or both. If love is forbidden but sex is permitted, the individual will be promiscuous. If sex is forbidden but love is permitted, the person may become a priest or care for orphans. Both are tormented by their awareness that others can enjoy sex and love.
Always	If that's what you chose to do then you can just spend the rest of your life doing it!	Parent prompts the young person to commit a sin then expells him or her for doing it.
Until	You can have the golden apple, but not until you've done this and this to earn it!	Person may avoid sexual contact until after marriage ceremony or may not date until father or mother dies; can't ask a girl for a date until he has X money in the bank and so forth.
After	You can enjoy yourself for a little while; but look out, the bad things will come!	Once you have children, your troubles begin—results in fear of pregnancy.
Over and Over	There you go again! You almost made it, is only.....	Person tries again and again but never quite makes it. Person may come close to orgasm, but drifts back down again without release.
Open End	Detailed instructions as to how to live life up to a certain age or retirement, but no instructions about how to fill time before death. Always so as mother tells you!	Person regards sex as an effort or an obligation; as they grow older they use age as an excuse to avoid it. Lack of programming for this time period results in individuals drying up and fading away.

Berne outlined thirty or more games and others have added to his list. Among the patients who enter family therapy there may be players who use any of them. There may even be someone who plays a brand new game! However, as TA therapists have built successive years of work with families, there has emerged a family album of favorite games and these are the ones a family therapist sees most often.

Game Play—from Light to Heavy

All games, these and any others you may encounter, may be played in varying degrees of intensity. Light games help maintain the Not OK posture but still enable the players to function in the real world, whereas heavier games absorb an increased amount of energy and thus greatly restrict nongames activities. The heaviest games require total involvement and may result in homicide or suicide.

Games played within a family setting attain an intensity that is seldom reached in games played with co-workers, schoolmates, or others outside the home. Furthermore, the roles within the games often rotate, giving the family game a higher number of possible variations. Because people within a troubled family all usually play two or three chosen games and have done so over a period of years, games can be initiated swiftly with only a word or two, a look, or a gesture. A game can be concluded just as quickly with an instant payoff all around, or it may continue as a running game that never really ends. Usually, people identify their own games very quickly as they are described by a therapist or as they read general descriptions of common games in any of the books about TA.

There is a real danger at this point that novices in TA will "call" the game play of other family members, and this almost never has the hoped-for positive effect. It usually only serves to further alienate the gameplayer. Instead, the newcomer to TA needs to hear about and become familiar with the notion of the *antithesis*. An antithesis to game play begins with a clear understanding on the part of the responder, or player B, precisely what player A, the initiator's, opening move is, from which ego state it comes, which ego state it is intended to attract, and what player A hopes to get from the game. Thus, the diagraming of game play in therapy lays a firm foundation in the minds of gameplayers from which they can begin to move into game-free life. Player B also must decide he or she will not engage in the game.

The Adult of player B must first recognize what player A is doing and decide not to join in the game. Next, still working from the Adult, player B uses a specific question in response to A's opener. This question is spoken in a family tone; it acknowledges the presents of A (A's worthiness, and so forth), but it firmly declines the game gambit. Examples of these questions are included in each description of a family game in the following section.

When player A hears this question, one of two things happen. If A is also interested in becoming game-free, he or she may respond with the Adult directly to the question. The game has thus been aborted, and these people are on the way toward phasing out games. If, however, A is not yet ready to try being game-free, he or she will try to escalate the game. An example of this is found with Jason and Martha (chapter 6). Player B again can remain friendly but firmly decline the game invitation by restating the chosen question and offering some reassurance to A's frightened Adapted Child at the same time. A hug at this point may be more eloquent than words.

This moment, however, is not the time for an analysis of the game. That is wisely left until the patients are calmer, perhaps not even until the next therapy session.

Most important, when a family decides to use these antigame strategies, they stand an excellent chance of attaining a game-free relationship very quickly. By working together and using the agreed-on antithesis for their games, they offer each other mutual support during the transition phase. The Adapted Child can become quite anxious if games are stopped abruptly without the use of antithesis behavior. Protection, permission, and potency offered by the therapist are also vital at this time. More will be said about these latter strategies later.

Kick Me. This game is an all-time family favorite, with the children in the family usually acting as instigators. It can be played to yield any of the negative-stroke transactions that result in hurt, depression, and other rackets. Betty Moulenarie, in the guilt racket family (chapter 5), played Kick Me with her mother and father regularly.

Kick Me isn't limited to children, of course. Richard (chapter 6), played a form of Kick Me when he tells his wife he will be home at seven and then shows up at eleven. Alza, of the anger racket family (chapter 5), played Kick Me primarily with her father.

In its standard form, Kick Me begins with a provocative act. The initiating player always knows exactly what kind of act will provoke a *kick*. Richard knew that in calling Eileen and telling her he would be home at seven, then actually arriving around eleven, would always inflame her. She then could be counted on to give him his kick. Richard both said and did something, but Kick Me can be initiated with a look or gesture, too. The provocative act comes from the Adapted Child ego state and attracts, or *hooks,* the Critical Parent of the other player. The kick is then delivered by the Critical Parent and both players collect their favorite brand of stamps (anger stamps).

One way to abort this game is for the player B to restrain his or her Critical Parent response and try to entice the Adult of player A. Player B might respond, "Did you want to make me feel angry?" (in a friendly tone of voice). When player A is a young child and player B is the real parent, a hug or tickle to coax out the Natural Child may deflate the Adapted Child and substitute a positive stroke for the expected negative one.

The therapist will usually use an Adult-hooking question in response to a Kick Me opening. He or she may then go on to explain that a person initiates this game to provoke a negative reaction because it keeps him or her from realizing their own sadistic urges, that is, urges to be cruel and hateful.

Children who initiate Kick Me will probably stop spontaneously when the relationship between the parents improves. From the young teen years on, however, there seems to be a solidifying of the ego states, and behaviors like game playing are not dropped so easily. When Betty (chapter 5), began to get better, I asked her, "What happened in the past when you did that?" (following a Kick Me-initiating behavior). She described the bawling out she had received earlier. Then, I asked, "Well, what do you think will happen this time? Is that what you really want to happen?" As she considered this and realized that she did have the option to avoid provocative behavior, she gradually gave up this game, but not before she picked up the habit of stopping and asking herself, "Is this what I really want to happen?"

NIGYYSOB. The companion game for Kick Me is, "Now I've Got You, You Son of a Bitch," or *NIGYYSOB.* Some times player A, the Kick-Me initiator, will save up his or her stamps and cash them in on NIGYYSOB, pouncing on Player B for revenge. More often, however, it is player B acting from the Critical Parent ego state who stars in this game. As with Kick Me, the game is started by player A acting from the Adapted Child and committing a provocative act. This time, however, player B's Critical Parent goes all out, venting rage far in excess of that warranted by the original act. A rather mild misbehavior may serve as the excuse for a general attack on player A's entire way of living. Betty's mother, Joanne, played this game (chapter 5) at least part of the time during the period of greatest stress. Eileen also used this game against Richard (chapter 6), particularly when he provoked her in minor matters around the house. At those times, she vented freely the anger and frustration built by their generally unsatisfying relationship.

NIGYYSOB, then, is characterized by a minor provocative act, an overinflated angry response, and the collection of angry payoff feelings. As with Kick Me, this game can be stopped if player A decides not to commit provocative acts in the presence of player B. When Betty decided to do the things her mother asked her to do and to do them pretty much in the way her mother described, she eliminated those behaviors that triggered NIGYYSOB. Richard also modified his general behavior around the house, and, in addition, he made very careful agreements with Eileen as to what he would do and when he would do it. Then, of course, he did what he agreed to do.

Having a clear understanding of exactly what each person expects and then holding to that understanding helps to eliminate the probability of starting a NIGYYSOB game. For the therapist, this means stating very explicitly what he or she expects from a patient and what he or she will do for that patient. These efforts may take some time and some careful thought. I once had an older colleague who made it a practice to greet a new patient and immediately outline the behavior he expected from all patients. Only after these ground rules were acknowledged and agreed on could he proceed to take a case history.

If, in spite of all these precautions, a game of Kick Me or NIGYYSOB does occur during therapy, the therapist can sit quietly until the blast is over and then ask, "How do you feel right now?" or turn to another member of the family and ask, "How do you feel when (Mom, Dad, or whoever) talks like that?" The therapist can also ask the player, "Who talked like that to you in the past?" Any of these questions can involve the Adult and result in more information to plug into the patient's understanding of what is going on when these things occur.

Why Don't You, Yes But. This game is another classic family favorite. The real parents in the family may initiate it under the subtitle of *I'm Only Trying To Help.* In this version the real parent, using Critical Parent, offers advice to others in the family. The motive here is to keep the others, usually younger family members, passive—that is, to rob the others of initiative. Thus the parent says, "You really should wear your Mary Janes to the party, dear." To which seven-year-old Janey replies, "But Mother, everyone else will be wearing tennes!" Mother is implying that Janey couldn't possibly choose the appropriate shoes, that she is inept in such matters. Janey naturally must defend herself, and this takes energy. The necessity for this defense drains her energy, and she becomes more passive, which is what Mother wanted in the first place.

Played in full form by adults, *Why Don't You, Yes But* goes like this. Player A opens play by saying, "Oh, dear, I just don't know what to do about my saxophone...." This is usually accompanied by a helpless look sagging shoulder, even teary eyes. The opener coming from player A's Adapted Child is designed to hook (or stimulate) the helpful or Nurturing Parents of whoever is handy. Player B then responds with, "Why don't you take it to Mr. Small at the music shop?" This is a suggestion phrased as a question. Player A responds to the suggestion, "Yes, but he's so expensive." Player A's response always acknowledged that player B's suggestion is valid (Yes But) and then states why it won't be followed. It's significant that player A leaves open the possibility for more suggestions, which player B or others then go on to make. Each one will be declined in the same way. When all the Critical Parents have suggested everything they can think of, they simply retire from the games leaving player A to collect his or her payoff, with a small smile of triumph that no parent can tell her anything. One way to abort this game is to look player A in the eye and say sympathetically, "Hum, what are you going to do about your saxophone?"

After diagraming and discussing this game with a family one day, the mother immediately launched another round of play. After several moments she giggled nervously and said, "Oh, Doctor, I hope I'm not 'yes butting.' " This gave me a chance to note that her comment was coming from her Child, and that this was not all bad—in fact, not bad at all. It's not necessary or even very functional for a patient to try to stay in his or her Adult all the time. After all, it's usually the Child who motivates game behavior, and we need to observe this in action to identify it.

Furthermore, it is in the Child that redecisioning occurs—that is, deciding to change the life position or life plan (Goulding 1972, Goulding and Goulding 1976). Thus, it's vital to acknowledge the importance of the Child's role from time to time. It's also helpful for the therapist to listen with and be aware of the reaction of his or her own Child.

The woman who observed her own "yes butting" had been actively fighting off everyone including me. I reminded her that this was what the Yes But really meant and thus accomplished. One way for the therapist to avoid being drawn into this particular game is to avoid the notion of helping the patient and instead elicit an analysis from the patient himself or herself.

When I acknowledged her Yes But and pointed out again the way it shut her off from others, she said, "You mean everytime I Yes But I'm fighting you off?" This question showed me that she was fighting submission to my interpretation of her fear of submission. By playing this notion back to me as my interpretation of her behavior, she was staging a last-ditch effort to avoid submitting to the notion and/or my interpretation of her behavior. A therapist needs a patient's Adult to resolve this behavior, and he or she may ask a question such as, "Can you hear yourself?"

People who use the Yes But game dare not submit to anyone else's ideas. This fear of submission may originate from different episodes in the past, but in general the fear stems from a feeling that self will disintegrate and be lost if submission occurs.

Along with the fear of submission is a fear of penetration. Women will sometimes find themselves "frigid" and find sexual penetration unpleasant if tolerated at all. When men feel a fear of submission, they usually ejaculate prematurely.

Oddly enough, it is often these Yes But patients who request hypnosis during therapy. Of course, hypnosis is almost total submission. Asking for hypnosis signals the basic conflict between fear of submission and a longing for total submission.

A request for hypnosis may come via a more intense version of Yes But called *Do Me Something* (DMS). In DMS, the patient invites the therapist to take a more active role, to "do something" in the therapy. Jenny (chapter 6) played DMS; she was hospitalized with depression when I first met her. I remember her sitting up in bed, eyes brimming with tears, saying "Oh, Doctor, you've got to do something...." In the pattern of this game player A never tells player B what it is that he or she is to do but becomes angry when player B fails to do it. In the family setting or between a couple, this results in player A collecting an unlimited number of disappointments or depression stamps, and player B obtaining guilt or depression stamps as well.

I've often seen a couple one or two times and then received a call like this. "We've decided to stop therapy, doctor, you're not really helping us." This move is a subtle version of DMS. If they don't hang up right away, I can mention this game and suggest that it is what might be happening. Usually, such a couple can be encouraged to come in and find out more about the game and continue their therapy.

Joanne (chapter 5) also played DMS in therapy sessions when she said to me, "Doctor, these sessions ought to be more *productive.*" I responded with a question to her Adult, "Well, which do you want more, quantity or quality?" She thought for a moment and said, "More quality, I think...." Her Adult was speaking again, but the pattern was pervasive, and she returned to it again and again. Each time I repeated that key question. Finally, on the seventh or eighth pass, she interrupted me laughingly. "Yeah, I know, quality or quantity." Joanne understood the game with her Adult, and she could readily abort the game when her Adult was hooked with the question.

Uproar. Any two people who want to avoid sexual intimacy may play *Uproar.* Either spouse can start play, and any tiny, even imaginary, event cited as "cause." Player A charges, "You're a lousy housekeeper, there's dust an inch thick on the top of the hot water heater!" Where upon player B roars back, "Well, if you made enough money so I could have cleaning help like Sally does, it wouldn't be there!" From then on, the battle may escalate until the couple has emptied each other of their garbage bags of complaints. The final move is when one or both leave the room going in opposite directions and slamming the door or doors behind them.

As we will see, Jenny (chapter 6) had a strong fear of submission and of sexual intimacy. So did Jack, but to a lesser degree. The game of Uproar for them took the place of sexual excitement and freed them from a need to submit. Since they did really care for each other, they were quite amenable to using the Adult-hooking question to break up this game. Either one might say, "You hurt my feelings, was that your intention?" Along with this, they were practicing use of their Nurturing Parents. Jack, in particular, learned to offer Jenny reassurance frequently and warmly, so that in time she was able to accept it. At the same time, she ended her negative relationship with her mother, was upset less often, and had more energy for Jack. As their fears of intimacy and submission subsided, so did their need to play Uproar.

Courtroom. In therapy, Uproar can escalate into another game called *Courtroom,* in which the therapist, or any other third person, may be cast in the role of judge by the spouses. I remember one afternoon a new couple came into my office, and before he sat down the man said, "She's a mess, the house is a mess, and she won't have sex with me." The wife quickly replied, "He should talk! Always leaving his clothes right where he drops them! Hangs his wet towels over the top of the door! I'm a mess? He's a mess!" They then both turned and looked expectantly at me as if to say, "Okay, Judge, who's right?"

I nodded and invited them to sit down. Then, I explained that it's not part of my role as a therapist to act as a judge. Furthermore, I'm not going to judge or blame anyone in my office. That's one way to handle Courtroom. Another way is to calmly state, "You're both right" or "You're both wrong" and then ask how they feel about either statement. At this point, the game usually escalates into Uproar, with the partners openly fighting each other. In Courtroom, the fighting is detoured or routed through a third person. It is crucial in couple or family therapy to get these people to transact with each other, so that the games, transactions, and payoffs may be observed directly.

Furthermore. Another variation of marital fighting is *furthermore.* This game is from Adapted Child to Adapted Child and characteristically begins with a "you...." accusation like, "You never take me out anymore!" To which he responds, "Who would? You look like some dame from the late night reruns!"

This "you-you" sparring may go on for years, apparently without interruption. Payoffs can be collected after each exchange. As an ongoing game it becomes a very rigid, nonproductive way to structure time. When a couple seems to be operating in this pattern, you may want to invite the children to come with them for a therapy session. The children can then be asked, "What do they (the parents) do when they aren't talking like this (playing Furthermore)?" They will know, of course, and be able to provide revealing insights to the daily life of that family.

In this game the Adapted Child is trying to get a Nurturing-Parent response from the spouse but is never successful. Each partner is trying to change the other into the mother or father they didn't have or who was unsatisfactory in some way when they were real children. Since neither player is going to come on as Nurturing Parent, the therapist can begin to break up the game by saying, "Okay, let's limit this to one complaint at a time." Then, he or she continues by translating the "you..." into "I feel..." and "I want..." and so forth. Thus, the woman who said, "You never take me out anymore!" could be translated by the therapist, "Did you mean you would like to go out some evening?"

When one spouse is hurling accusations at the other in this way, you can be sure that the one under attack isn't listening. The object of the accusations is planning what he or she will say in counterattack. This is done in defense of their own egos. The pattern can be treated with an antithesis, which again is a hook to force an Adult response. The therapist can turn to the attacked one and say, "What is right, or true, about what your spouse is saying?"

If a couple is playing Furthermore and Courtroom extensively, they can be given individual appointments on alternate weeks. When they are separated, they are forced to talk about themselves and that particular game is defused.

Uproar, Courtroom, and Furthermore are all games involving verbal battles—they are fighting games. *Sweetheart* and *If It Weren't for You* are conversational games usually played out in a well-modulated, social tone of voice. The voice may be edged with bitterness as the game becomes more intense, but it will not altogether lose that conversational quality.

Sweetheart. The game of *Sweetheart* is initiated by Player A because he or she is feeling on the defensive in the social situation. Ralph Johnson (chapter 5) often began the therapy hour with just such a play. "Say, Doctor, I gotta tell you about what happened the other night. Sally (Mrs. Johnson) got into a real wingding with her mom. Why, before they were through, Mom chewed her out, but good, for the way Alza's behaving. Told her she was a rotten mother and stuff like that. But Sally, did she tell her to buzz off? Not on your life...just stood there and took it nice as a pie, didn't you sweetheart?

In the beginning play, an anecdote is told describing something that happened to the Sweetheart. This story is essentially true, but highly unflattering if not downright embarrassing. The concluding phrase is always a request for agreement from the Sweetheart. And the Sweetheart always agrees first, because the story is mostly true and there doesn't seem to be any point in not agreeing and second because the telling of such a story helps the "Sweetheart" maintain her or his Not OK position.

Sally was collecting anger stamps as her payoff from this game. She planned to cash them in on a divorce, as she told us, "in a year or two." When Ralph heard this, he was shocked into action. We diagramed the game and talked over it's dynamics, and he quickly activated his own Adult to knock off this game.

If It Weren't for You. The conversational game of *If It Weren't for You* was originally identified as one played by women as they talked about their husbands to other women. However, it may also be played by men discussing their wives or parents discussing their children. In all cases, player A has chosen a mate or children to restrict his or her activities and prevent him or her from participating in something feared. Thus, a man marries a fragile woman, who is frequently ill and then complains, "If it weren't for Helena,

I'd be off in the back country fighting right now!" Helena and her delicate health give him a built-in, lifelong excuse not to participate in rugged outdoor activities. The men he works with all enjoy this kind of leisure-time adventure, but he really doesn't like to get sweaty and dirty.

The therapist working with families will undoubtedly hear this game again and again. It is seen when a family enters therapy with a child as the identified patient. "If it weren't for Christopher, we'd have a very happy family." All the blame for dissatisfactions within the family is heaped on the scapegoat, the identified patient.

When this happens, the parents are, of course, denying their own problems and their own responsibility. If they have been scripted to have an unpleasant, nonintimate family, they must create less a child who will keep the battle going, keep everyone at their distance. Alza and Betty (chapter 5) did yeoman service in this role. As the therapist begins to deframe the identified patient, this game will be exposed.

Once parents begin to acknowledge their role in shaping the child's behavior, they usually drop this game and get into the reasons they needed to use this strategy to keep the family operating in a particular way. As with all game behavior, it is not enough to "understand" the game. Unless the need for that game's payoff is eliminated, play will escalate in intensity or shift into another version of the game.

More sex games. Although all game play helps the players to avoid intimacy with each other, several games specifically aid participants in avoiding sexual intimacy. As mentioned, Uproar is often played in this context. Another common sex-voiding game is *Rapo.* In this game, the player A, of either sex, behaves in an openly provocative manner and appears to invite sexual overtures from player B. Now player A is only doing this as a cover for feelings of sexual inadequacy, but player B would never guess it from the visable and verbal clues. Naturally, player B says, "Why not? Let's do it!" Whereupon player A is indignant, outraged, and so forth. A full description of the play of this game is found in chapter 6 along with further background material.

Who Needs You? Another primarily antisex maneuver is *Who Needs You?* However, in this game both players, a married couple, began their relationship with feelings of personal inadequacy in sexual matters. Later, one of the pair decides that sex is okay, but the other half of the duo is still unsure. The more aggressive partner then goes out and finds sexual expression with someone else. The key scene in this scenario is when the aggressive partner comes home, tells the spouse all about how it was with a stranger, and ends by saying, "So, who needs you? Chapter 6 provides an example of how this game played itself out in the lives of one couple and what they did to stop play.

Some sexual games are quite straightforward; they simply help the players stay out of bed with each other. However, others have a rather kinky twist like *Make Someone (Often Mother) Suffer.* In this game players not only avoid having sex with each other, one of them also ends up physically battered. The Hoffers played this one, the full details of which appear in Chapter 6.

You and Your Goddamn Parent! It's been my experience and that of others, as well, that family members need to be cautioned regularly to avoid accusatory name calling, once they are familiar with game theory. It's wise for the therapist also to keep this in mind, for it's so tempting when you hear two people engaging in any of these classic dialogues to shout, "Stop, you're playing a game!"

At home, the scene may begin with one family member delivering a lecture to another. The listener then responds, "There you go again, you and your goddamn parent!" The first speaker can then come back, "Well, there has to be a little Child around in order for a Parent to come out!" Both players can collect an anger stamp from this exchange. I tell them not to use the jargon at home because it's usually taken as an accusation if somebody calls a game.

For this reason, I've suggested again and again that the therapist draw a diagram of the game transaction when he or she hears one.

Get the patients to help fill in the words over the arrows. By the time the diagram is finished and all the exchanges discussed, most patients will say "Uh-huh, yeah, that's what we were doing all right." They will call their own game.

To abort a game in midplay the therapist can use the Adult-hooking question, "What do you think is happening?" I find that after I've done this several times with a family and perhaps talked about doing it, they begin to pick it up and use similar questions among themselves. But, they can not do that comfortably if the need for the payoff is still very much present and they are not yet moving toward a new OK life position.

Corner games. No family album of games would be complete without a mention of Corner games. In this game, the intent of player A is to maneuver player B into the Corner, where he or she is damned if they do and damned if they don't. Mother might say solicitously to Dad, "What would you like for dinner dear?" If he tells her, the next response from her will be dramatically different in tone, and ego state, from her initial question. "Don't tell mewhat to cook—I work hard enough all day for this family without criticism." Or, if he simply responds that he doesn't care, anything will be fine, her Child can wail, "You won't even answer a simple question...." He can't win a positive stroke either way.

Some people add another dimension to this game, creating a much heavier payoff. In this version, the contradictory messages are given along with an injunction from a survival figure that this contradiction can't be discussed. The only way to live with this incongruency is to become crazy or schizophrenic (Bateson 1956). Parents who play this heavy Corner game regularly with their children create schizophrenic people.

In this transactional pattern, a father known to be sick might ask his child, "What do you want?" Again, the child will be damned if he or she asks for something and also damned if they don't, but the critical difference is that the child doesn't dare comment on this conflict because any comment might make the father sicker. Thus, the child draws a negative stroke and permission to be crazy.

The Wallace family, described as having a hurt racket (chapter 5), used this game between mother and child. Families operating with a fear racket also may use this game. It rarely occurs in anger or guilt racket families.

Persecutor-Rescuer-Victim. Karpman (1968) is credited with first recognizing the *Persecution-Rescuer-Victim* triangle in games. As you will see, the hurt family (chapter 5) played regularly and, at times, constantly in this triangle. The idea is that the players can switch from one role to the other in the triangle (see Figure 7). Since

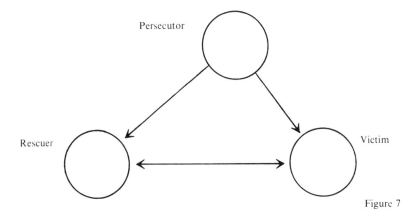

Figure 7

games are cyclical in nature it's hard to say just where the game starts. It requires at least two people and can be played by three or more. Once a player enters a round, that person may operate from all three roles before that round ends. That is, in the hurt racket family, if Dad chooses to *Rescue* Sally he will later usually also become a *Persecutor* and also a *Victim.*

The Persecutor-Rescuer-Victim triangle is so pervasive in its milder forms that once one becomes aware of it, it's possible to observe it being played everywhere. For example, Judy, a student and mother, says to her neighbor-friend Sue, "Arragh, I've got a midterm tomorrow." She might here be seen as Victim. Sue, aware that caring for two-year-old Tom will not be conducive to studying, offers a rescue, "I'd be glad to take Tommy to my house for the afternoon." (Sue is the Rescuer.) "Oh, would you?" Judy sighs in relief. "Here's some extra Pampers, he seems to have diarrhea today." Sue has slipped into the Victim position. Now, she's stuck with changing an afternoon's worth of smelly diapers. At this point, Judy is now playing Persecutor.

Depending on her own mood, Sue might then indulge Tommy in usually forbidden sweets or not bother with a nap to make the afternoon easier for herself and, in doing so, move around into the Persecutor spot, with Judy again, mildly, the Victim. Sue will have her chance to cash in on being the Victim when Randy comes home from the office and she tells him about it. Perhaps she will graciously allow him to Rescue her by taking her out for dinner.

In its very mild forms, like this one, Persecutor-Rescuer-Victim can be aborted either by Judy proposing a trade of services contract in the first place to free her afternoon for study. She is also all responsible for arranging her life so that she can adequately take care of both her child and her studying. Or, Sue might have also offered to take Tommy on the condition that Judy return the favor in a way that was genuinely helpful to Sue.

When triangle switches occur in their more serious forms, as in the Wallace family, players need to recognize the pattern and also work toward an understanding of why they are interacting in this way. When someone appears to be needing a Rescue, the would-be or former rescuer might say, "You seem to be having a problem, how do you plan to handle it?" Then, if the person who could be a victim asks directly for a very specific kind of help, the rescuer can decide whether or not to give this help. If specific help is given, it is not a Rescue. The key notion in a Rescue is that the provider does what he or she thinks ought to be done for the victim—that is, the Rescuer projects a personal view of the problem. This view and the solution may be quite different from the victim's perception of the problem and choice of solution. It is this "Mother knows best" attitude that automatically turns the Rescuer into a Persecutor. Moreover, because the rescuer is doing what he or she *thinks* is best for the victim, rather than what the victim really *wants*, the strokes resulting from the transaction are likely to be negative or at least not as good as the Rescuer thinks he or she deserves, thus putting the latter in a Victim spot.

Once people visualize this triangle and understand the roles, they can become very alert not to appear a Victim in the presence of a person known to enjoy Rescuing. In other words, each of the players in a family can begin to take responsibility for arranging their affairs so as to avoid being considered the Victim of their circumstances.

OK, Wise Guy. Individual patients and patient-families often try to play the game of *OK, Wise Guy* with the therapist. It is the opposite of "Gee, You're a Wonderful Professor." In OK, Wise Guy, the patient feels attacked by the therapist's Parent. Usually, he or she will hear this "criticism" as if the real parent of the past were speaking. Perhaps the words spoken by the therapist elicit the *rubber band* response (Haimowitz 1971) that replays parent words of long ago—that is, the feelings of the Child part are reactivated. When this happens, the patient will say, in effect, "OK, if you're so smart, what do I do about it?" The question may be stated more subtly or veiled with other phrases, but this is the essence of it. Of course, the Adapted Child of the patient is speaking.

The therapist who was originally speaking from his or her Adult then needs to get the conversation back into the Adult frame by hooking the patient's Adult. "What is the Parent in your head saying now?" Or, "What ego state did you think I was using just then? What made you think so?" or other similar questions designed to get the patient to observe what is going on.

The preceding, then, are the games I see most often in working with couples and families. They structure a great deal of the day-to-day conversation between people in a home. Along with identifying the game, working out antithesis questions, and agreeing to knock off game play, people need to rediscover the potential for candid dialogue as they move toward a more intimate family relationship.

A WORD ABOUT STAMP COLLECTIONS

The image of *trading stamps* as the feeling payoff of transactional games started with Eric Berne's first writing about games. The notion has been expanded by other writers in this field. Different people have named the varieties of stamps that can be collected according to their own view of the process.

When we talk about families according to their *Rackets,* I find it convenient to identify a stamp associated with each of them. This is not to say that people in any one racket family are limited to collecting only their own variety of stamp! They can and do collect whatever looks good at any given time. Most of these stamps serve the purpose of maintaining the Not OK position.

Some writers have also identified the "gold" stamps, those that help maintain the I'm OK position. Those are the ones people pick up from intimate, accepting behavior in game-free relationships.

Fear stamps. Fear stamps are collected by those in the fear racket, and I think of them as yellow. They can be injuncted by parents who say, "Be careful, Watch out!" or "What if." When I hear these phrases repeated several times in a conversation I am certain that the speaker is flipping the pages of a fear stamp book. A really grand collection of yellow stamps can be turned in on another round of clinging or dependency.

Guilt stamps. Guilt racket people collect these blue guilt stamps. Once I was asked to meet with a father and son at the hospital. It seemed that the son, who was a voluntary patient, was afraid to come to my office. When I entered the son's room, the first thing the father said was, "That must have been a nuisance to drive over here, Doctor." This remark was designed to make the son feel guilty and it worked. Blue guilt stamps can be turned in on a depression and withdrawal. A really big collection can net the saver withdrawal to a mental ward or even total withdrawal via suicide.

Anger Stamps. These bright red stamps are collected in anger racket families by those who have been rejected or put down. Sally Johnson, who bore the brunt of her husband's put-down game, Sweetheart, collected this variety. She planned to cash hers in on a divorce. An anger stamp collection can be converted into a guilt-free blowup, of course, at any time.

Hurt stamps. Purple hurt stamps are collected and savored for the pleasure that these individuals derive from being hurt. They come from being rejected or put down in any of the same ways that anger stamps are given. Purple stamps are, in the main, collected for their hurt value, but they also can generate some feelings of anger. When a player decides it's time to cash in his or her stamp books, the prize may be a blowup that combines hurting and anger.

Awful stamps. Another very common variety of stamp collected by people suffering depression or paranoia are the awful stamps, which are brown. People who collect them seem to view the world as though it reflected the color of their stamps. Everything is miserable to them, which really means shitty.

Among the people who seek help from those of us in any of the various counselor, therapist, and advisor roles, we can expect to find the Not OK Adapted Child actively engaging in a variety of ulterior transactions or games designed to promote the collecting of negative payoffs or stamps required to maintain that feeling of Not OK.

WHERE DO WE GO FROM HERE?

Over the years, those working with TA principles began to notice that individuals who clearly had Not OK Adapted Child parts did not necessarily relate to others in the same way. They also did not share a generally similar view of life.

Frank J. Ernst, Jr. (1973), observed this phenomenon and found these dissimilar attitudes toward life could be generalized in what he called the "OK Corral." He named four principal life positions, each of which describes the way the individual feels about himself and also about others. The position also tells what that person's attitude toward life will be.

The optimum position is *I'm OK—You're OK*. Persons in this position carry a "let's get on with it" attitude about life.

The life position of many people I meet in therapeutic settings is *I'm Not OK—You're OK*. This may also be referred to as the depressive position. People who adopt this position can be seen withdrawing from others and their attitude characteristically is "I'll get away from...."

Another life position that I sometimes see is *I'm OK—You're Not OK*. These people may also be thought of as somewhat paranoid. They choose to "get rid of others."

There is a fourth position that Dr. Ernst includes in his description, but people in it rarely seek therapy. That position is *I'm Not OK—You're Not OK*. People who operate from this position are said to "Go nowhere." They end up in places like San Quentin, the city morgue, or the county mental hospital.

Once a life position is assumed, the individual is committed to maintaining that position—committed, that is, until he or she chooses to assume another one. As mentioned previously, it is a basic premise of TA that everyone enters life in the I'm OK—You're OK position and everyone can return to that position at any time. As the choice of any of the other positions is reversible, no one need be locked into any Not OK slot. Thus, the overall goal in TA therapy is to guide individuals and families back into that original position of I'm OK—Everyone Else Is OK, too.

WHY TA?

The general goal of helping people feel good about themselves is not new. Why is TA more effective as a therapeutic method? Why do I use it and recommend it to others? I already suggested that it is easy to talk about, the vocabulary is simple, and patients can become conversant with the concepts from the first interview. But convenient as each of these elements may be, they would be worthless if the method as a whole did not have anything more to offer.

In a sense, Transactional Analysis is a middle ground between the analytic tradition with its emphasis on psychic mechanisms, drives, transference relationships, and a tendency to focus on deep-level resolution of the patient's conflict on the one hand and the behavior-and communication-oriented approaches that characterize most family systems work today. TA adds to the analytic approach an emphasis on understanding the connections between an individual's intrapsychic realities and his or her current transaction with people, often those in the family. TA adds to the behavior- and communication-oriented approaches that characterize most systems work today. TA adds to the analytic approach an emphasis on understanding the connections between an individual's intrapsychic realities and his or her current transaction with people, often those in the family. TA adds to the behavior- and communication-oriented schools a theory of psychic functioning that permits inferences as to the deeper causes of observed behavior, thereby providing therapists with more ways and levels of intervening to change behavior.

possibilities for being objective and precise in this area of family behaviors did not exist before the inception of Transactional Analysis.

The following lecture on TA is one taped from an actual session with a family. It is a single parent family without the mother speaking; there is one brother and one sister.

A SAMPLE INTRODUCTORY LECTURE

I thought that I would just introduce you to a few things about Transactional Analysis. Some we have already read, and now we will talk about it. This Parent, Adult, and Child are not the same as id, ego, and superego. Have you heard of these? They are Freudian concepts—that is, that there's an ego; something unconscious, the id; and the ego has something to contend with, the superego and external reality. The Parent is more under the influence of the superego. The thing that is different is that the Child means an actual child, what you wanted to do, what you were like as a Child. And it doesn't mean Childish, but childlike. Childish is a criticism by the Critical Parent. Anyway, why bother with this at all?

Well, this is a sorting system in which you can think, act, feel, and behave in at least three different ways, since everybody has a Parent, Adult, and Child. Parent and Child are from the past. These are called ego states, which mean that they lie within the ego. These are called ego states, which means that they lie within the ego. There are three parts that everybody has, unless you have brain damage. So why bother with this at all? The reason is that, if you understand yourselves in these terms, you have three choices as to how you think, act, feel, and behave.

other two. The Adult is simply a computer. It feels very little except certain kicks out of sports or something like that, whereas the feelings are in the Child and Parent, and they are both from the past. The Parent knows what is right and wrong and good and bad and what you should do and what you ought to do and must do. Since the Parent knows what's right and wrong, it has the moral values. Go ahead and ask questions if this is not clear as we go along. However, we don't use the word mature because everybody has a little boy or girl inside of them called their Child. Everybody has a conscience, or Parent.

Brother: Conscience is theParent sort of. It's got the moral standards so that it knows what you should do and criticizes.
Doctor: Right.
Sister: When the Parent is talking to a little person is she talking to the Child or Adult?
Doctor: Could be all three. It depends on what the transaction is like.

Brother: If they are bitching at each other could it be both parents
          fighting back at each other or the Parent and Child
          fighting?
Doctor: Well, we'll get to that in a minute. We haven't gotten to a
          transaction yet.

The reason for using the sorting system is that you can choose
how you think, act, feel and behave if you do use it, unless you are
using it in a crooked way to hide something. Berne, who was the
early writer in TA, would talk about these states in the ego—the
Parent, Adult, and Child—as actual phenomenological realities.
You can look in the phone book and get the Parent and probably
you can get the Child from the phone book also. In other words, a
Child living in a home lives with Parents in a house, and you can
look in a phonebook and find the phone number of the Parent and
reach the Child. The thing is that in the Freudian concept of superego you can't find the superego in the phone book. They are
abstractions. Berne used to say that these ego states are realities.
You can actually see them. He took them from group therapy and
found out that people can come on and respond in these three
different ways. So if you're going to use it, how do you tell which is
which?

Well, the Child or the Parent might say something is awful,
where the Adult would say it's unfortunate. The Adults computer-
ize their logic and are able to figure things out.

Brother: By contamination you mean that Child and Parent are
          trying to interrupt the thought?
Doctor: It's not contaminated by other parts of the personality.

You see the circle is around the Parent, Adult, and Child; sometimes the Child and the Adult can override, so that this portion of
the Adult is confused and can't think logically. So, one way to tell
the difference between Parent and Child is, Did the Parent, did
your mother or father actually say that? Did you do that as a child
or didn't you? Did you want to do that as a child? Are you making

an objective appraisal of reality? That would be Adult. One way to tell is by history, Did you do that, or did they do that. The other way is voice tone. If you listen to yourself you will hear different voice tones.

Brother: When I'm in a childish mood I have kinda a squeaky voice.
Doctor: Childlike. You said childish.
Brother: When I'm in a Parentlike mood, I'm ready to chew up my sister. Doesn't that mean because my mother chewed me up first?
Doctor: Yes.

So we have history, voice tone, and posture, so you can tell when different parts are plugged in. Somebody saying you'd better do that and wagging a forefinger, that's Parent; and somebody jumping up and down saying well, whoopee, that's Child. Somebody talking with a relatively level head can be considered Adult. The most important way to tell the difference is the vocabulary. So that what words are used or actually transacted, that's more important. If Parent knows what's right and wrong, then you should, you must, you have to, you've got to, you're supposed to, you better, don't do that, stop it, etc.

Brother: That's like in my German class. We're learning all those phrases.

You see the Child would say I should, I must, I have to, I ought to, whereas the strong You is usually Parent unless it's a mocking Child state—like, aren't you supposed to do it this way? That would be Child. Since the Adult is a computer, any thing that sounds computerlike ccʻld be Adult, really meaning being correct or incorrect. So if the Parent and the Child get mad and the Adult doesn't and the Child and the Parent can say it's awful, the Adult would say it's unfortunate. What other words might be considered

Adult? Words like worthwhile, practical, feasible, workable, sensible, desirable could be considered Adult.

Now suppose I say to you, "What time is it?" and you say back to me, "The time is 4:30." That's a stimulus and a response. That is, something is exchanged between the two different ego states. This is a transaction (see Figure 8).

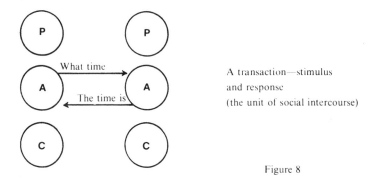

A transaction—stimulus and response (the unit of social intercourse)

Figure 8

Brother: Can there be a transaction between an Adult and a Child?

Doctor: You mean between the same person?

Brother: No. Between... oh yes. How can someone send an Adult response and actually expect to get an Adult Response back?

If you will notice the two arrows in Figure 8, arrow to arrow are parallel; you can have a crossed transaction. For example, a guy says to his wife, with his Adult, asking for information, "Where are my shirts?" She responds with her Critical Parent, "You should know where your shirts are." You notice here that the arrows cross (see Figure 9). The crossed transaction stops the communication on that level. Usually, the Child can be hooked by the Parent's statement like that and then get mad. This leads to the game of Uproar.

Parent to Parent could be a fight, or it could be two old landladies saying how awful juvenile delinquents are. Or Child to Child could be, "Yum, Yum, this ice cream is good." "Yes, it sure is."

The Child is the best part of you. You can't have any fun without your Child. It's also the part that is most mixed up. You can't solve

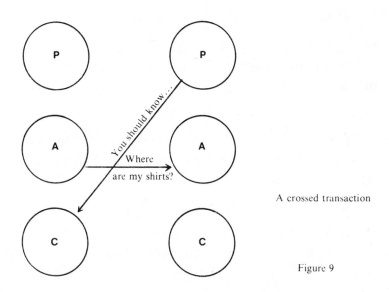

A crossed transaction

Figure 9

logical problems without an Adult, and you can't raise kids very easily without a Parent, because it's actually been shown that a Parent ego state just doesn't know what to say if the Parent died say, when a child is fourteen. However, when you're raising your kids you probably wouldn't know what to do from your Parent ego state after age fourteen anyway. The Parent comes from the actual parents.

Brother: Don't say that, I'm fourteen today.
Doctor: You are.
Brother: Today is my birthday.
Doctor: Happy Birthday. I'll try and get a Child goodie for you.
Brother: Junk!

Let's see now, we have transaction on a parallel, we have a crossed transaction, we have complementary or parallel. So we get into a transaction that makes it a little more complex, which you probably already know. The Parent part has a Nurturing Parent

and a Critical Parent. And the Child has an Adapted Child and a
Natural Child.

Brother: Is there something like quite a few adaptations or just one
          adaptation just the full thing?
Doctor: No, there'd be a lot because the Critical Parent says a lot
          of things.

The Adapted Child does what the Parent wants him to basically
or has some reaction to what the Critical Parent says. If the Critical
Parent says, "Sit down and keep still," usually it is a compliant
Adapted Child that will do that. The Nurturing Parent hugs and
gives positive encouragement. The Natural Child just has fun and
doesn't really care what the Critical Parent says. I think that in the
Games People Play book Eric Berne uses the example of a Nurturing Parent with a Child who is having a fever; the parent brings a
glass of water to the child.

Now, these transactions we are talking about between Adult and
Adult meet a certain need for a person. That is, a person needs to
be stimulated or recognized, and these transactions do that, so do
speak. They stroke the other person. They are positive and negative
strokes. Like, "I like you" is a positive stroke; and slap is a negative
stroke. The strokes are actually used as the words stroke because
you can usually tell how people would treat a baby if you listen to
them talk. You can listen with your Child and figure that out. It's
the Natural Child that's creative, intuitive, and spontaneous.

The id, or unconscious wishes—that is, certain primitive things
that are sexual—are, according to Freud, a seething cauldron of
wishes, like a boiling pot. Whereas somebody's actual Child, if it
tends to be Child part, if it tends to be age four, will have a behavior
and a set of feelings that would reproduce what would have
happened at age four. That's why it's called the Child. The Child
part can vary in age; it can return to earlier feelings or it can feel
relatively adolescent in feelings.

The next thing that I feel is useful is the time structuring, and
then after that script or life planning injunctions. TA moves from

structural analysis of Parent, Adult, and Child to transactional analysis, which is the actual transaction that goes back and forth between ego stages, game analysis, and script analysis. It doesn't always go orderly, in that way. Anyway, if you want to talk about time structuring, there are only a few different ways that you can structure time. Entertainers are paid a lot to help people structure time. But the first way of structuring time would be a ritual. That goes like, "Hi," "Hi," "How are you?" "Fine, how are you?" "Fine." "Good-bye." "Good-bye," in which two people haven't really said anything to each other that is meaningful, but they feel better because they stroked each other. So, if you said, "Hi," to somebody and they did not say "Hi" back, you'd wonder whether they were mad at you. Then, there's an activity. That means programming external reality, and the best example of that is work. You can withdraw—that is, not transact with anybody else and still have transactions in your head. Your Parent could be talking to your Child as in, "You should not feel pain." That would be a Parent and Child in your head transaction. Pastimes, which mean activity structured around certain fields of interest—like sports cars, swimming, horseback riding, and stuff like that. These are pastimes. It doesn't mean that an Adult can't enjoy them, but you're no good at a party without pastimes.

Brother: Pastimes, is that what you have before games?
Sister: Or is it like having—
Doctor: No it's small talk.

If you've ever been to a party, people will talk about sports cars and something like that. They are trying to feel the other person out. The Child part is going to see if they are structured around the field of material you know like General Motors. I like Ford better than a Chevie. Complete this in twenty-five words or less.

Sister: What about reincarnation? What happens to your Parent, Adult, and Child if you've been reincarnated?
Doctor: That's an unanswerable question. No one knows.

Sister: But what about reincarnation?

Doctor: That's an unanswerable question. I'd prefer not to talk about that right now. Is that okay?

The next way to spend time is intimacy, and that means a candid Natural Child to Natural Child, or Adult to Adult exposure of the Child's feelings. What intimacy means is game-free behavior. So that leads us to, What's a game? Kick Me is a game. That means somebody provokes the other person to get mad, and then they get mad when the other person boots them.

In order to be a game, it doesn't mean it's silly because it's a game. People can get killed with games. A game has to have two things: It has to have an ulterior transaction, and it has to have a payoff. So, if we draw two people here and they are going to play a game, we draw their Parent, Adult, and Child parts (see Figure 10). Let's see what would be a game and what wouldn't be. Suppose, on the social level the Adult to Adult transaction would appear to be coming forth. Suppose Joe says to Mary, "I've got a terrible problem. I've got a bunion on my foot and I don't know what to do

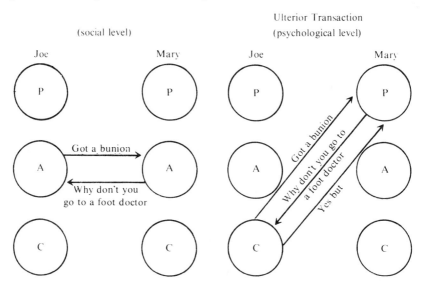

Figure 10

about it." Mary says, "Why don't you go to a foot doctor?" That sounds sensible as it sounds Adult. She is giving him a gimmick. The con is that he's got a terrible problem. So that the reaction is, "Yes, but, I've already been to a foot doctor." "Then why don't you go to a surgeon?" "Well, yeah, but I've already been to a surgeon." That keeps on, on that level. What the meaningful level of this, the psychological level really, is Critical Parent to Adapted Child, so that the psychological level here is the meaningful level. That is the ulterior transaction.

Sister: What would it mean if Mary were to say, "What do you want me to do about it?"

Doctor: Yeah. That's Adult.

Brother: That depends on the voice. What would you do if—I went up to my mother one time and she was really hurting and I said I had a hurt toe and it was in a cast and she said, "What the hell do you want me to do about it?" That would be a Parent wouldn't it?

Doctor: Yeah. That's Critical Parent.

If someone said planning, "I've got a terrible problem, I've got a bunion on my foot," and you went back at them with your Adult, like, "What are you going to do about it?" I mean neutral, not Critical, and not excited or laughing or crying like a child. But what are you going to do about it. That would send an Adult Stimulus and hook their Adult, hopefully, and make them think about what they're going to do about it. Because there is also a payoff here. The Yes But fights off and the payoff up here for Mary is, "People are ungrateful for my help."

You see, "I'm only trying to help" is a game that for most people says, "Why don't you?" "Why don't you" is a suggestion, not a question. If you said, "Why haven't you gone to a foot doctor?" that's Adult. So there's a payoff, and there's an ulterior transaction, so that is a game. Suppose it was the other way around, and Joe said, "I've got a bunion on my foot," and the response was, "I know a foot doctor on Foothill, would you like to go to him?"

Again, that is a request. There is a game formula which goes like this. There's a con that "I've got a terrible problem, I've got a bunion on my foot"; plus a gimmick, which is, "Why don't you go to a foot doctor?"; leading to a switch, "Yes but, I've already been to a foot doctor"; leading to a payoff, which is, "No Parent can tell me anything" on the part of the persons whose Child is plugged in; and "People are ungrateful," which is the payoff for the Parent. These payoffs leads to certain feelings, like the person who gets a payoff with people who are ungrateful for my help. They get an unpleasant feeling or Racket. What happens as a result in the collection of the payoff is a collection of an unpleasant feeling, like fear, hurt, guilt, anger, anxiety, shame, disgust. Here people are ungrateful. Mary is "only trying to help" winds up feeling disappointment so she is in the disappointment racket. The person who winds up with their Child part saying, "No Parent can tell me anything," winds up with "You can't make me submit," and "I'm not going to submit." So what happens here is that these games advance the script. The script means a life plan, like kill yourself at age fifty; or be a doctor, or a lawyer, or be a businessman, businesswomen; or it could be like kill somebody else. People take certain life positions like they're okay or they're not okay, and this resides in the Adapted Child. That position tends to get reinforced by the games. In other words, if you play Kick Me, you're going to get to feeling Not OK because you are going to get booted by your mom, and then you're going to feel mad and disgusted and hurt; but largely anger is your payoff.

Have you seen a script matrix? Do you want to try this? If you draw your own Parent, Adult, and Child out on a chart and that's you, and you put a pen around you and take your two parents and their Parent, Adult, and Child, you can figure out part of the script by what messages they're actually giving. Like in the case of an alcoholic, usually both parents will say, "Don't drink"; and the hooker is that strokes from Child to Child, that is, from your actual mother's and father's Child part are about ten to twenty times stronger than the antiscript, or counterscript, messages, "Don't drink" (see Figure 11). In other words, the mother might really be

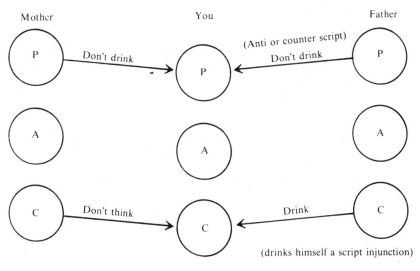

Figure 11

saying to you, "Don't drink." (Your mother doesn't do that, but an alcoholic's mother might.) And father then might show you how, by actually drinking himself. In other words, the Child thing to identify with is the actual drinking to solve the problems. The script message is from here to here—that is, the Child part of the parent going to your actual Child part. Okay? So this is a script Matrix. There are a number of negative injunctions that can occur from the Adapted Child like, "Don't be," "Don't exist," "Don't have sex," "Don't have fun." They are all negative injunctions and they are powerful. So that's a script matrix. Any questions?

Brother: No. That's like you're in the middle of it, and they are telling you what not to do and...
Doctor: Who is?
Brother: Your Parents.
Doctor: Telling you what not to do about what?
Brother: About anything that they don't want you to do.
Sister: Like what happens if there are two different opinions.

Doctor: Two different what?

Brother: Opinions. Like when one parent says, "Do...."

Sister: And the other parent says "Don't...."

Doctor: Then the Child is in trouble. If the two parents disagree on their Critical Parent part, they may be fighting through the Child.

Brother: Yeah.

Doctor: It would be "Pony Express." Like mom says, "Go tell your father this," and your father says, "Go tell your mother this." That's called Pony Express. Remember, games advance the script. Okay, That's it for today.

CHAPTER   2

Using TA Concepts
with Other
Therapy Methods

Many practitioners in the helping professions have already received training in family systems therapy of one kind or another or have completed the traditional program for psychoanalysts. How can the fundamental concepts of Transactional Analysis supplement and amplify these other therapy approaches?

Transactional Analysis and family systems therapy share some basic premises. Both voice a strong predilection to working in the here and now. Of primary importance is an awareness of what is happening in the real world of the patient today. Both also deemphasize the delving into the childhood of patients. A total replay of early experiences does not play a primary role in either therapy. And finally, both approaches also favor a short-term intervention by the therapist. The therapeutic experience is usually envisioned as taking weeks or months, but not years. Families normally enter either of these therapists as a result of the referral of a child who is said to "have" or "be" a problem.

Within the field of family systems therapy there are several distinct groups, each with their own view of the family and their own style of therapy. Salvador Minuchin, with his analysis of family structures, and Virginia Satir, with her identification of communication patterns, are two of the acknowledged leaders in the family systems movement, and we will be looking at some ways that TA ideas can be added to or used along with their key concepts to further enhance the therapeutic possibilities. In doing this, we are giving the reader a pattern that may then be applied to any other family systems therapeutic method. I believe that the vocabulary of TA and its concepts can be added to those of other therapies to further clarify what's happening in the lives of patients and open the way to the consideration of more satisfying options.

TA AND THE FAMILY STRUCTURES APPROACH

Salvador Minuchin, the acknowledged leader in the family structures sector of family systems therapy, is given credit for identifying and labeling the two-person grouping within the family as *subsystems*; for picking out and describing the divisions between such subsystems as *boundaries,* and for noting the temporary alliances in which an action from one may pass through another on its way to a third person as *detouring.* These key concepts are those that we will discuss and relate to the general principles of TA.

To be sure, Dr. Minuchin in his book, *Families and Family Therapy* (1974), has a great deal to say about normal families, too. He describes how families change as they pass through developmental stages, gives examples of episodes in distressed families, and shares clinical techniques that the therapist may use in working with family groups. It is important reading for anyone entering this field.

First, let's consider *subsystems.* According to Dr. Minuchin, a subsystem may be formed in a family when two or more members join forces for any reason. These subsystems may be mother-father, child-child, or parent-child. Such pairing, or groupings, are formed on the basis of generation as in parent-parent, or sex as in mother-daughter, or by activity like kite-maker (father) with kite flyer (daughter). We can describe this graphically by using some PAC diagrams (see Figure 1).

Sometimes a subsystem gets together only occasionally for a specific task such as repairing a bicycle. Or, such groupings may be more or less constant through many different activities, as in the case of two close-age siblings who sleep, play, and attend nursery school together.

The division between the subsystem within a family Minuchin calls *boundaries.* These boundaries tell who participates in a subsystem and what it is that they do. When these dividing lines aren't clearly understood, problems arise. In a subsystem of mother-son involved with bicycle repair, the attempt of two-year-old Jenny to join the subsystem will bring about firm redefinition of its boundaries!

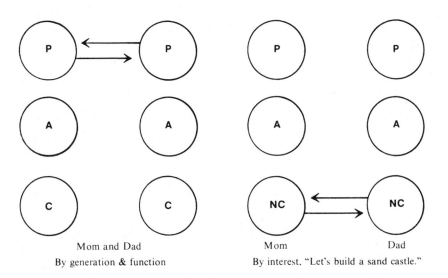

Mom and Dad
By generation & function

Mom   Dad
By interest. "Let's build a sand castle."

Figure 1

The concept of boundaries between family systems within a fully functioning family can be shown with the diagram in Figure 2. Notice that these possible transactions are parallel and therefore complementary. Thus, they can proceed indefinitely.

Sometimes, however, the subsystem of mother-child becomes a constant one, day in and day out through a variety of activities, rather than a transient one related to short-term functions. The boundary of their subsystem may then be termed *rigid*, and we view them as being locked into a partnership.

This statement might certainly have been made to describe the subsystem formed by Phil Rathrone and his mother Diane (chapter 5). When a rigid boundary is erected, the others in the family, in this case the father, become *disengaged*. Using the theories of Transactional Analysis, we may talk about how this boundary problem got started, how each member of the family is keeping it going, and what their options are for cutting it off, thereby freeing them to move on into other relationships with each other. This situation may be shown via the diagram in Figure 3.

Detouring, Dr. Minuchin's third key concept, identifies what happens when a conflict between two family members is fought through a third person. Transactionsl Analysis calls this a Game, "Let's You and Him Fight" (see Figure 4). We will see this happening in the Wallace family (chapter 5).

Another version of detouring is found in the case of the child who goads his or her parents into fighting with each other to escape being *Blemished* (Berne 1964) by one or the other of them. The game of Blemish is finding faults with another person. Figure 5 diagrams this process.

This is the way it happened in the Alexander family: The father, Gus, and the mother, Ruth, both had very strong vocal Critical Parents, but it was Gus who particularly relished a good round of Blemish. He played with anyone who was available, but his favorite co-player was their seven-year-old-son, Tim. When I met him, I learned that Tim had never played easily with other children and now in second grade was frequently the center of class disturbances. Gus never missed an opportunity to correct or call attention

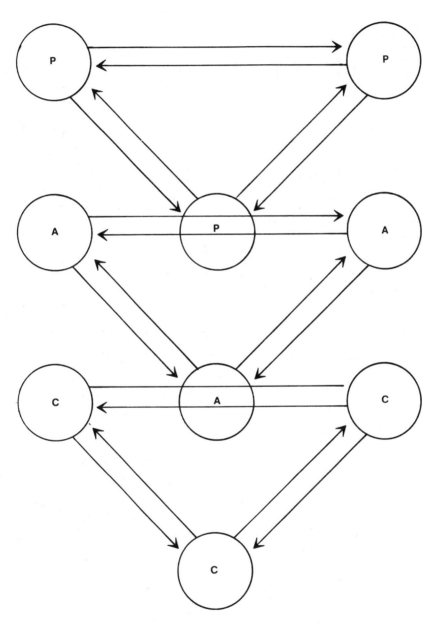

Figure 2

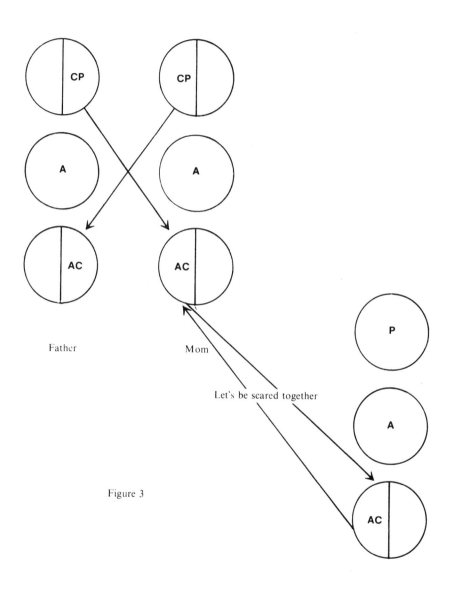

Figure 3

Figure 4

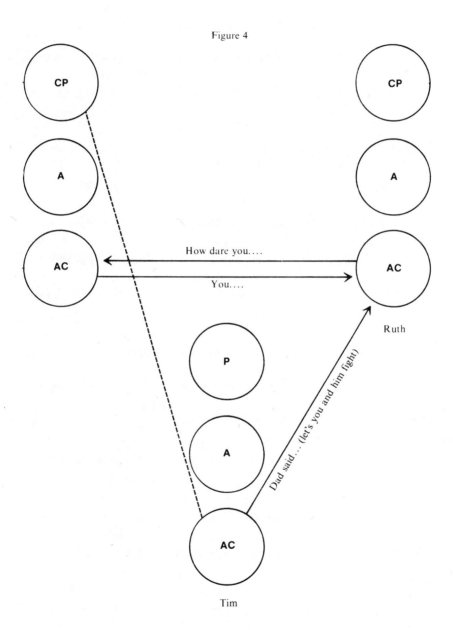

to his behavior, and Tim spent more and more time playing alone in his room. However, he couldn't keep out of sight all the time, but he did discover that it was safe for him to be in the presence of mom and dad when they were fighting with each other. No one bothered to Blemish him then. To insure parent fighting, he made a point of repeating to Ruth some version of an earlier real or imaginary conversation with his father in which Gus stated an opinion known to be different from Ruth's or something similar that would guarantee her attack. He might also use the same tactic in reverse when alone with his father. When he did this, he could rest assured that for the next several hours it would be safe to wander through the house unmolested, as Gus and Ruth would be too busy fighting between themselves to notice him.

The situation in the Alexander family is another example of detouring because Tim is routing his anger toward his father through his mother and vice versa as well. Since he is a young child and less powerful than the adult parents in his family, this process serves him well in discharging the anger he feels but is impotent to adequately express.

In the case of Mark and Emily Wagner in *Families and Family Therapy* (Minuchin 1974), Mark and Emily considered themselves a normal family and were interviewed as such. Minuchin did uncover some difficulties they had experienced in establishing the boundary of their new family. In discussing Emily's earlier life at home, the alliance between Emily and her mother came to light. It seems that this alliance was used by her mother to detour her own anger toward the father through Emily letting Emily's voice show anger.

Emily began smoking at age fourteen and was allowed to smoke openly in front of her mother, although her father had expressly forbidden such behavior until she would turn sixteen. There were apparently many times when her mother covered for Emily's action when these acts were in violation of father's rules. In return, Emily talked rudely to her father until she saw that he had become thoroughly upset. When she was fifteen, he became angry enough to strike her one or two times.

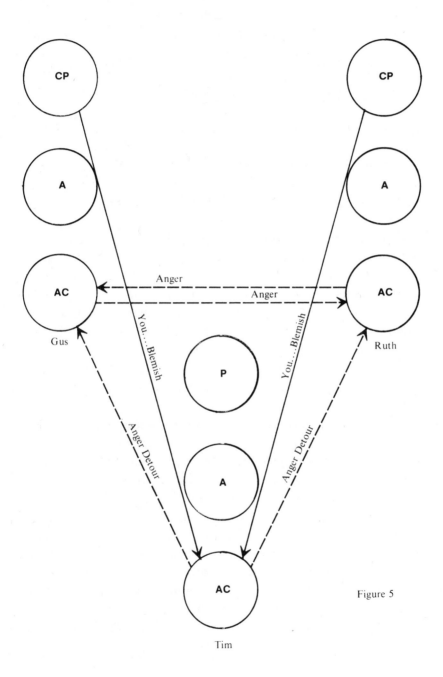

Figure 5

As Dr. Minuchin viewed Emily's family of origin, he saw that the normal husband-wife conflicts spilled over into the arena of parenting. "Parental authority was split and each parent attacked the other spouse through their daughter. The mother encouraged her to disobey the father; the father attacked her when he was angry at his wife" (Minuchin 1974).

Looking at the same family situation with the labels of TA, we might see the following: Mother's Adapted Child making a temporary deal with Emily's Adapted Child who then does the thing mother would like to do in defiance of father. The latter act hooks Father's Critical Parent, who then rages and storms at Emily's Child.

It may be further presumed that Emily is playing Kick Me to her father's game of NIGYYSOB. She is collecting anger stamps which she can turn in on a free blow up at her father later. This picture also shows a mother and father who may be avoiding sex or intimacy by playing a version of Uproar (Berne 1964) through Emily. The Parent messages coming to Emily say something like "be a lady, behave properly." However, the scripting coming from the mother's Adapted Child is obviously in conflict with that. It might be "Do whatever you like, but make sure they don't find out!"

In this particular case, Emily escaped the transactions with her parents when she married Mark. As noted, they considered themselves a "normal" couple and had in fact made some specific behavioral changes with the help of a marriage counselor to avoid a replay of this same act in their own family.

The use of the PAC diagram to show graphically what happens when a subsystem is formed, a boundary erected, or a detour effected gives therapist and patient a clear visual picture of what is going on. The addition of the game theory to the concept of detouring helps focus attention on why an individual uses the detouring technique and also what might be used instead to achieve more generally satisfying results. Thus, these TA principles can be used to complement the family structures concepts of subsystems, boundaries, and detouring.

TA AND THE FAMILY COMMUNICATIONS APPROACH

In recent years, many people have studied and commented on the importance of patterns of speech between family members, but Virginia Satir is perhaps one of the most highly regarded authorities in this sector of family therapy. *Conjoint Family Therapy* (1964), *People Making*, and her other book contain much of value to the family therapist. Ms. Satir's key concepts regarding communication are *congruent* and *incongruent* communication (1964). We will consider how these concepts relate to TA.

When writing of communication between people in the revised edition of *Conjoint Family Therapy* (1967), Ms. Satir is referring to the words the speaker chooses to express his or her ideas, the non-verbal clues that accompany it, and any other words that the speaker uses to modify the message. These latter modifying messages may tell more about the literal message or about the relationship between the speaker and listener.

In the case of *congruent* communication, all the messages, whether they are verbal, nonverbal, or verbal motifying, more or less agree. There is no real contradiction between the speaker's literal message and his or her body posture, for example, or facial expression or tone of voice. On the other hand, if a communication is *incongruent,* one or more of the accompanying messages seriously contracts another. Thus, the speaker may say, "Of course, I want to go to the movies tonight," with downcast eyes, drooping shoulders, and a dull tone of voice. All the nonverbal clues suggest that going to the movies is the last thing on earth the speaker would choose to do, yet the literal meaning of the message affirms the opposite. The two messages don't agree; they are incongruent.

Let's consider first the speaker's choice of words, or the semantics of the communication, and see how this fits with the Transactional Analysis view. Ms. Satir divides speakers into those she says are *functional* communicators and those who are *dysfunctional* communicators. An example of a functional communicator is one who when asked to clarify an earlier statement says, "That's the way I see it. Perhaps you don't share my view. How does it appear to you?'' The language used here clearly reflects and Adult ego state.

When a dysfunctional communicator is asked the same question, he or she respond, ''That simply is the wrong thing to do. You know quite well what I'm driving at,'' or something similar. These responses suggest the Critical Parent ego state. Thus, the notion of a functional communicator and a dysfunctional one could be shown via the PAC diagrams in Figure 6.

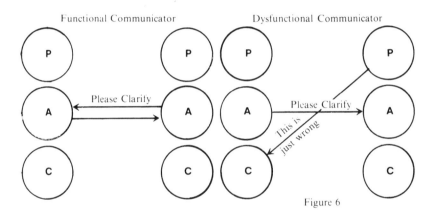

Figure 6

Functional communicators may, of course, speak from any of the three ego states, Parent to Parent, Adult to Adult, or Child to Child (see Figure 7). Dysfunctional communicators may also use all three ego states, but their transactions will usually be crossed. Thus, a Parent remark might be answered with an Adapted Child response, or an Adult remark might yield a Critical Parent rejoinder and so forth.

For example, a person says, ''The newspaper is on the porch.'' It sounds like a piece of data, doesn't it? It might be coming from the Adult ego state, but, it was said in an irritable tone of voice. What then? A dysfunctional communicator when asked a similar question might choose from several possible responses, among them,

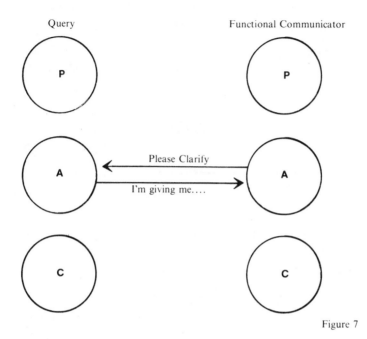

Figure 7

"You know perfectly well what I mean." As I said, "women are...." "That picture is not only ugly, it is positively revolting." "Why get so picky?" All of these responses suggest the Critical Parent ego state. Thus, the notion of a functional communicator and a dysfunctional one could be shown via the PAC diagram in Figure 8. The latter is, of course, in TA language, a *crossed transaction*.

Now, let's look at the notion of *metacommunication,* or the incongruency of nonverbal messages and see how TA relates to it. The term *metacommunication* is a broad one and includes all those qualifying phrases and gestures that go with ordinary speech—the friendly smile with a warm greeting, the angry glare with an explosive epithet, and the like. The metacommunication that is significant therapeutically, however, goes beyond the spoken word or differs in some way from it. It might look like the diagram in Figure 9.

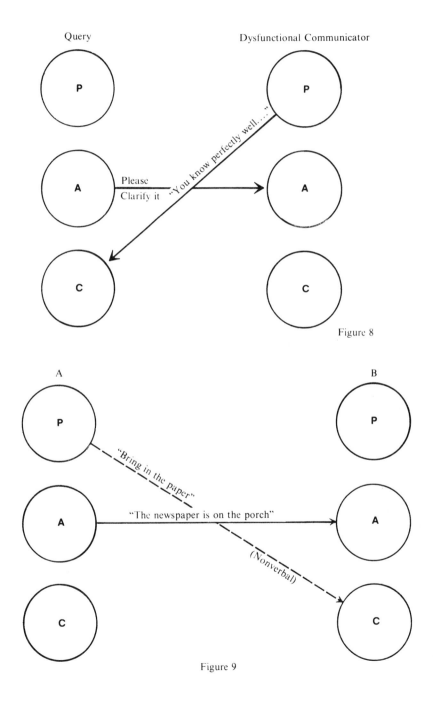

Figure 8

Figure 9

Person B in the situation diagramed in Figure 9 now has a choice. How to respond? Will the Adapted Child be hooked with this veiled Critical Parent message? or will the Adult choose to disregard it and respond directly?

Messages between family members that leave the receiver wondering what's going on and how on earth to respond may then be semantically unclear and may also carry with them metacommunications that are confusing or contradictory. This kind of communication then can be called incongruent or dysfunctional. The sender of such messages is, for one reason or another, deliberately making it hard for the receiver to respond and particularly hard for the receiver to respond in the way the sender wants him or her to. In other words, the sender chooses the message to insure a negative stroke payoff or another trading stamp of whatever variety he or she is collecting. For example, an incongruent dialogue between husband and wife about going to the park can be diagramed as shown in Figure 10. On the literal level it sounds like her Nurturing

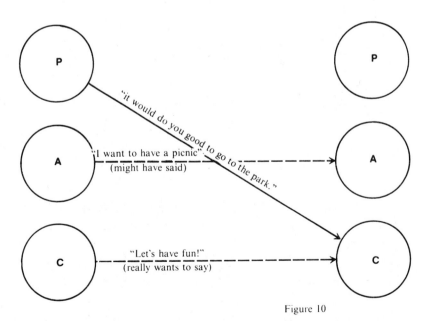

Figure 10

Parent, thinking of his well-being, is suggesting an outing. She doesn't tell him how she feels about going on a picnic but the two other messages are distinct possibilities.

Ms. Satir suggests that the husband then needs to check out with the wife what it is she does mean. He might then say, "Do you want to go to the park?" Now, this seems to be a straight Adult to Adult question and would often produce a straight Adult response, "Yes" or "No." However, the wife in this example is a dysfunctional communicator, and she responds, "No, I just thought we should" (see Figure 11).

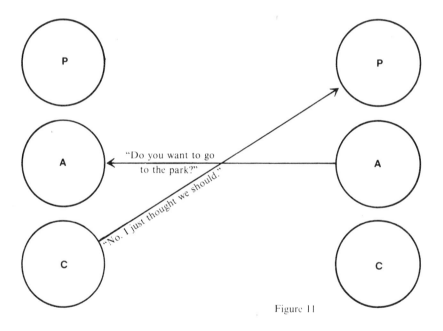

Figure 11

What happened here? At the outset of this conversation the wife wanted to go on a picnic. Incongruent communication does not then pass data clearly back and forth between the two people. It rather is an exchange of words that seems to end in a feeling exchange rather than in any action, at least not an action described by the words. The wife in this example can collect some more persecuted feelings as again she will not get to have any fun. But, the husband here responded in a fully functional way. Where did it go astray?

Let's look again at that from the wife's point of view. The Adapted Child of the wife has expanded and completely decommissioned the Adult. Thus, when the husband queries her Adult to Adult, his message is not received. Instead, she picks up his words as though they came from his Parent to her Child, and her response then is thus to his Parent (see Figure 12).

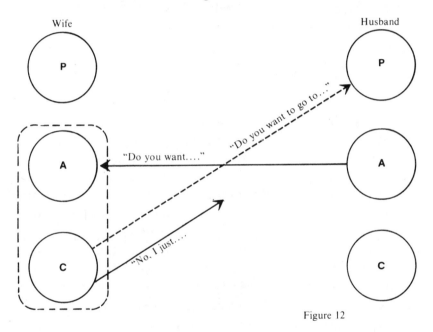

Figure 12

If the couple, just discussed, were in therapy we might analyze further their transactions or communications and learn a great deal about their relationship. However, simply working with this example and these diagrams, aren't the options obvious? Isn't it easy to see exactly what is going on? Isn't it apparent how such simple diagrams can be used to further clarify the relationships between people?

The preceding discussion suggests some ways the theories of Transactional Analysis can be used to amplify and depict graphically certain key ideas in family therapy developed by Dr. Minuchin and Ms. Satir. Of course, similar examples might be written to accompany the work of Ackerman, Whitaker, Pittman, or any of the several dozen leaders in this field. Perhaps, some diagram can be used to illustrate specific concepts considered particularly helpful in yet another therapy school. Taken together and used thoughtfully, these different views of how family relationships work can enhance the effectiveness of those working with troubled families. And a way to help distressed people move into less painful, more growth-oriented roles is, after all, what you and I are looking for, isn't it?

TA AND THE PSYCHOANALYTIC APPROACH

Although Transactional Analysis and psychoanalysis are outwardly quite dissimilar in their approach, I nonetheless believe that each can be complementary to the other and enhance the success of the patient's therapeutic experience. My own background and early training was in the psychoanalytic method of therapy, and after nearly fifteen years in family therapy practice I continue to affirm the importance of this training. For those unfamiliar with the principles of psychoanalysis, I recommend reading Ralph R. Greenson's *The Technique and Practice of Psychoanalysis* (1967). It is in very readable prose and provides a thoughtful discussion of this approach. Of course, the collected words of Sigmund Freud, the founder of psychoanalysis, are important reading as well.

By psychoanalysis is meant the process involving one patient and one therapist meeting three to five hours a week for about five years or more. During these meetings, the therapist stays in the Adult ego state, almost always neutral, and sits in a chair behind the patient. The patient assumes a supine position on a couch and has no eye contact with the therapist. The couch is used to induce the patient to return to more childlike feelings and to reexperience early conflict. The patient is encouraged to say everything that is passing through his or her mind, to fully express these Child feelings and conflicts. The goal of psychoanalysis is to bring the patient's unconscious into the conscious. Once in the conscious and verbalized to the therapist, the unresolved feelings and conflicts can be resolved.

Trained individuals working with the psychoanalytic method employ their understanding of a number of psychic mechanisms to further a patient's therapy. Among these are several that are particularly important and will be helpful for those not trained in psychoanalysis to be aware of and to understand. Again, a working knowledge of TA can be used to further amplify each one. Perhaps of foremost importance is an awareness of *defenses*—particularly those associated with *isolation and splitting*. In addition, we will consider *transference,* both *countertransference* and *crossed transference*. It is also important to consider dreams and dream analysis and some additional comments on the traditional diagnostic terms of this approach as they relate to TA.

Over the years my colleague who worked exclusively with psychoanalytic techniques have occasionally chided me, charging that TA is "too superficial and oversimplified." They allege that a patient could spend treatment hours "intellectualizing" and be simply reinforcing the defenses. These defenses are unconscious mechanisms that protect the self from anxiety, guilt, shame, or disgust. I would have to agree that such a scenario certainly can occur during the course of treatment with Transactional Analysis techniques. However, if the therapist is aware of this possibility, there is no reason why a defense need persist or interfere with treatment. An awareness and consideration of patient defenses is essential for anyone working in this field.

Isolation is one defense in which the effect is *separated* from the thought associated with it. It is possible that the Adapted Child can ask questions that sound Adult. When I sense that this is happening, I have several options. One is simply to explain that people often ask questions like that when their Adapted Child part is feeling anxious. I tell the patient that this kind of talk is a protection or defense. The burning question then is, "What is it that your Adapted Child is scared of or anxious about?" And, depending on the history of the patient, I may ask it simply and directly.

There are times, however, when a blunt question like that will only increase the feelings of anxiety in the Adapted Child. Then I choose what I think of as *Child language*—that is, short, simple words, and I avoid all TA or psychiatry terms as we talk.

Thus, when the therapist recognizes that a patient is using the defense of isolation by playing the game of *Psychiatry* during the treatment hour and describes this behavior to the person helping him or her understand its origin and how it works, the door is open to explore the fears and anxieties of that Adapted Child. It is an opportunity to discuss with him or her the fear or loss of self and the fear people have of the power of their own emotions. As mentioned, the self seems to be located within the Adapted Child; therefore, a defense designed to protect the Adapted Child is in fact also protecting the self as well.

The exposing of defenses, then, can be a positive move toward a time when defenses are no longer necessary. Defenses can serve another positive role in therapy, too, by providing a respite or breathing space following a very intense feeling oriented exchange. When people express strong emotions, relive painful scenes, or tap repressed feelings long out of awareness, they may need to drop into "safe" territory for a while. This condition is my cue to draw elaborate diagrams on my chalkboard, introduce hypothetical transactions, and the like. The therapist, then, may initiate or play along with a game of Psychiatry (talking about psychiatric concepts as an academic exercise) even though it is used as a defense, when it occurs following a period of intense interaction.

Again, an awareness of defense is often helpful, as one may be functioning with positive therapeutic value. The therapist may actually strengthen or support such a defense. For example, I once worked with a woman who was very fearful of dependency. She suffered from a peptic ulcer and during the course of therapy underwent a mastectomy. As the time for her surgery approached, she often joked about it and generally denied the gravity of the situation. Following her recovery and return to therapy, she laughingly showed off her "fancy new boob."

In this case, it seemed like a wise idea to support her defenses, so I complimented her and told her she was handling a difficult situation in a very good way. This pleased her and stroked her Child, which was frightened of dependency. My approval reassured the Child that it was acting in an independent and self-sufficient manner.

The play of Psychiatry in the absence of any intense interaction is one form that the defense of isolation may take, but there are others as well. Whenever a patient uses therapy time to talk in vague, intellectual terms about life, people, the times, or even themselves, that person may be using the defense isolation. He or she is isolating the feelings from the thought or ideas. The therapist can effectively respond to this defense in much the same way as suggested for the game of Psychiatry. People can use the structure of PAC to reinforce isolation. For instance, "I think my Child resents that interpretation, Doctor." Here the patient is afraid to be openly angry.

It is the Critical Parent to Adapted Child dialogue in the head that reproduces the actual parent to child relationship from childhood, as shown via the diagram in Figure 13. This Critical Parent injunction would result in an Adapted Child part inhibited to some degree in expressing anger or criticism of other people. Again, the vocabulary and the diagrams of TA serve both patient and therapist

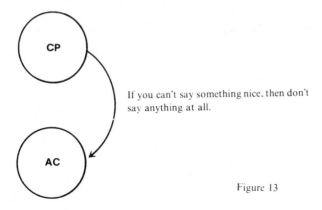

If you can't say something nice, then don't say anything at all.

Figure 13

in clarifying and describing visually the very important mechanism of the defense of isolation as it may be seen in any of several forms.

Psychoanalysis may charge that TA fosters at least one other defense, *splitting.* The defense of splitting involves an inconsistency in the patient's thinking or feelings about a single idea or particular person. It's true that part of the TA theory describing the Parent ego state divides it into two parts, or splits it. Thus, the theory of TA would appear to encourage the defense of splitting or active, separation of introjects (Kernberg 1976).

People who are particularly inclined to use the defense of splitting are those who might also be identified as borderline. Those working in psychoanalysis have for many years divided their patients into three categories—neurotic, borderline, and psychotic. Generally, patients considered *neurotic* are suffering from a serious internal conflict, but their perception of reality is still intact and they function in the real world. At the other end of the spectrum, *psychotic* patients cannot function in the world, have lost touch with reality, and also suffer major internal conflicts. *Borderline* patients still function in the world, but their reality-testing or perception may be, at the time, impaired, and their inner conflicts may be more severe than those of the neurotic individual. Thus, counselors and others in the helping professions often encounter people who might be labeled neurotic or borderline and may work with those individuals in the therapeutic situations. Truly regressed psychotic patients probably will require hospitalization and treatment by a psychiatrist, or they may receive care from a family therapist to avoid hospitalization.

To understand something of how this mechanism of splitting might occur, we need to consider again the two aspects of Parent ego state and the two or more aspects of real parents. As part of the normal part of growing up, the emerging adult in our culture recognizes that his or her real parents did good things and bad things in the process of parenting, but that both the good and bad stemmed from the same person. Mommy was nice sometimes and other times not so nice, but Mommy was still always Mommy. Some new adults are able to feel that Mommy can be an Adult friend even though she wasn't an ideal Mommy, and others decide that they never want to see Mommy again. In either case, there is no doubt that Mommy has two or more sides to her nature.

In Transactional Analysis, we ask people to consciously consider their own Parent ego states in two parts: Nurturing Parent and Critical Parent. Further, we talk about the real parent as having both a nurturing component and a critical one. For the borderline person who is having difficulty integrating the different parts of the real parent, this may represent an "out" or an excuse to continue splitting the Parent. The therapist might hold that suspicion when a patient persists in dividing the Parent, particularly at inappropriate times. We need to remind patients that the Adapted Child is dependent on receiving the same message that it always has from the internal Nurturing Parent and Critical Parent in order to maintain it's identity and to prevent diffusion of self.

In such a case, I might say, "I think you're afraid to keep your Parent ego state as one mass because if you look at it as a whole ego state your Child would be upset. It wouldn't know if it felt good or not good." Again, the aim of the therapist is to find out what the Child is afraid of.

As the patient comes to understand the how and why of this defense, he or she can use the awareness of the Nurturing Parent to promote feeling good; that is, an individual can call upon the internal Nurturing Parent to stroke the Adapted Child. This move reduces the need to attract Nurturing Parent strokes from others and leads to the possibility of more OK behavior and feelings. There are, of course, other identifiable defenses, but the general pattern will be the same.

A defense may also be spotted because it is somehow inappropriate or incongruent. Thus, if a patient has talked about the present and suddenly switches to talking about the past and continues to remain in the past, he or she may be using a defense. Once a therapist recognizes a defense for what it is, he or she can evaluate the situation and decide whether to support it for the moment, move toward more patient understanding of what is taking place, intervene with Child-hooking language, or analyze the defense in some other way to help the patient identify the fears of his or her Adapted Child.

Other psychoanalytic friends accustomed to working with the process of *transference* have expressed their doubts that Transactional Analysis can really cure people, since TA does not appear to acknowledge this process. By transference, using Greenson's definition (1967), is meant the process by which a person experiences feelings, attitudes, defenses, fantasies, and drives toward a person in the present that don't fit him or her but are instead really a replay of reactions originating in regard to significant persons of early childhood. When a psychoanalytic therapist works with an individual patient the patient is allowed to transfer to the therapist all those feelings from the past and deal with them in the present. The therapist working with families and employing TA methods doesn't specifically elicit transference, but it happens nonetheless as does countertransference and crossed Child to Parent transactions. The use of PAC diagrams is helpful in visualizing how this occurs. For example, a patient can react Parent to the therapist's Child: "Doctor, you're not taking care of yourself."

Transference is a reaction that some people have, wherever they are, without knowing it. I worked with a family once in which the mother had a particularly low opinion of men based on a low opinion of her father. She said to me, "You men are all alike. None of you are worth much. All you have on your minds is sex!" This case was a classic example of transference. Mom transferred her dislike of her father onto me, the male therapist (see Figure 14). Later she used Jimmy, age ten, as an excuse to end the relationship. A woman like this probably transferred her feelings about her father in the past onto any slightly older man she encountered anywhere in the present.

In working with couples, we can observe and work with crossed transference (see Figure 15). A husband almost always transfers to his wife most of the unresolved feelings he has about his mother, and, in turn, the wife transfers her residual feelings about dad onto him. We will see this in the case of the Hoffers (chapter 6). It enters

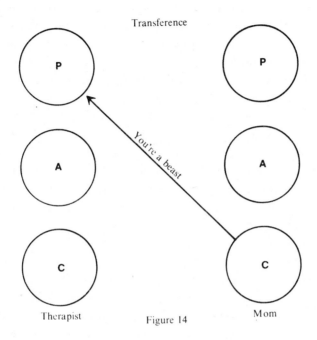

Transference

You're a beast

Therapist Figure 14 Mom

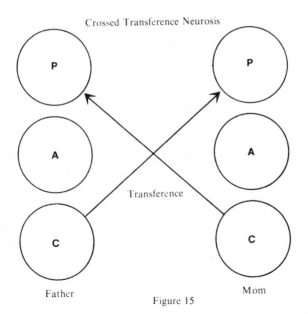

Crossed Transference Neurosis

Transference

Father Mom
Figure 15

into the mate-selecting process, of course, as people select mates on whom they can transfer these feelings.

In my office, a husband may actually behave toward his wife in the same way he, as a child, behaved toward his mother, or wanted to behave towards her. We can also observe in a wife's behavior toward her spouse a replay of her earlier life with father. This result is another added bonus of working with couples rather than individuals. The transference already exists between spouses; all we need to do in therapy is observe or identify it and analyze what is happening. With individual patients, it may take more time to establish a transference.

An important factor, then, in resolving a couple's dilemma is the unraveling of this crossed transference, each spouse getting free of the left over bad feelings about the opposite sex parent. These leftover bad feelings must go, as they get in the way of intimacy for the couple. If Betty is transferring some anger originally felt toward Dad, who ran away with his secretary and never validated her as a woman, onto David her husband, that anger will cloud her response to him. David will be unable to clear himself, even though he is existing in the present and stands fully ready to acknowledge and approve of her womanness.

In a sense, this is another view of the process of integrating that bad mommy and good mommy to create one person who can then be an older friend or not—but in either case a whole being. This process of integration of the Parent may come to people in different ways. Often its genesis is unknown, it simply emerges into the consciousness one day. But, there are times that are especially favorable for progress in that direction; one such time is when a couple is uncovering their scripts and script injunctions.

Countertransference or the emotional reaction of the therapist to the patient that is in some ways similar to the parent of the past may occur when the therapist uses his or her Parent to give a patient permission or protection. However, this behavior is not unconscious. The therapist chooses deliberately when and how he or she will assume this role of parent. Knowing what is transference is useful to TA therapists.

The psychoanalytic tradition emphasizes the importance of dream analysis, and this area should not be overlooked by those working in TA. There is no doubt that dreams, particularly those remembered later during the day, are important. They tell us what the Child part is up to. From dreams we find out what it is that the Child really wants or what the Child is most afraid of.

Sometimes the Parent is so severe it won't let the Child have a dream. When a patient reports, "Oh, I never dream," I suspect that this statement is true, and I usually share my thoughts with the person. Together, we may find a way to get the Parent to let up on the Child and allow dreams to appear and not be made unconscious so quickly. This process reduces the need to repress—that is, to make feelings and thoughts unconscious. Although Transactional Analysis may appear to be concerned largely with activities in the real world, material from dreams and the unconscious also play an important role. The material we examine in working out life scripts probably also comes from the subconscious.

Therapist accustomed to working only in the psychoanalytic field may wonder how the familiar standard diagnoses translate into Transactional Analysis. Let's look at some of them.

Hysterical and phobic reaction. Hysterical and phobic individuals usually play the game of Rapo. They are seductive, in an attempt to reassure themselves that they're not afraid of being seductive. This may also be considered a fear of being seductive with the Adapted Child. Usually, they are partially fixated on the oedipal phase, or hung up at being afraid of and yet wanting genital activity.

Depression. The payoff among those involved in the anger or guilt racket is depression. There is a strong Not OK feeling in the Adapted Child usually reinforced by both the internal Critical Parent and the Critical Parent of the spouse.

A woman came to my office one day complaining of depression, and when I asked her if she had been treated for depression at any other time in her life, she ran down a long list of therapeutic experiences. After concluding her list of psychiatrists, hospitalizations, and electric shock treatments, she said, "Oh, doctor, I've tried everything! What else can I do?" "Well," I replied, "have you tried Draino?" She then laughed with her Natural Child, and I then knew I could talk to her Adult.

Depression is essentially a dialogue between the Critical Parent and the Adapted Child. Usually, the Critical Parent is saying such Not OK producing messages as, "There you go again," "You're a failure," "You have no character," or "See there, you failed again." The Adapted Child part responds by feeling Not OK. Sometimes the Adult can be aware of the dialogue, and sometimes the Child is so depressed by influence from the Critical Parent that there is no dialogue.

In the therapy of depression, without the restructuralization of the personality, there can be reprogramming in the dialogue messages. The way to cure a depression is to get the Adult plugged into recognizing the Critical Parent, and by this Adult endeavor the Critical Parent is decathected, or unplugged. The next stage in the therapy is to have the Nurturing Parent talk to the Adapted Child, in such a manner that the Adult programs the Nurturing Parent to say, "It's all right, you can take it." "You're OK, you can take a break." "You're doing all right, and there is no reason to feel like a failure."

The therapy of depression, transactionally speaking, can take place by the Natural Child talking to the Adapted Child. The Natural Child says, "This is no fun. Let's have some fun, and there is nothing to be glum about." In both approaches, whether the Natural Child or the Nurturing Parent speaks to the Adapted Child, the Adult must watch the Adapted Child to see how the Adapted Child receives the Nurturing Parent or the Natural Child messages. If the Child is "yes butting," discounting, or not believing the stroking from the Nurturing Parent or the encouragement from the Natural Child, the Adapted Child obviously can't feel differently. When this happens, the Adult can step in and acknowledge the Adapted Child's feelings, and the Nurturing Parent or Natural Child can then try again. It is important to recognize the Not OK or worthless feeling of the Child.

Telling a person that he or she feels worthless, empty, helpless, or hopeless also helps to increase the empathic understanding that the therapist has, although it doesn't change the dialogue in the depression. In addition, it is important to get the spouse to stop reinforcing the Not OK messages from his or her Parent ego state. Although the therapist may empathize and the spouse may offer support, the most effective force in relieving depression is activation of the internal Nurturing Parent. When the Nurturing Parent can be programmed to send encouraging messages to the Adapted Child, the Critical Parent is decommissioned and the Adapted Child feels less Not OK.

Obsessional states. People in obsessional states may exhibit a wide repetoire of games and payoffs. If they are intellectualizing, they may play the game of Psychiatry. They find it almost impossible to get at their feelings, and for this reason profound change may be very difficult to effect. Since they are inclined to intellectualize and isolate, very small words or "child language" may help to effect emotional understanding.

A good illustration of an oppositional obsessional person was a man I saw recently. As we talked, I noticed that following every comment I made, he responded, "I don't think it's that, doctor. I think it's this." After several rounds, I told him he was focusing on what was wrong rather than what was right in what I was saying and, therefore, was competing with me. The man thought about it for a while, looked up and said, "You know, I think you're wrong about that." I laughed, which was very therapeutic for him. With my laughter as a spotlight, he finally noted the contest in action, and after a few more moments he joined me in laughter.

Manic-depressive. The manic-depressive individual also has a Not OK Adapted Child and will actively look for negative strokes. In the manic phase, this individual feels super OK and elated, but the Critical Parent part is saying in effect, "Wait until I get a hold of you." Later, the Critical Parent comes back with dialogue to the Adapted Child, leading to the depression phase, or internal negative stroking. The Critical Parent will say, "You're Bad." "You've done it again."

Borderline states. There will be a lot of anxiety or intense feelings in the Adapted Child parts of borderline patients. As mentioned, borderline patients may use the defense of splitting. They may also do a lot of projecting of their own feelings onto the therapist or anyone available. It is particularly important in working with such an individual to involve the spouse because the projections may otherwise be construed by the therapist into, "that's the way the spouse really is."

Delusional psychotic reaction. A paranoid schizophrenic personality plays a Kick Me game of a higher and finer nature. This patient will attribute abuse as coming from other people, whereas he or she really harbors hostility. However, since the patient puts the hostility onto the other person, he or she feels justified in abusing the other person and gets kicks in return. The delusion is the false belief that others are persecuting. In these cases, the therapist may need to put new Parent injunctions into the head of the patient. This move, however, is only necessary if there are deficient existing ego states that enable the person to do socially inappropriate things.

Whatever the labeling system, the pain within the patient still cries out for healing. The behavior the patient employs to shield and maintain that pain may go by different names, yet all keep him or her from being fully alive. To guide people into new behaviors that free them to grow and live with less pain, therapists and others in the helping professions are commissioned to draw on the understanding of all those working in this endeavor, whether they be trained in Transactional Analysis, family systems therapies, or psychoanalysis. The goal is worthy of the best from all.

CHAPTER 3

Some Basic
Considerations
Concerning Families

It's my belief that either family therapy or couple therapy or both is indicated whenever a person comes to me for therapy and is currently a part of an intact, cooperative family situation or living arrangement. Sometimes a family or couple initiate therapy together, of course, but often they need to be encouraged to come. My encouragements along this line are usually pretty strong. Whenever there is a tie to the family of origin in the case of an individual patient, an attempt should be made to include the other members, even extended family members.

This dictum holds true even if the connection between an individual and his or her family is only financial. For example, when I was called to the hospital to talk with Lavinia, age twenty-one, who was in a suicidal depression, I found out from her that her mother and dad lived in a nearby county; a sister worked and lived in the next county; and a brother had a job in a neighboring state. I then worked toward arranging at least some sessions in which Lavinia, her sister, and her parents were present. If the brother had been in town for a visit, he could have been included once or twice in therapy during the course of treatment. Thus, people can and do function together as a family in therapy, even though they no longer live in the same domicile, or perhaps even see each other often.

Of course, therapy is not necessarily limited to biologically related families. Foster families, adopting families, and other sorts of family groupings are just as much at risk, if not more so; and the approaches and concepts of family therapy apply to their needs as much as they do to conventional biological families.

A LOOK AT A HEALTHY FAMILY

Healthy, happy, growth-nurturing families don't walk into my office seeking therapy. I do, however, often say "Goodbye" to families like that at the conclusion of a successful therapeutic experience. That is, after all, the grand goal of family therapy. We must therefore keep a mental picture of that fully functioning family as we counsel families in distress.

The parents in healthy families get along well with one another and feel themselves firmly entrenched as a couple and as a coalition or alliance within the family group. They have fun together, as shown by Natural Child to Natural Child interaction. Sometimes they nurture each other—Nurturing Parent to Child. Communication between husband and wife is, for the most part, functional and congruent. They communicate clearly about the world's demands on them and about ongoing events—Adult to Adult.

As they care for the children in the family, they are allied and in agreement most of the time in their own Parent ego states. This enables them to act effectively, firmly and consistently in socializing the young. Their Adult states will exchange data on how to apply the force of their Parent states to each child's behavior or needs. In doing this they will be scripting the child, by their own example, to be pleasant, happy, have fun, and not collect racket feelings or play games. If that is happening, it isn't necessary for parents to feel they must always say brilliant things to an upset child or answer every question in the best possible way. They can set aside the notion of becoming "perfect parents." Figure 1 presents a diagram of the functioning, healthy family, and Figure 2 shows the Child maturing and the Parent and Adult expanding.

The really important question of childhood, "How do I grow as a happy fully human being?," will be answered by continual demonstration. And as the mother and father give due emphasis to the solidarity of their relationship and its importance to them, they are showing clearly the boundaries between the parent system and the Child-Child subsystems. The child, or children, know beyond a shadow of a doubt they don't have a quasi-oedipal victory.

The ongoing Natural Child to Natural Child communication between parents demonstrates that Mommy is enough woman for Dad and Dad is enough man for Mommy. The Child part of the young child then feels secure in his or her own sexuality because there is implied stroking for that sexuality in the same-sex parent getting along well with the opposite-sex parent. The message is that the child will grow up and find somebody outside the family as their husband or wife. As the child matures, this message will be amplified and related at all areas of life.

As the child-raising years are completed, the growth objectives of parenting, differentiation, individuation, confidence, and eventual separation will have been achieved. An autonomous, clear-thinking, free adult will have developed.

This description does not mean to suggest that the fully functioning family does not experience problems, face crises, react to internal and external pressures, or the like. These processes are part of the human condition. It simply means that when a family is operating from the "Get on with it" life position, its members do just that. When problems come, they are dealt with or worked through. When grief comes there is a time for grieving and then resuming a new or altered life pattern.

Families pass through many developmental stages from marriage to death, and each brings changes that must be absorbed. Each day

The Functioning, Healthy Family

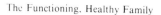

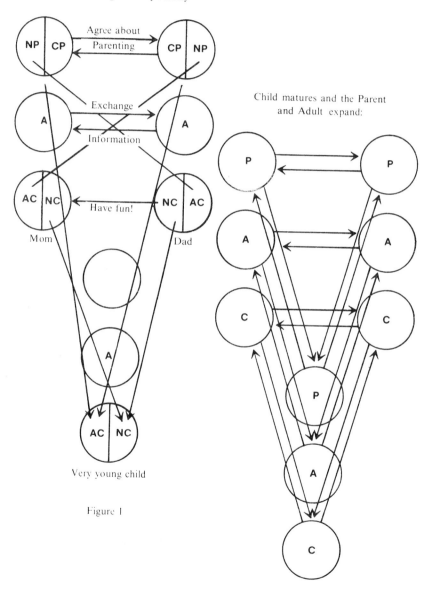

Figure 1

Child matures and the Parent
and Adult expand:

Figure 2

may bring new demands, new adjustments in relationships, and its members continue to grow and blossom as long as they live.

WHEN THINGS CHANGE

But being a functional family seems to be a monumental challenge today, even for couples who do not feel any particular pain in their twosome relationship. When a child is added to the system, husband and wife become Dad and Mom, and the fat hits the fire! The pain and conflict that remained hidden during the couple period often surfaces again. These mothers, fathers, and children then are the ones the family therapist meets. Their family system is not healthy, happy or growth-nurturing.

With the birth or adoption of the first child, each new parent pulls his or her bag of parenting injunctions off the shelf and rolls into action as *Mom* or *Dad*. Two different styles of parenting may thus be activated, along with all the remembered feelings of what it was like to be a child and any unhappy feelings about the opposite-sex parent. These hangovers of unresolved anger toward the real father may now be projected by the new Mom on the new father in her family, and vice versa. A day-by-day replay of the scenes that took place in both original households twenty or thirty years ago commences.

Mom and Dad feel the pain first. Dad is accustomed to being the full recipient of her Nurturing Parent; but suddenly that's all lavished on the new child, and he's left out. Mom may feel abandoned when Dad showers attention and affection on the newcomer. The more strongly the Adapted Child parts of either spouse need that reassurance and nurturing, the greater becomes the distress between the couple in a dysfunctional family.

A latent sexual problem may also become severe. If one spouse has already picked up on any excuse to avoid sex, the advent of a child yields a bonus "twenty-four-hours-a-day excuse," and sex may be successfully avoided altogether.

It's interesting that the more dysfunctional the couple relationship, the more the mother and father are likely to deny their own problems. It's almost always in the child, or children, that the first pain symptoms are seen and recognized. Usually, it is these symptoms, along with a referral by a physician, pastor, or teacher, that bring a family into therapy.

Several years ago, I saw a young couple, Samantha and Tom, along with their three-year-old son, Brian. Brian's pediatrician had referred them to me after treating his many allergies, asthma, and general nervousness. As we talked, it became apparent that their sexual adjustment was very limited, they fought and played Uproar constantly, and Tom drank heavily. Apparently, they could withstand the stress or their own difficulties with each other, as they had been married three or four years when Brian was born. However, when the effects of their distress began to be visible in him, they acknowledged that something was really going on, and they were willing to attempt change.

Over the course of several interviews, I discovered that both Tom and Samantha had loved the parent of the same sex more than the parent of the opposite sex. Samantha and her mother were very close, but her father had been away a good deal on business. When he was at home, she remembered only his lack of interest in her, his closeting himself in the study with "work" when she wanted his attention. As she grew into young womanhood, he was simply too "busy" to support and validate her emerging sexuality.

Tom's ties during childhood has been with his father—a warm nurturing man. It seemed that they shared not only hikes and Boy Scout projects but also confidences. Tom got very little approval of his masculinity from his mother. As an adult, Tom felt that he had to have sexual relations often to support his own feelings of masculinity, and Samantha didn't want to have sex at all. Brian, of course, provided a "twenty-four-hour-a-day excuse." At night, Brian would not sleep, except in his parents bed, and his allergies and asthma attacks kept her busy during the day.

Brian, with his allergies and asthma, was labeled "sick," and it was ostensibly out of concern for Brian's sickness that this family came into therapy. Other couples bring their children into therapy wearing tags of "bad," "crazy," or "stupid." Whatever the label reads, such children often provide the needed impetus to move a couple toward a reconsideration of their own life positions and scripts. At the outset of therapy, however, almost all parents insist that it is only the child who needs help. Initially, most mothers and fathers maintain that they have no problems themselves and that they can't see why their child should either.

The denial of complicity, in the extreme, came one day from a father who called me and asked me to see his daughter who had already been diagnosed as a schizophrenic. I said I would see her only on the condition that the whole family also came into treatment with her. He started to give me a series of reasons why this was unnecessary, culminating with, "It's a good marriage we have, you know." I persisted, "Well, why don't you talk with your wife and the other children and set a time when you can come in to talk?" He replied, "But, Doctor, I can't. We're separated."

THE FAMILY IN DISTRESS

I've talked about the fully functional family and the goal of family therapy, but what of that family in distress? It's the one the therapist meets in a counseling office. What can he or she expect to see? Which things are important to watch for?

As with the functional family, parents of the family in distress will each have a full set of ego states, and the therapist needs to note which states are used most often. He or she will soon see that the use of particular ego states follows some obvious patterns that quickly becomes predictable. These patterns are almost certain to be repeated by nearly everyone in the family group. The Parent to Parent agreement found in the healthy family may be totally absent or quite weak. The Adult to Adult exchanges of information may or may not be free and clear. But Natural Child to Natural Child play is likely to be limited.

The transactions that stand out most clearly are usually those from Critical Parent to Adapted Child or Adapted Child to Critical Parent. When there are children in the family who are old enough to take an active part in therapy sessions, look for partnerships between the Adapted Child parts of one or both parents and the Adapted Child of the real child.

Some time ago, a particular nonfunctioning family presented themselves in therapy. They came bringing their son Samuel as the identified patient. It seemed that he was always late for dinner, did poorly in school, and fought with his mother. As they walked into my office, I was struck by the physical appearance of the group. Father and son were both rather lean with angular noses and unkempt straw-colored hair. Sam Dunnington was a thirty-five year-old version of nine-year-old Samuel. Samuel's eight-year-old sister, Joanie, was a plump and round-faced girl. And Joan Dunnington, the mother, was an older, slightly more overweight Joanie.

As we talked, I found that Sam had separated from the family some weeks earlier, after a series of particularly bitter fights with Joan. He moved back home with his own mother and took a job as an auto mechanic in that town. Apparently, his mother welcomed him back and was willing to pick up after him and care for him as she had done when he was a little boy. Although he now lived some miles from my office, he agreed to come with the family to therapy each week.

Joan was working full time as a fifth-grade teacher. She got up, took care of the children, went to work, returned to care for the children and the home, but rarely found time for any recreation or fun.

When I asked them what they would like to talk about in therapy, the father shifted the question to Samuel and asked, "What would you like to talk about?" I quickly interjected, "Hey, how do you feel when your father puts you on the spot?" Samuel replied, "Lousy!" To which Joanie shouted, "You don't talk, you always hit."

Throughout that first session, Sam repeatedly jumped on Samuel, Joanie and Samuel played Uproar with each other, and

Joan glared angrily at them all. It seemed likely that this family's racket was anger, and although Sam and Joan did not fight in front of me, I could guess that the children's enactment of Uproar was a delayed replay of games they observed between mom and dad.

The next time I saw them, Sam was half an hour late. Joan then told us that he was also late for visits with the children. Sam, however, staunchly refused to let the discussion focus on anyone but Samuel. He reiterated his complaints about Samuel's lateness and then blamed it on the child's friends. Throughout all this arguing, Joan seemed to abdicate her mother's role entirely. She neither defended her son nor joined in the criticism of his behavior. She seemed to leave all the parenting to Sam.

The picture began to shape up that neither of two Adults really wanted to parent children. Sam generally avoided parenting by living with his mother, and Joan avoided it by passing the job over to Sam whenever he was available. It looked like they both had been scripted, "Don't mature, don't grow up." Their life position seemed to be "I'm OK, You're Not OK." Hence, they seemed to be "getting rid of" each other. In a quick glance at the observed behavior of father and son, it was easy to see that Samuel was following a scripting from Sam's Adapted Child that said, "Be just like me," as exemplified by their names. Both were habitually late, and both structured a lot of their time with verbal battles or Uproar. I imagine that similar behavior patterns also existed between Joan and Joanie.

This environment was certainly not a growing one for either parents or children. I didn't once observe even a hint of Natural Child interaction and rarely got an Adult response or question from any of them. Most of their transactions were coming from their Adapted Childs, with an occasional Critical Parent remark.

WHY THERAPY WITH FAMILIES?

We all have our biases, and there's no sense kidding ourselves into thinking that we're totally objective about everything. My particular bias in this area of therapeutic practice is toward working with families. This conviction is based on my own experience. However, the advantages of working with whole families, over working with individuals only, is well supported by the research of many others in the field.

The first work with families grew out of work with disturbed children, many of whom had been diagnosed as schizophrenic. (Bateson et al. 1956). There was a very small degree of success as therapists treated these children individually, particularly when the children remained in their own homes. Children who were moved into institutions seemed to improve only to regress again when brought into contact with their families (Bowen 1960).

Further research with the families of schizophrenics led workers to conclude that the family is a cohesive, rule-governed system, which generates a homeostasis among its members (Bateson et al. 1963). This homeostasis is an enduring, predictable pattern of behavior with its own internal stability. The existence of this homeostasis makes it very hard to change one individual's behavior and maintain that change if the rest of the family system remains the same. It follows then that if an individual is to be "cured," the entire family must cooperate in effecting that cure and altering, in someway, the homeostasis. My own experience corroborates this view, and along with it I've observed a number of very practical advantages to family therapy.

It's cheaper. The most basic and practical argument for seeing families rather than working only with their identified patient is that long-lasting change is effected with fewer visits to the therapist's office. It is far more costly in both time and money when the child is sent to a child therapist, and the marital couple to an adult therapist. If the homeostasis of a family must change to allow the individual, who is said to have the problem, to become problem-free, everyone in the family needs to work together to arrange that change—which, in turn, will affect them all.

It lasts. Over and over again, children who were thought to be "cured" by individual treatment while they were growing up seek psychotherapy for themselves as adults. One reason is that the treated child retains the understanding that he or she has an internalized disorder. Thus, as an adult when things go wrong, that individual can pick up again on the notion and head for the therapist again. If in childhood that same person had gone through the therapeutic experience with his or her family, he or she would know that it was the whole family who owned the problem, not just one member.

It helps the marital couple. Individual therapy for a child encourages parents to think that everything is being taken care of and that they are free of any responsibility for the transactions that produced the disorder. This conclusion means they'll go on doing the same things over and over again. Family therapy has the potential of helping them to identify the basic areas of conflict within their transacting as a couple.

It prevents further damage. Treating the whole family equilibrium forestalls more severe or future psychiatric disability in children who have so far shown no symptoms or in children yet unborn. There is now evidence that the same psychiatric disabilities that are not treated may be continued for several generations. Transactional Analysis therapists believe that they have been very successful in mapping the specific dynamics of such "family parades" (Berne 1971).

It provides firsthand data. The therapist working with a whole family can see for himself or herself how the parents relate to each other and to the child or children. This information does not have to be relayed to the therapist through the patient, as happens in individual therapy. Furthermore, the therapist's observation is not limited to how the patient interacts with peers as is often the case in a group situation. Thus, the available data may be much more complete because two or more people will be on hand to amplify it.

When I saw Martha Anderson, who was then nineteen years old, and her parents, Martha was having dreams in which there was something black coming over her face, but she couldn't relate this to anything. Her mother revealed that when Martha was a baby and cried, the father got angry about the crying, and she, the mother, put a pillow over the child's face. The girl was under three years old at the time this original event took place, and there's no way I could have retrieved the explanation if I'd been seeing Martha alone.

New data can be brought to the attention of everyone at the same time. Having an entire family present has some advantages in assessing the varying perceptions members may have of any event in the past or present. Questions can be phrased so that everyone answers them right in a session. For example, if one child seems to be constantly staring at me, I can ask each family member what he or she thinks this means. "What do you think Johnny is saying when he is staring at me?" Perhaps, Mother will say, "Oh, he likes doctors." Another will have a different comment and so on. I will also ask Johnny, "Why are you doing this?" This process leads to an understanding not only of Johnny's reason for staring at me but also, usually, of how consistently and totally the others hold widely divergent perceptions of one another's thoughts, feelings or wishes. These divergent perceptions might not normally be revealed in an individual interview.

It employs positive group pressure for change. Another kind of event that takes place in a family session is the exposure of one member's behavior. Several years ago, I saw the Ellerton family. Matt Ellerton, the father, was fiercely competitive and contentious. This behavior came on full force when I directed any sort of question toward him. If he had been an individual patient, I would have had to deal with this oppositional quality again and again. My reaction to it as a single individual, out of any social context, would have had a very limited effect, and Matt's behavior would have changed very slowly. With the five other Ellertons as allies, however, there was the potential hope for a faster modification.

I sensed that the other family members were uncomfortable with Matt's behavior. They grew edgy and angry whenever I questioned

Matt. One day, after a question to the senior Ellerton followed by his usual contentious response, I asked the others how they felt about their father's behavior pattern. As they answered, he saw how their Parent, Adult, and Child ego states were reacting to his behavior. He then acknowledged with his Adult the validity of the family's reaction; this recognition proved a potent force for change.

It opens the way for a change. There is strong evidence that individual therapy for a child intensifies the family system rather than changes it (Montalvo and Haley 1973). According to this theory, the identified patient's "illness" serves an important role in the whole family system, and as long as that person is in treatment the notion will persist that only he or she is "sick." Thus, in order to save time and money for our clients, effect long-lasting changes for the better, resolve marital difficulties, and prevent the recurrence of problem patterns in the future, I am convinced that it's appropriate, whenever possible, to see whole families, rather than individual "problem" children.

CHAPTER 4

A Plan for
Using TA
with Families

The transition from therapy work with individuals using other methods to therapy with families employing TA may represent a major shift both in the philosophy and the daily routine of the therapist. But it is a transition that can be made quite painlessly if some thought is given both to the physical fact of working with several people, rather than with one, and to the practical use of these techniques during therapy sessions.

When I was far along with psychoanalytic training, I assumed that I would work with individual patients. Most therapeutic work was carried on in that way in private practice. Indeed, my initial contact with private patients was with individuals. Work with families began around 1957, and I read with interest the reports of those who tried it.

In the spring of 1963, I scheduled my first family session. Today, my practice is divided about evenly among individuals, groups, and families, but I have grown to prefer working with families. The potential for a lasting "cure" and a state of "lived happily ever after" is greatly enhanced when all members of a family system join together in this task.

As I prepared for my first session with a family my questions were, "Where do I begin?" "Why there?" I suspect whatever a therapist's previous experience or understanding of other family therapy systems is, the question remains essentially the same. How does the TA family therapist get started with family therapy? What kinds of things can the therapist do to promote an effective therapy? How will everyone know that the therapy process has been successful? What happens in TA family therapy that's different from the work with families done by Satir, Minuchin, Ackerman, Wittaker, Sager, or Pittman? These are the questions we will be working with in this chapter.

Not all the strategies I use as a TA family therapist are significantly different from those used by any family therapist. Here, I'll call them by their TA names to unify the vocabulary. For example, Virginia Satir (1965) said that she is practicing "ego enhancing." She tries to take some of the tension out of an initial interview by pointing out a positive characteristic of a child in the family. Using TA terms, I say that I'm sending a Nurturing Parent (positive-stroke) permission to the family parents to see their child as OK. The activity is similar, and the intended outcome much the same in both systems.

Other strategies not only carry TA labels but also are more specifically TA-based. A prime example is the general practice of teaching the basics of TA very early in therapy. To my knowledge no other family therapy approach has TA's commitment to giving the basic tools to the patient, or patients, right at the start of the process, partly because no other family therapy system has such a simple and teachable set of concepts with which to work.

GETTING STARTED WITH A FAMILY IN THERAPY

I arrange strategies and plan my line of questioning to achieve specific goals, depending on who appears for the first interview: the couple or parent, alone or with children; the degree of crisis present; and the apparent level of anxiety in the group. My goals for the first three session are:

1. To help the family to relax and begin to trust me.
2. To ask, What do you think the problem is?
3. To lift the blame frame from the identified patient if there is one.
4. To teach the basic notions and vocabulary of TA, so that they can be put into action by everyone to observe and understand the patterns of behavior.

Help Everyone to Relax

When a family group enters my office, my immediate task almost always is to help them relax, feel safe, and begin to trust me a little. What better way to promote good feelings than with humor? Take a seemingly banal question, and answer it first yourself, giving a funny twist. One I like to use goes like this: "What did you want to be when you grow up? You know, I always wanted to be a lifeguard. Yeah, a real lifeguard...in a car wash!" This tactic is guaranteed to get at least a guffaw or two and opens the way for others to respond humorously as well.

Humor loosens up the Child ego states of most or all of the family members and that loosening up is an important, serious condition of change and receptiveness to what you plan to say later. In the use of humor in therapy the therapist must be aware of patients who will take the laughter with their Adapted Child as though they were being laughed *at* rather than *with*. Greenson (1967) told how he allowed mirth to occur between himself and his patients. But, he insisted on analyzing how the patient reacted to his laughter. He

believed that he was safeguarding the patient's rights by listening to
and carefully observing the patient's response to laughter.

A good many years ago, when I was starting in family therapy
practice, I had rooms adjacent to those of another psychiatrist. One
hot afternoon, the air-conditioning failed, and we were forced to
leave windows open and our doors ajar. My family came in and
settled quietly into their chairs, and then we all heard a loud burst
of laughter from across the hall. The family in my office giggled
nervously. "My family can laugh louder than yours can!" I hollered
to my colleague. And, on cue, they all laughed and laughed. From
that moment on, they knew they had permission from me, at least,
to play. Honest laughter and good-humored playfulness go a long
way toward enhancing the effectiveness of the therapeutic process.

A lack of humor, on the other hand, can prevent healing from
happening. A few years ago I worked with a family who brought in
their daughter Sally. Sally was a very tiny girl with a huge fearful
Adapted Child. She said she didn't know what she should talk
about or do in family therapy. I wound up referring her to a Child
analyst. Today I know better, and I owe my experience to Sally.

The child analyst kept up an unrelieved attitude of grave serious-
ness with Sally. He probed her thoughtfully and constantly, until
she was literally scared out of therapy. Fortunately, the family had
continued working with me, and together we arranged for Sally to
return to our sessions. This time I did a lot of joking, and we all
shared a number of good laughs. In a few sessions, we found out
why she had problems letting her Natural Child out, and she
improved rapidly.

Although we may easily agree that it's far more pleasant to spend
the therapy hour exercising our wit and laughing with our patients,
it is therapeutically sound and practical as well. When an individual feels or displays tensions, anger, or anxiety the Adapted Child
is using most of the energy. In this situation, the Adapted Child
may contaminate the Adult and prevent it from thinking clearly. A
good laugh activates the Natural Child, and the Natural Child
begins to draw energy from the Adapted Child, thereby causing it

to shrink. The Adult is then free to process data and think clearly again, as shown in the diagram in Figure 1.

Another way to help a family relax and become comfortable is to take a family history. Some therapists arbitrarily begin all family therapies in this way, and I've found that it serves several positive functions. First, it continues to promote a comfortable feeling among family members. Most everyone can respond without distress to the simple routine questions like, "Where were you born?" "Where did you go to school?" Second, I find out quite a lot about the family that will be directly useful as we talk about life scripting. Finally, children love to hear the story of their family, as well as of

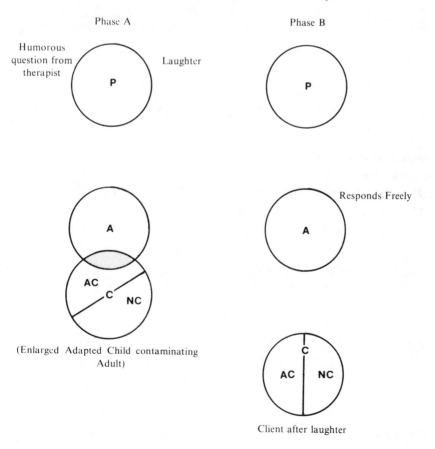

Figure 1

themselves. I have a feeling that they often find out more about their beginnings in one of these sessions than they knew when they entered my office.

During the initial interview, the therapist needs to be alert for ways to give positive strokes to all the family members. Positive strokes from the Nurturing Parent of the therapist help deactivate the overanxious Adapted Child, again freeing the Adult to talk and think clearly. The cooperation of the Adult is essential as therapy begins if the patient is to fully work out his or her therapeutic experience.

One way to ensure positive strokes for the young children in therapy is to get down on the floor and physically pat or stroke each one. If there is a baby, this is the time for "kitchy kitchy cooing" or whatever affectionate game the therapist enjoys playing with babies. If I physically stroke the children, it means that they are getting some strokes, and they can worry less about the parents blowing up at each other.

With older children, the therapist can give positive strokes by complimenting them on the way they answer the questions. I use my Nurturing Parent to tell them that they have given very good answers to my questions.

I use my Nurturing Parent to give positive strokes to the parents, too. Over the years, I have observed that nearly all parents are extremely worried that in family therapy they will have the finger pointed at them as lousy parents. In our American culture, it seems that parents are expected to live for their children and to somehow be "perfect parents." To relieve this worry, I use my Nurturing Parent to say things like, "Parents rack their brains trying to please their children," or "Most parents do the very best job of parenting they can." Later, after we have talked about ego states, I stroke parents by noting when they are talking from their Adult and saying, "You're coming on Adult now." Most parents are pleased to be told this.

At this beginning stage and later on as well, both parents and children need to be reassured and reminded that nobody is going to be blamed in this experience. However, each one must also understand that he or she alone is responsible for all of his or her own transactions.

Questioning in Therapy

Beyond helping the family group feel comfortable in the therapy situation and reviewing with them what events in their lives led up to their appearance in my office, what do I do, what can you do, to move the therapeutic experience along? There are several general lines of questioning to choose from and perhaps you will come up with others as well. Here are three I find helpful along with some ideas about why I like to use them.

What do you think the problem is? This question is directed at one or all the children in the group. I like to begin with them because they usually have a very clear idea about what's going on, and their perceptions provide a good starting point. In addition, I've observed that my simply questioning a child in this way, treating him or her like a thinking human being, and listening thoughtfully to the response, also gives that child a strong positive stroke. Sometimes a parent will jump in and answer for the child. This response is, of course, a *discount*. A *discount* means being nonreceptive to transactions. Usually it can be avoided by explaining first that one ground rule of therapy is, "Every person speaks for himself or herself."

Are you angry? Another line of questioning that I often use is specifically designed to uncover the racket feelings in a family and find out how they are handled. Although these questions may be quite serious, I consciously ask them in a casual offhand voice, and people generally respond quite directly, without feeling threatened. For example, if it appears that anger might be a family's racket, I'd ask, "What can you do to make Mom angry enough to kick you?" Or, in a family where I sense a guilt racket, "How do your parents control you?" "Do they make you feel bad?" "Who feels most Not OK and feels hurt a lot of the time?" When there is a very anxious feeling surrounding a family, I might ask, "What are the things your parents threaten you with that make you frightened?" "What do you do with your fear?" These questions will help bring the family's fear into focus if that is their racket.

As various family members respond to any of these or similar questions, I listen and make mental note of their use of these key feeling words, anger (angry), guilt (guilty), fear (afraid), and hurt (hurting). They will keep popping up in the conversation like billboards announcing the theory of rackets, and these same key words will help point the way toward a more comfortable family relationship.

What's the contract? Among the questions the therapist will ask a family during the initial or early interviews are the ones that will lead to making a "contract." The *contract* is a key factor in TA therapy. It helps define the course of the treatment and also lets everyone know when the therapy course is completed. In my experience, people often find that as they progress in their understanding, they want to renegotiate their contract; but this initial contract is a necessary starting point nonetheless.

One way to ask a contract leading question is, "What whole-family problems needs to be resolved?" Usually, the therapist will get some sort of sensible answer. The therapist then guides the family members to state their responses to this question behaviorally. For example, members of a family may initially say their goal or contract is to get the identified patient cured or taken care of. The therapist then works toward a broader perception of the family's problems by focusing attention on the family's pattern of interaction and level of happiness. Soon, a contract can be stated that contains certain goals for other members or areas of family life, or both.

The primary goal of family therapy is the healing of the home environment for growing. The therapist neither hopes that the marital partners will continue to live together nor that they will separate, but rather that whatever they decide to do, it will be less painful. The amelioration of some of the pain will, in many cases, also make the relationship more stable. In the case of older teenage children or young adults who are still "stuck" in the family system, the therapist may well be primarily an advocate for that child, and the goal may be to break the family apart to allow him or her to individuate.

By asking these or similar opening questions and by consciously stroking each member of a family, the therapist helps the family to relax. As family members begin to feel less tense, they also find out that they can relax and still be safe with the therapist. The beginning of this kind of trust between patient and therapist is essential to the therapeutic process.

As children and parents respond to my questions, a spontaneous dialogue usually develops between them. By listening carefully with my Child, I can often spot the family's favorite games, which in turn help suggest the family racket. And people who have not engaged in a real dialogue for days or weeks may suddenly find themselves talking to each other.

Drop the Blame Frame

Often when a family comes to a therapist or counselor, the parents will insist that one of the children is or has "the problem," and he or she is the identified patient. Sometimes it may be that one spouse carries that label rather than a child, but most often one child is considered the owner of the problem. Then, along with making the family comfortable in the therapy setting and finding out more about each of them, I look for ways to deframe the identified patient, or to drop the *blame frame*.

One day, a family came in to see me with the father, John, complaining loudly that he couldn't see what earthly good it would do to have all of them trekking into some psychiatrist's office each week when none of them had had anything to do with Joey's problem. It seemed that Joey, then ten years old, was getting very poor grades in school. Joey's dad used these grades as evidence that the boy had a "problem." When a parent presents a situation in this way, he or she is projecting everything from the entire family onto one child. In reality, the family has everything to do with Joey's "problem."

In the case of this particular father, I suspected that his projection indicated his own paranoia, and later interviews corroborated this diagnosis. I might say to Joey's father, "Sometimes parents feel pretty helpless when a child has consistently poor grades. Is that the way you're feeling about Joey now?" Encouraging or allowing the parent to express his or her own feelings about the "problem" draws that person into the action and reduces the glare of the spotlight on the identified patient.

Another maneuver that helps lift the blame from one individual is to point out the difficulties that other children in the family are also having, if they are. Perhaps a brother or sister is acting withdrawn in the therapy interchanges or is giving evidence of feelings that bother him or her by body language or facial expression.

Both of these deframing strategies and other similar ones bring the whole family into focus as sharing joint ownership of "the problem." This stage must be attained before the healing process can really begin.

Sometimes, when the frame is dropped from an identified patient, that individual is reluctant to rejoin the family. Often this child will need a lot of positive stroking through several sessions before he or she can be a part of the family group and contribute to the therapy.

As I've said, the therapist needs to give each family member positive strokes, particularly at the outset but also throughout the therapy process. The identified patient may continue to need a special quota of these strokes. When parents bring in such a child they often think of him or her as bad, sick, crazy, or stupid and they have been thinking about that child in those terms for months or even years. It will take a concerted effort on their part to turn this thinking around. Thus, it's also important that the parents learn to stroke the child again.

Usually the therapist can initiate this change in parental behavior by giving the mother and dad permission to see their child as OK. This act does not mean that the difficulties the parents associate with this child will either disappear or are to be ignored; it simply means that they remember that he or she is, after all, a basically worthwhile—OK—human being, with or without some transitory difficulties. I might say to John, for example, "Joey really is a nice boy, you know." As I comment on what a nice child they have, I'm using my own Nurturing Parent to give these parents a positive stroke and permission to regard their child as "nice."

Give a Brief Lecture on TA

Building a rapport and trust with a new family group and drop-ping a blame frame from their identified patient may proceed simultaneously and extend over several interviews, but there is some basic information about TA that I try to give a family the very first time we meet. Of course, in crisis situations we will deal with the crisis first and then talk about theory. But at either the first or the first relatively calm session, I give my "thirty-minute lecture on TA."

For this introduction to Transactional Analysis, I choose from among the concepts described in chapter 1 and put together a lec-ture of around thirty minutes in length (see chapter 1). This lecture always begins with an explanation of the PAC diagram and the ways we identify each ego state. I continue with examples of straight, or parallel, and crossed, or crooked, transactions. I often conclude with a mention of the ways time may be structured and a brief note about game play.

Following this brief talk, I invite patients to ask questions about any area they find particularly interesting, and I also urge them to read one or two other books on the subject. At this time, patients need to be cautioned not to talk "TA" at home. This lecture is, after all, only a first briefing; and although these concepts appear very simple and are, in fact, quite easy to understand, it's desirable to find out more about TA before applying labels to people and their behaviors. As discussed, it is such a temptation to shout, "That's a game!" or "Stop coming on Critical Parent!" These re-sponses simply don't promote good feelings between people, even though they may be accurate assessments of the situation. The novice needs to learn about positive antithesis strategies and to acquire a fuller awareness of his or her own ego states before using TA language or techniques with the supervision of the therapist.

CREATING THE ENVIRONMENT FOR HEALING

As the therapist begins work with a new family, it is important, as mentioned, to consider saying those things that will help the family relax and begin to understand what therapy and transactional analysis are all about, and creating the environment for healing is the first stage of a family's therapy through TA. But what of the nonverbal strategies as therapy begins?

Take a look around the room. How are the chairs arranged? In my office, I have a rather comfortable black naugahyde covered chair that I usually sit in. I sit a lot as I work, and I like to sit comfortably. The other chairs in the room are a collection of folding metal card-table-type chairs, some metal and plastic armless ones and a couple of old wooden office armchairs. Who will sit in which chair? Who will sit next to whom?

As a family returns to my office two or more times, I notice that they develop a liking for a particular spot and often return to about the same place each time; some people seem to find one kind of chair more comfortable than another. But I note particularly the people who again and again choose to sit next to each other. These pairings often represent an alliance or subsystem within the family.

If that alliance seems dysfunctional as we find out more about what is going on in the family, I will ask those people to separate physically during the hour. This maneuver can be strikingly effective when it's used at a particularly strategic juncture, as happened with the Rathorne family (chapter 5). During the first ten or fifteen sessions with this family, the son, Phil, always sat between his mother, Diane, and father, Bert, although just a little closer to Mom. Mother and son reassured each other during the hour with shared eye contact and small subtle gestures of alliance. As we established verbally what was happening in this family and I began to see that Phil was moving toward breaking out, I changed this seating arrangement. I asked Phil to join me on one side of the room and shifted the parents' chairs so that they had to look more toward each other. By moving Phil close to my chair I gave him the protection he needed to begin to move away from Diane. Then, by forcing Bert and Diane to confront each other without Phil between them, I got a flurry of the transactions I knew would come between her Adapted Child and his contentious Critical Parent. A couple of sessions with this seating arrangement left no one in doubt as to what the situation between that husband and wife was.

The physical arrangement of the room therefore plays an important role in creating a setting for families with children of about twelve years of age or older. Children need to be at least that old or perhaps a little older before they can sit quietly and carry on a discussion, particularly one dealing mostly with abstractions.

If the children are younger and are not too disruptive, they can play with toys such as Tinker Toys, cars, trucks, dolls, or a blackboard while the discussion is in progress. The therapist needs to be alert to their play, however, and to talk with them about it from time to time. All play, drawing, and other nonverbal ways of communicating ideas are important to the family system and the family script.

As the younger children play, the therapist can sometimes spot the way the sibling subsystem in the family works or observe the child's reaction to the parental coalition. For example, during the first session with the Grovner family, mother and dad cuddled and smiled at Carol, who was then four and a half years old, and she played happily with the Tinker Toys during most of the hour. As she fitted and refitted the pieces together, I could tell that she was listening to and aware of our conversation. The ten-year-old identified patient, Laurel, was depressed and sat quietly in her chair. There were no affectionate gestures or smiles passing from either parent to this daughter. Thus, the structure of this family was very apparent right from the first meeting.

Occasionally, an older child is drawn to the toy box and plays to avoid answering questions. If it is apparent that the child is able to discuss or respond but is using a play to avoid doing so, this tactic needs to be called to his or her attention. This effort may be a starting point for more discussions that include him or her.

Remember the therapy, if it's effective, results in changes in both attitudes and behavior. People may learn a new way to live, and there is always some fear of that new way. Resistance is to be expected. It's a myth that in family therapy parents will be cooperative and willing to further the therapy for the sake of the problem child. Although they may be in considerable pain, it is a familiar pain and they have built this family system themselves. It contains their rules for living, and any new ones or new behaviors are bound to be threatening.

The system, then, cannot be expected to change just because "it" spends some time in a therapist's office. The role of the therapist is likely to be very active, particularly in the beginning. If the therapist initially appears passive, he or she is likely to get sucked into the family system as a "sibling." Such a situation will not further the family's therapy.

When a school-age child is the identified patient, he or she will naturally be involved in a number of the initial sessions. As the parents begin to see some of their responsibility for the family system, the child may be excused and perhaps brought in periodically with the other children.

If the child is under four years old, it is not necessary for him or her to be present for all sessions. I do like to bring children of that age in from time to time when gains are consolidated or when there is new behavior on the part of the parents.

In families where parents are fighting a lot, I see no point in having the children observing this behavior. When parents play games with really angry payoffs, no real resolution or exploration is taking place. These games must be broken up before there can be observations I might want children to see. When the sexual problems between a couple are in focus, I excuse the children for a while, or set up extra couple-only therapy sessions in addition to the ongoing family session.

Ideally, both parents and all the children come in for the initial interview and continue to appear together throughout the therapy except under the conditions just noted. However, sometimes one spouse refuses to come or simply fails to show up at the appointment time When this happens, I usually call the absent spouse on the phone and encourage him or her to come in next time, saying, "You know your contribution is important to the whole family." This move works in ninety percent of the cases. When it doesn't, I write to the absent spouse, again inviting him or her to join the family in therapy, reminding him or her that when one spouse does not participate in such a venture, the family is usually divided by separation or divorce, or the son or daughter won't get better.

Occasionally, one family member becomes determined to drop out of therapy and neither my phone calls not my notes effect a return. Oftem such an individual simply won't listen to the others in the family of the therapist is a setting where everyone is present. This person may come around after one or two individual interviews. The matter that is troubling such an individual may well be best discussed privately as when a father or mother is secretly involved with someone else. Exposing the others to this information may not serve the therapeutic process at all, particularly at that time. Thus, individual sessions may be indicated when one family member refuses to participate with the others in therapy.

REREADING THE FAMILY SCRIPT

With a warning to the reader in mind that the stages of family therapy being presented are hardly ever as distinct as they are made out to be here, I will now explore what I consider the second stage of a family's therapy through Transactional Analysis. The family is now well acquainted with the therapist and knows the basis of TA (through the introductory lecture and various sublessons I've given along the way, as well as review as a particular concept comes up). Usually, at least one family member (except in extreme cases) has gotten good at spotting some of the major games, and we've been over the racket or rackets being played in the family several times. We may have begun discussing the injunctions or rules of the family system, although this concept will still seem fairly abstract to the average family. However, I'm coming to have a fairly firm idea of what the injunctions are, and I have a fairly good map of the family system interactions, which I've begun to share via my blackboard.

Along about the tenth to the fifteenth interview, I'm ready and the family is ready, in terms of comfort with me and with TA, to push for some real changes in both social behavior and feelings. This next part of the process gives the family a much deeper insight into their problems and usually also finds the basic family pains or fears brought much closer to the surface. Consequently, although the potential for real changes is there, there are increasing risks of losing one family member from the therapy, of losing the whole family, or having one member demonstrate very frightening behavior. If change does begin to occur, the protection I give will be extremely important, because the family and its members will be venturing on to a new strange "life territory" with a change of feelings, attitudes, and behavior, and they'll be very anxious as a result.

One day, a young colleague of mine delivered a particularly brilliant analysis of a family's games and concluded with a mention of games and scripts he felt could now be given up. When he stopped talking, the husband looked at him and shook his head sadly, "See there, doctor, I must get a divorce because it really is all my fault. I start all these games." The patient took the therapist's brilliant discourse as a bawling out of him.

Another time, when I had patiently led a family through an understanding of some of their difficulties and drawn a first tentative script matrix for them, I had a similarly surprising response. Instead of acknowledging this new insight, the mother came on with her Adapted Child and said, "Doctor, should I talk about my parents more?" I then asked, "Which ego state said that?" We reviewed together the language of the different states, and she concluded that it might have been her Child. I pointed out to her that this response was a tangential and indirect acknowledgement of the new insight by her Adapted Child. We went on to talk about what an Adult response and what a Parent response might have been. By reviewing the language of each ego state, we drew attention away from her Adapted Child and avoided discounting her.

In the two cases just mentioned, both my colleague and I thought our patients were able to handle more information with their Adults than, in fact, they could. When patients are able to accept and integrate new understandings, however, observable change often results.

One day, a couple with whom I'd been working for several months came to a particularly significant new understanding of their scripts, and as they basked in the glow of their new found wisdom, he turned to me and said, "I see now where this came from and how that fits in and which messages came from Mother or Dad. But, Doctor, if I got all these messages from them, where did they get them from?"

Who scripted grandma? Who scripted grandpa? These questions are crucial, and they may lead to the integration of a patient's perception of his or her real parents. The answer to them can also move the blame from those who may still be living today to those who have departed from this world. This effort seems worthwhile, in my opinion, as the dead can rest peacefully within a blame frame. Far better that the dead wear such a blame frame than that it remain encircling those who still live.

Occasionally, I'm able to arrange interviews with three generations in a family, and we can discover the elements of their script parade right in my office. More often, however, the parents to today's parents live many miles away, and the connection must be made with phone calls, letters, or visits. When parents begin to ask the grandparents what the great-grandparents were like, a whole flood of interesting things can happen.

If direct contact can be made with the grandparents, their anecdotes about their childhoods almost inevitably include script injunction episodes. Myrna, who counted among her script messages the notion that children are a nuisance and a burden, found that her mother's earliest memories included scenes in which relatives were commiserating with the family over the misfortune of her birth. She remembers them saying, "Oh dear, another mouth to feed!" Myrna was fortunate in that although the relationship between her and her mother had been strained, they were still able to converse as friends. An afternoon of sympathetic listening based on Myrna's growing understanding of how scripting takes place enabled this young woman to consider carrying her blame frame out to the cemetery.

When Myrna returned to talk over this conversation with me, we found that we had five or six clear scripting scenes to examine. Looking at her mother's apparent script along with what we had discovered about Myrna's helped put the latter's in a new perspective. In addition, I suggested that she check out a couple of books that described the social history of the parts of the country where her mother was born and where the family lived at the time of Myrna's birth.

Social history is often neglected in our general school education, yet the lives of people are inevitably played out against the backdrop of the society of that time. An awareness of the economic climate, the issues of concern and the general mood of the times contributes to our understanding of "what made grandma say that?"

When direct conversation or communication is not feasible between a patient and his or her real parents, a study of the social conditions surrounding that parent's childhood and early adulthood may be the place to begin. The exercise of using the Adult to consider the parent as a human being living and working in a particular year or period of recorded history reduces the Adapted Child feeling response to some extent. The energy used by the Adapted Child to feel about that person now will not be available as the Adult will be using it.

We can then speculate on the basis of what the patient now knows to be true about life, raising children, relating to inlaws, and the like; and to imagine what it might have been like for the parent when the patient was born. Remembered remarks of the parent, long-forgotten scenes with grandma, and similar reminiscences help fill out the picture.

Although the change of feelings must occur within the Adapted Child, this process of finding out as an Adult about the life script of the parents often frees the Adapted Child to change its perceptions. As new understanding develops, the Adapted Child may feel a sympathy or compassion for the once blamed parent and then lift the blame frame and let it fall peacefully on the nonliving.

The awareness of the Adapted Child proves useful to patient and therapist in many ways. When the Adapted Child says, "I don't like..." or "I don't want..." it is a strong indication that the patient is anxious about something. This line of thought is useful to pursue because the Adapted Child collects anxiety stamps to prevent intimacy. The need for these stamps motivates certain games that keep people from getting close, and this collection promotes defenses.

Often, when couples have been practicing saying exactly what they want and negotiating and fighting constructively for a time, they may switch to a game or pastime. Such a switch happens when the intimacy or threat of intimacy is more than one or both partners can handle. For example, a couple may move into a Parent-Teachers Association (PTA) pastime discussing, "the children" in the abstract. They shift their dialogue from the less abstract, or more concrete and intimate, to the more abstract, for relief from the stress or nearness. When this situation occurs in the therapy session, we can identify it and talk about why the change occurred. This discussion often opens the way for acknowledgment of a basic fear or an insight into another script injunction.

ACTING AS AN AGENT OF CHANGE

The family, or couple, entering therapy does so because there is something about their life they want to change. Yet in spite of this apparent desire for change, patients employ a variety of defenses and cling persistantly to the old patterns. Change, when it does occur, must take place in the Adapted Child, not in the reasoning Adult. Therefore, the therapist acting as an agent of change will be using his or her own Parent to reach the Adapted Child.

The therapist brings into action the Three P's: *permission, protection,* and *potency* (Crossman 1966). This juncture in the treatment is critical, and it is hoped that by this time the therapist has built up that quality of potency between himself or herself and the patient. The therapist's Parent must be more potent than the real parent in order to undo the injunctions of the past.

Potency is built up over a series of meetings in many ways. Initially, the strokes given by the therapist help induce an atmosphere of acceptance. As patients test the therapist's theories and find them valid, credibility is established. A therapist's potency is further enhanced by the patients themselves. Patients, because they are operating from the Not OK Adapted Child position much of the time, cast the therapist in the role of powerful Parent. This is noticeable when the therapist hears the patient respond to a remark from the therapist's Adult as though it had come from the Parent instead. Such a person hears Adult data as Critical Parent accusations and responds in a hurt or angry way from the Adapted Child.

With this in mind, one can make sure there has been a good stroke directed toward the Adapted Child before attempting to contact the patient's Adult. At this time, when change is imminent or when the potential for change is felt, the Adapted Child grows more anxious and fearful. This fear needs to be brought out into the open and acknowledged. After all, the changes that may come will substantially alter every facet of an individual's life. This possibility is not a small thing; it will be, in reality, quite an earthshaking experience. Everyone is afraid of the unknown, and this new game-free life is unknown territory for all patients. It is reassuring to most people to simply know that their fear is shared by many others who have stood on the brink of a new OK life-style. They will be further supported by hearing that many, many people just like them have cast aside the old Not OK position, and are now thriving as fully OK people. To take those first steps into OK living, patients need the Permission and Protection of the therapist.

Permission usually means a Nurturing Parent exhortation on the part of the therapist for the patient to be allowed a behavior or feeling that was prohibited by the actual parent. For example, an actual parent saying with her Critical Parent, "You're selfish!" (see Figure 2). This remark could inhibit the child from asking for what he or she wants. The therapist later saying "ask for what you want or would like" is a permission (see Figure 3). It would hopefully undo the past prohibition, if it is more potent than that of the actual parent. Since this new script direction, permission, might make a patient's Adapted Child anxious or mistrustful in trying the new behavior of assertion, the therapist needs to be available for protection.

Protection means supporting the script change by reinforcing the permission and working through the difficulties that result from the permission. Thus, the therapist must be available for anxious phone calls. The therapist must be supportive, reassuring, and comforting with hir or her Nurturing Parent and must have empathy with his or her Adult. For example, "I know it's hard to

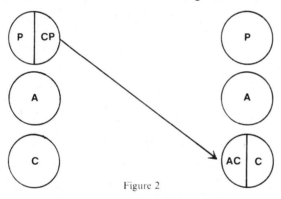

Figure 2

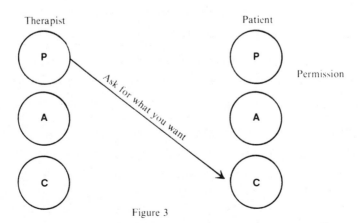

Figure 3

assert yourself" (Adult). A couple and family can be told to help each other with permissions and protections.

The therapist can discuss these concepts about self and the fears of the Adapted Child with patients, assuring them again and again, if need be, that the self will persist intact as the Adapted Child takes on OK-ness. The therapist, in a sense, will protect the self during the change. Then, usually via specific homework, the therapist gives permission to try some OK behavior. As the Adapted Child practices new ways of acting, a new confidence develops, and there will be an internal feeling awareness that all the therapist has said is true. The self will live and thrive in the absence of pain and the presence of OK-ness without diminishing or damaging self. Perhaps we can think of self as though, stretchy stuff. It can be either OK or Not OK and still contain the same unique "I-ness."

KEEPING SCORE

How can you tell if a family is progressing? What are the signs that the need for therapy may be over?

One sign that flashes for the therapist can happen after you've drawn the script matrix on the chalkboard. The family members, or couple, may say, "A-ha, so that's how it is! Thank you for showing us!" These thank-yous are usually voiced with much enthusiasm, as a sense of relief and freedom usually flows through a person when the script matrix is revealed.

Sometimes the contract appears fulfilled, yet the patient remains fearful and anxious. When this happens, it's usually time to amend that contract. Contracts are progressive and flexible, expanding as new needs become apparent. For instance, in some families the original contract may have been to "cure" the identified patient, but later on, when that person becomes free of the blame frame and more comfortable, the parents may recontract and focus on transactional differences between themselves.

Children are often the barometers of family feelings. They may get very upset with the changes that are occurring—but that's a good sign. It means that something is definitely happening. Again, when the children in the family have returned to more or less normal activities—working in school, playing with friends, eating, and sleeping—then the therapist can be confident that the family is healing.

Another benchmark to note is the session, or sessions, where the couple takes up most of the hour and the interactions with the children begin to taper off. Thus, they are taking responsibility for the transactions between themselves, as well as for the transactions with the children. If a family doesn't reach that point and yet there is no indication of impending separation, the therapy is for some reason not being effective. In that event, it's wise to buy consultation time with another therapist or two. Perhaps one of them will spot something that has slipped by unnoticed, thereby breaking the log jam.

"I want to try it on my own" is the cry of the Adapted Child when it senses dependency and has been scripted to avoid it. You'll hear it midway in the therapy, when the individual has perhaps been relieved of some of his or her pain and is moving closer to basic feelings. Of course, this same individual may say the same thing to a spouse or other family members whenever there is a sense of impending dependency or closeness. Unless this fear of dependency is unmasked, that individual will go on feeling uncomfortable. But beware of saying, "It's your Child that wants out of therapy." This response doesn't get at the feeling. Instead, you might say, "Your Child is afraid of being dependent." This names the feeling (fear) and the cause (dependency).

Redecisioning, or deciding to get on with it, must be done in the Child ego state. The Adult may intellectually consider making the change, but it is the Child who feels and lives it. The child, then, must rescript itself, usually taking new Parent injunctions from the therapist's Parent via his or her permission. To do this, the Child part must have a friendly divorce from the Parent ego state. The new Adapted Child will then feel free to disregard any Critical Parent messages that his or her Adult says doesn't fit the new life pattern. In the real world, this process is demonstrated when the patient can agreeably visit the real parents and not be influenced unduly by them. This result does not attack the real parents who did the best they could, considering their scripting.

If the therapist's potency is strong enough and the permission is taken, the risks for the Child part can be practiced in homework, so that the patient reaches the point where it is easy to do constructive things in his or her life. As this happens, patients will ask me, "How do I know when I'm well?" I then say Adult to Adult, "Well, ask your Little Kid if he or she feels comfortable with himself or herself, and that's your answer." Therapy is completed when all members of the family can use their Adult to report clearly what their Child and Parent feels. At that point, they are spontaneous and aware (Berne 1964) and can communicate feelings well and also tolerate differences. They use "I" messages when they tell each other what they want or like or don't like.

In a cured family, the games stop and there is no mutual exploitation or destructive gameplaying. The scripts are recognized and changed in order to put a new show on the road. They will be able to flexibly alternate their Parent and Child parts in parenting and with each other.

SOME OTHER THINGS TO CONSIDER

Here and there, a skeptical voice can be heard alleging that the therapist is merely a "rent-a-friend"; and in this culture where nearly everything can be rented for a price, how can the therapist make sure this doesn't, in fact, happen? In Transactional Analysis the contract provides a viable safeguard. As long as there is a straight contract between therapist and patient or patient family there is little danger of the therapist becoming just a "rent-a-friend."

Of course, it's generally desirable that the therapist value the patient as OK, but occasionally a patient may appear who is Not OK in the eyes of a particular therapist. You and I may subscribe wholeheartedly to the theory that all people as human beings are

OK, but in the case of Mommy or Herman or Mike, this OK-ness is somehow invisible. That patient should then be referred to a colleague. Every patient deserves to be viewed as OK by his or her therapist during therapy—not by every therapist, not necessarily by you or me, but certainly by one therapist.

Thus, that one therapist beginning work with a patient or patient-family and necessarily viewing those individuals as OK can hardly be called "neutral." Some people have claimed that the therapist must always remain neutral, but I don't feel that this either is possible or desirable in Transactional Analysis. Using this system, and particularly in working with families, the therapist brings into the experience much of himself or herself.

As I'm getting to know a family I often show them how I use my Adult in my own marriage or tell them an episode involving my own children to illustrate the use of the Parent ego state. Doing this seems to make it easier for the Child part of the individuals in a family to reveal themselves in therapy.

One day, we were discussing domestic interactions and I mentioned to the patient-family that I usually get up early in the morning but my wife likes to catch an extra fifteen or twenty minutes of sleep. When I do awaken and get up, my habit is to walk down to the kitchen and put on the coffee. My wife used to complain that I was making noises in the kitchen disturbing her sleep.

I then paused and asked the people in that family what they would have said to my wife. They responded with a variety of Parent and Child comments. I wrote each one on the chalkboard alongside of a PAC diagram. Together, we drew the appropriate arrows to indicate which ego state was responding, reviewing the principles of TA as we did this. Finally, when we had exhausted their responses, the mother turned to me and asked, "Well, doctor, what did you say?" I told them, as it happened that morning, I said, "What noise do you hear, honey?" It was a straight Adult question. It happened that with this family my personal anecdote hit the bulle's-eye. This wife had the same complaint about her husband!

Thus the therapist using Transactional Analysis with couples or families interacts with those individuals in some very positive ways.

He or she is very much in control of these ways, and they are carefully chosen for their therapeutic value. More difficult, yet vital to the process, is encouraging real dialogue between members of the patient-family. Often, these people haven't really talked to each other in years. They have carefully structured their time together to avoid any candid conversation. In such cases, the art of family conversation must be rediscovered and nurtured. It is truly exciting to see a family, previously riddled with pathology, change into a growth-nurturing, straight-transacting, and ego-enhancing system of development.

CHAPTER 5

Rackets
and
Families

In working with families in therapy, I've found that the identifi-cation of their games is often the first step in diagnosis. Along with this identification of specific games played within the family comes an awareness of the variety of stamps they seem to collect. Games and the kinds of stamps the players collect usually go in sets, and these sets, or groupings, are called *rackets* (Berne 1966). I've found that people who are associated in a family almost always share one dominant racket.

Therefore, each family in this chapter is identified by their rac-ket—guilt, fear, anger, and hurt. Following the initial diagnosis in each case and an analysis of how their family games provide each player with a continuous flow of the chosen stamps, we continued in therapy to piece together the life scripts of the parents and thus see why they needed to play in this racket. As the family members be-gan to understand how and why these behaviors were shaping their lives, we planned together some ways they could substitute other more satisfying ways of interacting with each other.

In the retelling of any case history, it often appears that this action takes place neatly, one step at a time, in an orderly progression; but such simplicity never occurs in real life. People acquire new information about themselves in the Adult, but change occurs in the Adapted Child. Thus, people don't think themselves into a new way of behaving. Rather, usually via homework, they practice acting in some new ways and find later that their thinking process has also changed.

To uncover and name the basic fears of the Adapted Child and use this information to provide the kind of reassurance that the frightened Adapted Child needs means that a lot of attention is focused on revealing the nature of those basic fears. The closer a family or individual gets to an exposure of these fears the more resistance and defenses come into play. This time in therapy demands more sensitivity and adeptness on the part of the therapist than any other.

With each of these families we will see how the successive stages of therapy occur, how the possibilities for change are recognized, and how these families move into game-free living. The PAC diagrams at the beginning of each case indicate the relative energization of ego states at the onset of therapy.

THE MOULENARIES, A GUILT RACKET FAMILY

Figuring out the Family System

Joe and Joanne came to me one afternoon, dragging their ten-year-old-daughter, Betty, by the hand. Joe had made the appointment, and he'd said on the phone, "Doctor, we've just got to have some help. Neither Joanne nor I can seem to get anywhere with her." I'd ask for a little more information on Betty and found out that she was irritable, uncooperative, and 'didn't seem to be very happy or enjoy playing or school much"—which I translated

The Moulenaries, a Guilt Racket Family

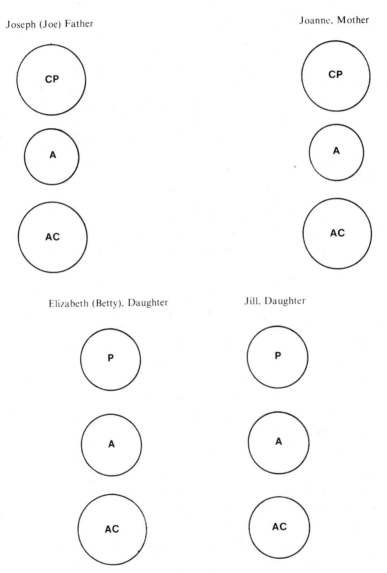

Figure 1

into depression. I also found out that the parents were both college teachers, and Joe, at least, sounded very rational, even when he was expressing his concern about his daughter.

The family wasn't facing a major crisis, and I didn't pick up hints of intense antagonisms between the parents, so I asked to see them all for the first interview. I quickly decided that they were "good thinkers," a characteristic that had already been suggested by their choice of occupation and Joe's level, rational voice on the phone. I therefore decided to give them the introductory Transactional Analysis lecture right away.

I was explaining the different types of time structuring and had gotten to withdrawal when Joanne broke in with, "That's what Betty was doing last Tuesday, and that's one reason we decided to come and see you. I came home at noon, and there she was, lying under the bed when she was supposed to be in school. She hadn't finished her homework and she didn't want to go without it done."

We'd just gone through PAC, and it was an opportune time to ask Joe and Joanne how they felt about this episode, so I did. Joe said, "Well, Betty should have gone to school even if she didn't have her work done. Betty, you should have told us that you didn't have it done." Joanne said, "Betty, you know you have to go to school, that's all there is to it. Maybe you didn't have your work done, but you have to do it, and you have to work out some way of getting the work done later."

Now I asked Betty how she felt because I saw her starting to bristle with her parents' comments. "I wish they'd lay off me," she began angrily, but then her mood changed. Her head dropped, her voice lowered in tone, and she said, "I know I should have gone to school, and I have to get my work done. I just feel awful bad about it, and I didn't want to go and have the teacher know I hadn't finished my work." She tapered off her statements in a discouraged, listless way.

I asked everyone to look at the blackboard again and gave them the job of identifying the ego-states active in this situation. I said, "What about those 'shoulds' from you, Joe, and those 'have tos' from you, Joanne? What ego state are those coming from?"

"Parent, I think," they answered, and I said, "Good, that's using your Adult! Betty, how about those feelings of 'awful bad'?" "Maybe my Adapted Child?" she asked.

I told her that she was right and added that all of us had been operating with our Adult and maybe some Little Professor (the Adult in the Child ego state) in categorizing the feelings and the transactions in this episode. In addition, I indicated that it looked like all of them could do that labeling very well indeed. As suggested earlier, this kind of immediate categorizing task gives a family in therapy something to do right away because the categories are easily used and everyone will usually apply them correctly the first time, giving the therapist some opportunity for solidly based praise.

At that point, our time together was up. I promised to continue the lecture and hear more about what was going on in their family in the next session.

Picking up the Family Racket

In the next session with the Moulenarie family, I finished the introductory lecture, with no particular comments or reactions from either Joe, Joanne, or Betty, and heard about another incident in which Betty had lost a coat. Joanne had bought it quite recently and had intended it to last for a couple of years. I got Joe's and Joanne's feelings again, "Betty should have been more careful" and "Betty, you just have to learn to remember where you put your things, and you have to keep track of them." Again, Betty bristled initially and then acknowledged with the discouraged downcast tone that yes, she *should*, and that she did have to do the things she's been asked to do.

The dominant racket or rackets going on in the family is one of the things other Transactional Analysis therapists and I seem to be able to pick up most quickly and easily from families in treatment. A racket, of course, may have individual adaptations but patterns of similar rackets will often be found in families that come from treatment, and the family itself can explore the hypothesis that different family members have learned rackets from one another. In the case of Betty's family, given the episodes of her behavior already described and her description of her feelings about them, I could guess that Betty's racket was guilt, leading to depression and a reinforcement of her conviction that she was Not OK.

Rackets, it now appears, can be maintained in at least two different ways, either via a process of complementary transactions that includes the bad feelings, or through the use of games, the payoffs of which add to the racket "stamp collection." Betty had been pasting blue stamps (for guilt and depression) in her stamp book for a long time and, in the case of the absence from school, had turned them in for a period of withdrawal.

Guilt racket people can generally be recognized by statements like, "I did something and I feel bad," "I don't and I feel bad," and "I know I should have." Body language shows a downcast head, sad face, and discouraged demeanor—these all being most noticeable when the unmet "shoulds" have been numerous and heavy. As most people who are guilt racketeers are usually somewhat depressed; I also look for the guilt racket if depression is part of a person's diagnosis when they come to me. Listening with my child helps too. I can often feel helplessness and hopelessness rising in my Child, as it responds intuitively to the members of the family present, picking up on the many "shoulds," "oughts," and "have tos." Of course, what my Child is feeling is likely being felt by the other Adapted Child parts in the other people present. To put it another way, the racket signals a particular type of transaction that is probably occurring between the Parent and Child ego states in the individual's head or between the Parent and Child states in the family.

With Betty's family, I could proceed to check out my hunch that a guilt racket and withdrawal would be shared by other family members as a form of time structuring. I listened for the transactions along the vector shown in Figure 2 and heard a lot of "should's" coming from Joe's parent, to Joanne's Child. Her Child seemed to respond with a hopeless feeling, and a lot of "I can't" and "shouldn't do that—be a serious adult." I also listened for

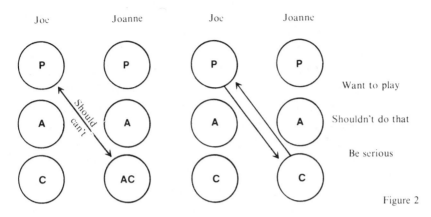

Figure 2

transactions in the vector in the relationship shown in Figure 3, and found the same have tos, which Joanne had issued to Betty on the subject of going to school and taking care of her coat, also, directed toward Joe's Adapted Child—usually disguised with a strong "please." Joe's Child either rebelled or complied very reluctantly. One of this methods was to delay doing something that Joanne's Parent had asked such as cleaning the bathtub.

But there were also transactions that began with Joe's Adapted Child seeking nurturing from Joanne's Nurturing Parent. For example, he'd ask her to cook him something special, but the return transaction almost always came from Joanne's Critical Parent and was a variation of "You ought to do that for yourself,

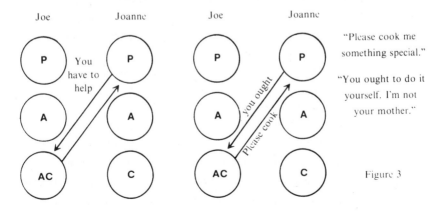

Figure 3

you're a grownup!" Joe's Adapted Child picked up disappointment stamps from these transactions and cashed them in for withdrawal from Joanne, a move that also served to get him away from some of the "have to" messages that were usually floating around in her vicinity. I even felt these "have tos," or rather my Child picked them up, in the transaction from Joanne's productivity-demanding Parent, diagramed in Figure 4. The way I handled this, incidentally, was to ask Joanne, "What would you define as quality?" (I only had to raise this question about twice and her Adult was

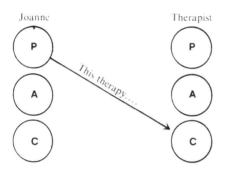

"This therapy has to be productive. We have to talk about a lot of things. We can't waste time. What have we accomplished now?"

Figure 4

hooked and came into action every time that Parent began to demand productivity. In a sense, this hook also got her Parent and Adult in agreement on the importance of the family's contract.)

I also found that variations of these transactional patterns were going on internally between Joanne's Parent and Child and Joe's Parent and Child states (see Figure 5), an example of the operation of what other Transactional Analysis writers have called the *Not OK circuit*. It isn't surprising that this state of affairs had become frustrating to Joe's and Joanne's Child states over the years; not only their own Parent ego states but also the Parent state of the spouse were putting on a lot of demands.

It appeared that Joe and Joanne generally tried to avoid as much interaction between their Child parts as possible, as well as interaction between Parent and Child parts, and had adopted a strong "thinker" orientation, which showed up clearly in the therapy hour (see Figure 6). They had what Berne (1961) termed an *excluding* Adult to Adult relationship; that is, they both would think logi-

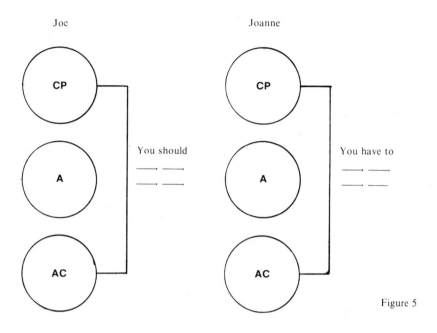

Figure 5

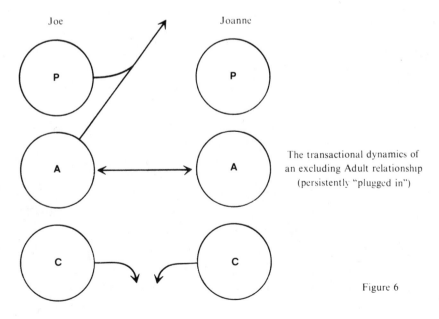

The transactional dynamics of
an excluding Adult relationship
(persistently "plugged in")

Figure 6

cally, at length, about their problems, playing with one another very little.

During the first four sessions or so with this family, I was particularly alert to their games and to how they were being played. Identification of the games proved important because they were for this family (as for all families) the reliable patterns of interactionthat the family had come to count on for getting the kind of feelings they wanted to collect in order to maintain their life positions with each other. As soon as I could have them recognize some of the games, I was able to get one or more of the family members to knock off the games, and, in a sense, this would unsettle the family system and create room for alternate behaviors.

Betty's major game, typical with children who are out to collect stamps of any negative variety, was Kick Me. In this essentially masochistic game, a person promotes negative strokes by acting in a way that has gotten negative strokes before. Children get to know their parents quite well in this regard. Betty's losing the coat was a Kick Me. Characteristically, she would not do what she was asked to do, would not put away her things, and would not clean up messes after herself.

Another game, usually initiated by Joanne from her Child, was *Look How Hard I'm Trying,* the dynamic of which is fear and expectation of criticism. One *of* the ways in which Joanne tried very hard was in keeping the house clean. This game, of course, gave Betty plenty of opportunity to play Kick Me through not doing her part of the cleaning and gave Joe plenty of opportunity to rebel against the have tos, by delaying cleanup help he was asked to give. Joe's Child knew how to take advantage of this and to give Joanne the disappointment stamps she was looking for.

In one session, Joe's Child designed an alliance with the Child parts of the daughters and said, "We feel she tries to keep the house too clean." Joe's Child couldn't complain openly, as we've suggested before, and this creation of an alliance fulfilled his purpose by detouring his feelings, through the two children (see Figure 7). This example illustrates that a game is *not* necessarily just

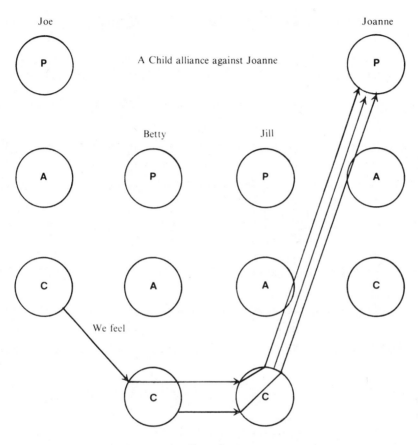

Figure 7

between two people, but can involve all the members of a family system. In this case, the con is on Joanne's Adapted Child.

The next step in the TA therapist's diagnosis of a family is to use his or her understanding of the dominant racket and the games being played together to work out hypotheses for the family's major script injunctions. The injunctions are usually uncovered later than are the racket and associated games because the former are more generalized life commands, which are less easily recognized by the therapist in the early stages of therapy and are certainly less approachable by the patient or family in the early stages. People must also have a little practice with listening to what the Parent in their head is saying before the therapist can get much material on injunctions. But getting at injunctions is also getting closer to the information that will hit people where they live and will promote the most change. An awareness of what the basic fears or hurts are that originally generated the injunction is a directive for a copying life attitude.

A view of injunctions as containing two parts is useful in helping the therapist see this connection. An injunction has a *command* section such as "Be Serious," "Don't Exist," or "Hurry Up," and an *implied,* or "because," section. In family system approaches, injunctions are called the basic family rules. A Transactional Analysis therapist can begin to focus on the family's injunctions if he or she reviews the racket pattern and the games being played with this question in mind: What order or command would generate these responses? To what demand are these patterns a conforming behavior?

In the Moulenarie family, I could review in my mind guilt stamps, disappointment stamps, and a dominant pattern of withdrawal as the behavior most family members were cashing their stamp collections in to get. The dominance of Critical Parent to Adapted Child interactions and excluding Adult tone meant that Child-Child interactions were getting left out and that Nurturing Parent to Child vectors were weak.

The script injunctions began to shape up like the following: "Do it by yourself." "Don't lean on anybody." "Don't expect anybody to help you." "Psychiatrists are crutches." And the family's behavior that I could observe seemed to be more and more like a response to these commands. At one point, relatively early in the therapy, the family was buying a new house, and Joanne was anxious about the financial commitment involved. As we talked about it, we found out that she had grown up in a dirt-poor family and had experienced deprivation to the point of fear of starvation in her early childhood. She was in tears one hour, feeling her fear at its worst. All the husband could do was lean over and reassuringly pat her shoulder a little. The injunction coming from her family shaped up as, "Be productive"—the source of the have to message her family and I have been receiving. Its because section was, "If you don't (aren't productive), you'll face extreme deprivation." The "Don't lean on anybody" injunction came from Critical Parent, and the because section of that injunction was, "They'll reject you and let you down."

As the Moulenarie family began to discover and talk about their script injunctions, I set up several interviews with the parents alone in which we discussed the couple's typical interactions. I drew them a Transactional Analysis picture of their relationship and we reviewed several situations in which one or the other of their Child parts had ventured to seek some nurturing from the other's Nurturing Parent or (very rarely) had tried to get some play, sexual or otherwise, going with the Child of the other. That venture from one of their Child parts was almost always not reciprocated by something from the other person's Child, but was instead met with some form of "stand on your own two feet" or "don't be dependent on me" command from the other person's Parent.

I drew to diagrams; one showed what one of their Child parts (at any given time) wanted, and the other showed what they really got (see Figure 8). "Why does that reaching out always get aborted?" I asked them. "When you see that other person's Child, why can't your Child respond?" When both of your Child parts want to play or when you feel like having fun, *What does the Parent in your head say?*"

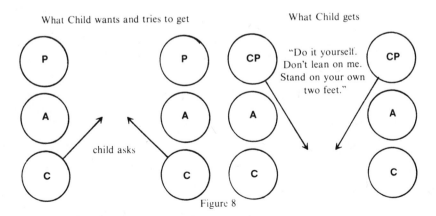

Figure 8

Joe thought for a moment and then said, with an intent and surprised look on his face, "It says, 'stay away, you shouldn't need anything from me, you should be grown up.' " "Who seems to be saying that?" I asked. "My mother," he said, tentatively.

Joanne replied, "Let's see. Stand on your own two feet, you have to do things yourself." Joanne paused and thought a moment. "I think it's my father, but my mother might have said something like that, too."

I find that these "Parent in the head" messages are usually relatively easy for people to spot once they become fairly familiar with PAC and have come to know how their own Parent comes on in everyday life. These messages are less powerful as life-shaping commands than those that Transactional Analysis gives the label of *injunctions*, or negative commands coming from the Child part of a person's actual parent. In fact, Wollams, Brown, and Huige in *TA in Brief* (1976) suggest that a negative stroke from the parent's Adapted Child may well be twenty times stronger than a positive stroke from the parent's Nurturing Parent or five times stronger than a negative stroke from parent's Critical Parent. If we assume that roughly the same is true for life-shaping commands, the rules that the Parent passes along to guide the living of life by his or her Child are much less powerful than injunctions from the Parent's Adapted Child.

I explained the differences between Parent commands and true injunctions to Joe and Joanne and asked them to settle back and think of their actual parents in a variety of settings at different times and try to think of what their parents had warned them against, had been afraid of themselves, or had showed their own Child feelings about strongly. I told them that the Gouldings, along with some other psychiatrists working with Transactional Analysis, believed that the basic injunctions come from the Child and always begin with a don't.

Joanne thought for a moment, then said, "The feeling I get is don't rely on other people, you'll be disappointed." Then, "Hey," she said, "I think when I ask Joe for something, that I'm expecting to be disappointed."

Joe thought for a few minutes and then said, "For me, I think my mother was giving me the message, 'Don't get close to me, I don't like you being a boy!' I don't think she liked my father very much," he added, and went on, "Is that why I feel awkward getting close to Joanne?"

"I think we know enough to talk about your scripts, now," I said, and got out the blackboard to draw some script matrixes. We took Joe's first and put down those messages he'd gotten from his actual parents' Adapted Child, as shown in Figure 9. We then drew

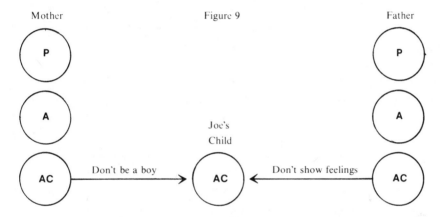

Joanne's (Figure 10), and finally we tried drawing Betty's (Figure 11). The latter was the blockbuster; Joe and Joanne in particular seemed almost stunned. They could see very graphically just how they were passing on some basic fear and avoidance messages without even knowing they were doing it. A lot of these messages were fears of dependence and the reinforcing Parental "Stand alone," and "be independent" messages from their own parents to Betty and her sister. Although Joe and Joanne were surprised by the depth of their own reaction, I often find that the drawing of the script matrix for the family members is a powerful form of insight for all the family members and is often the first real turning point toward change in the therapy.

With Joe and Joanne, we kept on discussing their parents and the messages they got in childhood until we were all quite sure we had

Figure 10

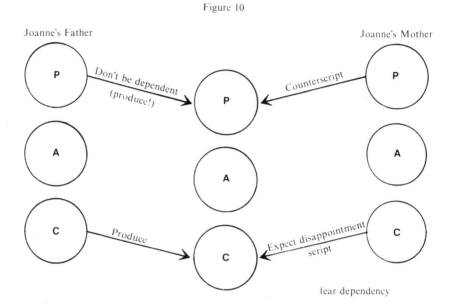

Joanne's Father

Joanne's Mother

Don't be dependent (produce!)

Counterscript

Produce

Expect disappointment script

fear dependency

Figure 11

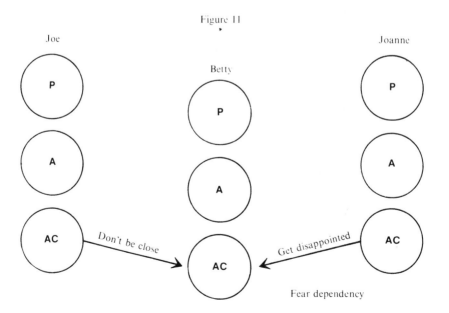

Joe

Betty

Joanne

Don't be close

Get disappointed

Fear dependency

covered this ground. However, we always related it to what was happening currently in their Parent and Child states. We tried to understand the behavior of their parents and some of the reasons for it, so that Joe and Joanne could see the origins of their own behavior and feel less guilty about it and so that they could act less as if they were being persecuted by the therapist or their children for the way they were acting as parents. We could also see that their parents had more reasons—economically, psychologically, socially, and culturally—for passing on those messages to Joe and Joanne, then Joe and Joanne had for passing them on to Betty and Jill. We were also able to see that even for Joe's and Joanne's parents, life according to those script commands might not have been the best possible or happiest adjustment; that is, even in that generation there were better commands to live by, and that Joe's and Joanne's grandparents had even played a role in creating and passing on some of the script messages.

As we shared what we'd been doing with the children, they were able to tell us very clearly how the basic script messages in the family had affected them. Betty said, when we asked her how she understood what we'd been talking about, "I don't feel like I can be taken care of, like that's allowed, so I get afraid of asking you two (Joe and Joanne) for help." This whole matter came up at a point where the family was considering quitting therapy. Later in this discussion it came out that they considered this because of the growing subconscious fear of dependency on me, then the younger daughter voiced the fear of disappointment that was the basic driver of that "don't be close" message in the family. Her point was, "If we don't come to therapy, I don't get to go to the bakery and have donuts."

With these realizations, we also began to get close to the real source of Betty's uncooperativeness. Not only did she see her father rebelling against Joanne's "shoulds" by not cooperating (the delay in cleaning the bathtub is the example we used), but she also could see that being uncooperative, in a version of Kick Me, was a way to get at least some strokes, negative though they were, in a family in which the members were scripted against closeness and support.

Now that we had at least a beginning understanding of the scripting in the family and some of the reason for the passing on of those "can't be close" messages, I could more easily prescribe *homework,* an aspect of Transactional Analysis therapy that Berne originated, both to keep people reminded of what they'd been concerned with between therapy sessions and to reemphasize their responsibility for changing life patterns they'd begun to decide were dysfunctional. One group of homework assignments, the major one, was part of a reconditioning process of practicing what the family members were afraid of, steadily raising the "dosage" as a new tolerance for the previously threatening behavior was established. "Practice being dependent," I said to Joe and Joanne, and we explored together how one of them might be dependent on the other. I then assigned a minimum of half an hour of such practice every week. The children's homework was, "Ask mother and daddy to take care of you." By assigning this homework, I was also giving a permission to do what they'd been injuncted against doing.

Another set of homework assignments had to do with Natural Child to Natural Child interaction between spouses. Once we'd found out what the fear was, we could easily ask, "What would your Natural Child like from the other person if the fear weren't there in the Adapted Child?" Of course, there was nurturing from the Nurturing Parent of the other spouse, but we also found out that Joe's Child wanted to be tickled, and Joanne's Child wanted to be hugged and held. Joe's father had tickled him, but his mother had projected a real fear of and reluctance to getting close in that way, leading to his tendency to withdraw from women.

I should emphasize that I might very easily have lost this family just at the point of getting in touch with their real feelings and fears if I hadn't been sensitive to their Parent commands against dependence and been able to infer (in Transactional Analysis terms from the logic of the script matrix and in the terms I learned from analytic training) the Child injunctions and associated fears concerning closeness. I had to assess what I understood of these fears in the context of their relationship we developed; that is, the closer the relationship we developed in therapy, the more their fears of being dependent on me would escalate. When Joanne began to question the effectiveness of the therapy, and said, "Sometimes I feel that psychiatrists are crutches. We ought to be able to work this out ourselves." I knew that a critical point was coming up, and it turned out to be the point at which I introduced the script matrix. After that, my permissions were the exact opposite of the injunctions. I asked them to practice being dependent on me, as well as on each other, to call me up if they were having trouble, to lean on me, and so on. The potency of these permissions depends, as usual, primarily on the Child trust in me as a Parent figure who can protect against the threats of a change while people were getting accustomed to it.

Throughout this stage of the therapy, I also had to deal with the persistence of Joe and Joanne's "thinker" orientation, their pattern of thinking at length, logically, about any subject that came up and their reluctance to play or to expose many of their Child feelings. A subinjunction in their script (part of the anticloseness theme) was not to show feelings. This subinjunction was another reason for their choice of strong Adult to Adult interaction. I had to continually fight their tendency to keep the therapy a thinking operation. I frequently reiterated that in their thinking postures they were a closed corporation and that when I tried to get at their feelings they saw me as a threat to the system. One way this came out was a running game of Yes But that Joanne and Joe played with each other and a variant of it that they played with me. Initially, Joe and Joanne would play Yes But back and forth, particularly about their parenting actions, with each of them trying to keep the other separated and passive. In their play with me, they were projecting their Parent parts on to me, experiencing me as their own parents from the past and taking many of the things I said as "why don't yous."

Beginning to see Change

At this stage of the therapy, I was also beginning to see some change in the family system or apprehension of change. Betty, off and on, played her Kick Me game harder, partly to test out what was happening and partly to see if her role in the family could be maintained if, after all, it was secure. This increase in symptoms on the part of a child is usually a good indication that the system is beginning to change in subtle ways and that for the first time the children are faced with the question, "Do we really want it changed?" Their increased acting out is an indication of their anxiety about a new role and of the loss of proven ways of getting strokes. During this stage in the therapy, when we really began to raise the anxiety level about what a new form of life would be, I could also see Joe's and Joanne's Adapted Child parts fighting to keep the old orientations to life.

The Guilt Racket Family

After Joanne, Joe, Betty and Jill, the younger daughter, had become quite conscious of the family's script and had been trying to practice more interdependency, they reached a point where they felt stopped. They knew that they had discovered some important things about their family life and history, but they did not feel quite whole and happy or confident in their new knowledge. In behavior, they had achieved a good social control level or cure; that is, they knew how to consciously avoid the negative interactions that had bothered them, but they did not know very well yet how to bring positive interactions into play. Their script contained a message about not showing feeling, I told them, and I made the point that they were still only letting me into their thinking lives.

The solution turned out to be a *family marathon* in the style that I use. I haven't found a continuous weekend marathon to be feasible. It's simply too hard to schedule. If I were to do this with every family, I would never see my own; I'd have to start family therapy with them, and my Parent says that would be "too much." So instead, I ask a family to sign up for three two-hour sessions a week for a couple of weeks. I found this tactic excellent for the Moulenarie family because in the first forty-five minutes I could begin to wear out their thinker orientation; and when they got a little tired, more Child began to come out where we could see it. We could spend a lot more time on the feeling level and follow a feeling through several family experiences and aspects in some detail.

Betty was the indicator that this schedule was successful. At first, she began to object to coming to the therapy. She was afraid of changing the family system, now that real change was starting. She even engaged in some fresh rounds of Kick Me and in other ways sought reassurance that a new alliance of parents wasn't going to leave her out in the cold. It was hard for her to see, as it is for many children, that a new arrangement may be better than the familiar one. When it comes to the crunch, the familiar is always preferred, as it is with almost all of our behavior patterns.

Betty signaled her concern one day by leaving a note on the kitchen table that she was failing in school. When Joanne came home, she saw the note and got worried. She asked Betty what was going on. Betty said everything was all right in school and she didn't mean to alarm her. I said, "Betty, you know that was being a very provocative child, you wanted your mother to be concerned. I think you're afraid she isn't going to love you and that you have to provoke some extra concern from her." Betty admitted that I was right and complained that now her parents seemed to be giving more attention to each other (another sharp insight for a relatively young child).

Joe and Joanne also showed some signs of strain. Shortly after our marathon weeks, they came in saying they'd read a text about therapists who told people just what to do in response to their feelings and they complained, "You tell us what we're doing, but not what we ought to do about it."

"You're making a last-ditch bid for dependency on me, aren't you?" I laughed, "Did you notice that you said 'what we ought to do'?" I got a sheepish grin in return and escalated their homework assignment of practicing dependence on each other. I also reminded them about what Betty had said about the effect on her of the system they had been using. We continued to work on practicing Natural Child to Natural Child play and Nurturing Parent caring and Parent to Parent collaboration on how they should raise the children. This strategy was the basic prescription for their future relationship.

I pointed out to them that one of the ways of getting rid of some of the old worries or power of the Adapted Child was to practice another ego state behavior, in their case Nurturing Parent, since by practicing that they reduced the energy available to the Adapted Child. I emphasized once, for example, trying things that used to make them feel guilty (a totally free, nonproductive time for Joanne), and I gave Joe the task of watching with his Nurturing Parent for Joanne's emerging guilt and then cutting it off by giving her permission to enjoy the nonproductivity. He was also to watch closely with his Adult to make sure that no one picked up the vibrations of her Productive Parent and tried to tell her that she "ought to be doing something."

It's pleasing to report that it wasn't very long before seeing that the parents' play lifted the depression from Betty and that she soon found that her mother and father could give her more stroking and nurturing when they were having fun with their Natural Child parts. I let them go with a provision that they were welcome to come back and be a little dependent on me if the need arose. I heard months later that they were still very happy and feeling free of their script with its demanding Critical Parent parts, which had cost them so much enjoyment. It was a satisfying way to end the case.

THE RATHORNES, A FEAR RACKET FAMILY

Bert Rathorne, a professor of science at a nearby state college, was sure that the problem with his son Phillip was chemical or physiological and at first would not admit that there could be anything emotionally or mentally (psychiatrically) amiss with him. The symptoms themselves were clear enough. Phil, at the age of twenty, had tremendous difficulty mustering the courage to leave home to go to work or to school. At the time we started our meetings, he had already been hospitalized several times for paralyzing attacks of

The Rathornes, A Fear Racket Family

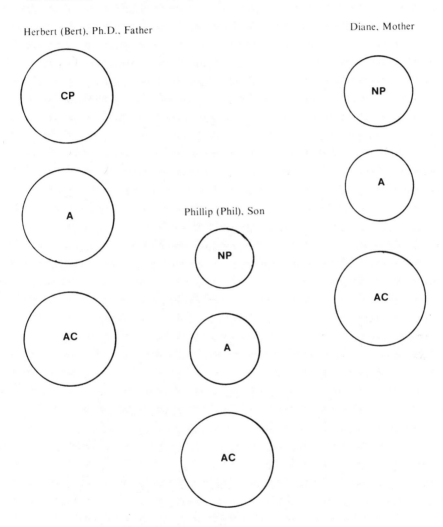

Figure 12

panic, which had occurred in various places away from his home. It was during the third of these hospitalizations that Phil's mother asked me to work with him, and I agreed, on the condition, as usual, that I would actually be working with the entire family.

For our first interview, I saw Phil alone at the hospital and rather quickly found out that the major current preoccupation of his Child, the preoccupation that was keeping him stuck to the house was, "What if when I'm walking around I panic, and get destructive, and smash a window or something worse?" It's become fairly well recognized in Transactional Analysis that a "what if" phrase is one key to a fear racket, and so those words caught my attention immediately. I filed them away in my head, and in my notes I decided to check, soon, to see if there were other "what ifs" being passed around in this family. However, there was a further dimension here because Phil was not voicing fear of an external threat, as much as the fear of his own feelings. I knew from my analytic training that one of the subjects of fear most likely to show up in anxiety (a generalized fear of something that can't quite be labeled or identified) is a person's fear of their own assertiveness, aggressiveness, or anger. It often comes from a young child repeatedly asking for things and a parent saying, in a tone which hints that something very important is at stake (usually that parent's feeling that they cannot provide or cannot give), "You shouldn't keep asking!" The child begins to feel that asserting or asking or demanding is going to rouse a hidden demon of some sort, but, of course, the child cannot know that the demon is usually that parent's own fear. Thus, the child learns to be afraid of exercising that assertiveness.

After we got Phil out of the hospital and I met with all three family members in my office, I began to pick up more "what if" messages. Bert's "what ifs" seemed to relate mostly to external threats—that is, to dangers from the environment. His father was always listing all the cautions and defenses that a person needed to exercise. We heard a lot about those when Phil expressed interest in getting a motorcycle.

Phil's father was very withdrawn, a personality type I think of as schizoid, but without strong externally visible symptoms. He rarely offered much on his own in the therapy sessions but instead communicated by writing out long discussions and arguments about what was going on and sending them to me in the mail. At one point, for example, he wrote up a long paper outlining all the reasons that Phil ought to be able to get out of the house and do things. His Parent message to Phil, albeit a relatively weak one, is diagramed in Figure 13.

However, it was understandable that Phil's Child didn't take it very seriously, since the other messages coming from his father were "What if. . ." (see Figure 14). Consequently, Phil had a lot of arguments about what he really should be doing mixed up with a lot of what ifs; the two could be seen as combining to make him fairly immobile. But these factors did not explain the fears of his own assertiveness or aggressiveness which I picked up in the first few interviews when we had discussed the kind of panic he felt in the outside world. Even though I couldn't easily explain those fears early in the therapy, I began to see another manifestation of them right in the sessions as I watched the sequence of interactions in the family as a whole.

Usually, the first person to pick up on any suggestions, explanation, or statement about the family's life or anything else, for that matter, was Phil's father. He's engage his disputatious Child and get into heavy sessions of Yes But, fighting off any direct approach to the family's feelings, any suggestion of closeness to Phil or his wife, Diane, and any idea that I put forth. Diane Rathorne would begin to build up resentment of his competitive Child, both because she couldn't get anything she said taken directly or seriously and because she could never get a firm point of view to depend on. The fun of the argument and the spirit of the competitiveness, as I have suggested, was the major point of the game for Bert.

But before Diane could built her anger up to the point of really blowing back at the father, Phil could leap in as the marriage counselor, temporarily relieving the growing anger between the parents by an Adult clarification of the matter. This behavior seemed cued by a certain level of agitation on the part of the mother. I suspected that her Adapted Child was calling Phil's Nurturing Parent for a

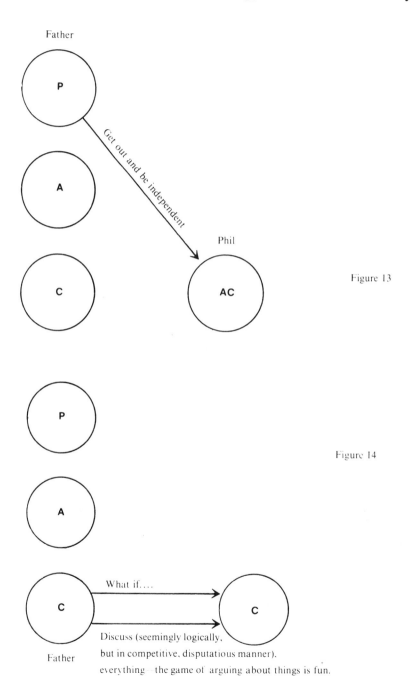

Figure 13

Figure 14

rescue, which Phil then provided. These steps, expressed in transactional diagrams, are shown in Figure 15.

After seeing the pattern repeated several times I asked myself, "Why was Phil doing this?" A possible answer suggested itself after Phil's mother sighed, "I don't know what life would be like around here without someone to make sense out of my interactions with my husband." There was the mother's motivation for keeping him around the house, but why did her son go along with it? I remembered his anxiety over his potential destructiveness were he ever to panic and release some feelings, and I quickly inferred that Phil's Child was programming his Adult to reduce the building anger between the spouses before it somehow exploded and caused that unknown, unexperienced disaster.

"What was the disaster?" I wondered. Diane was enlisting his aid to keep her anger from going too far. I thought about that and let my Child fantasize about being in her place. I played the father's transactions back and felt them with my Child. That constant argumentativeness, the Yes But, the fending me off, the lists of reasons for this and reasons for that, and a steady diet of those what ifs tantalized me (as the mother's Child), along with "be scared, be scared, be scared, but don't come running to me to be reassured." I began to feel totally alone (still as the mother's Child) as I was getting these messages (see Figure 16).

I began to feel angry at the father, and it struck me, "After thirty years like this, her Child must want to kill him." I soon persuaded the wife to have a couple of individual sessions with me, and lo and behold, my guess turned out to be correct. Of course, she was extremely afraid of that feeling, too, and at the same time she experienced it she also felt extremely dependent on this man, saw nowhere else to turn, and was prevented by the father's personality from getting close and achieving any comfort for her Child. As long as she could keep Phil in the family, she'd have a little companionship for her Child and help when she asked for it. She could keep just far enough apart from her husband so she wouldn't feel the death wish too often, and she could have her interactions with him interpreted so that she wouldn't feel completely alone.

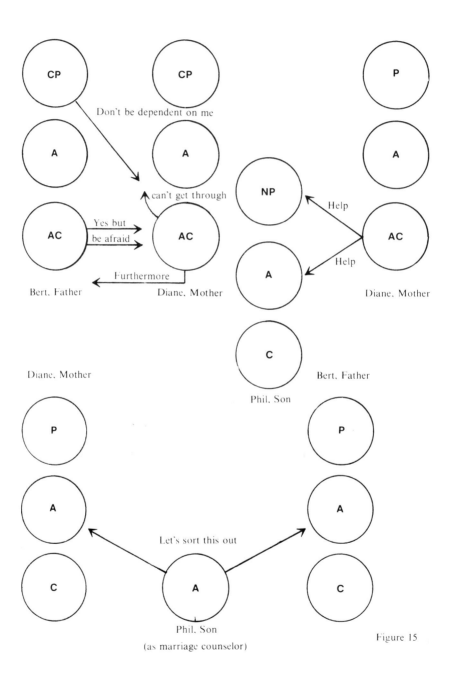

Figure 15

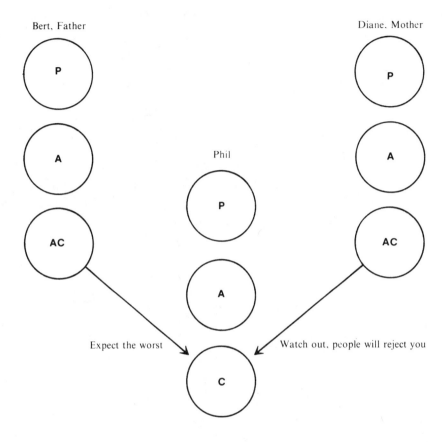

Figure 16

Phil, then, was collecting fear stamps of two kinds. Fears of the environment, which his father showed him how to collect, and fears of his own feelings, assertiveness, and aggressiveness, which his mother showed him how to collect. The mother's collection accumulated in two piles, on "What if I get angry and kill him," and "What if I kill him, or he dies, and I am left even more alone to face the world than I am now?"

Anxiety attacks such as Phil experienced are only one obvious manifestation of the fear-anxiety racket. I've seen other fear and anxiety collectors tensing up as their minds wander around for something to talk about in my office; their brows sometimes wrinkle and, of course, there are the what ifs. The games the Rathrone family played are to some degree typical of the fear racket in families. Why Don't You, Yes But is a game that keeps one person passive and the other person in a static role, dishing out the urgings (the Why don't yous, with the double-level "you won't, can't") for passivity and thus preventing someone with fears from actually going out and doing or trying new things that might raise the fears to consciousness. There is often a fear of closeness, particularly of potential violence or aggression by anothon, and so the game of Uproar is also important. In this family's case, Phil's mediation kept the Uproar at a fairly constant reduced level. He did not allow it to escalate to any really violent forms. Again, I asked myself, "What might have been the commands that would produce these kinds of actions?" and I got these Parental messages, "Be independent," "Dependency is weakness," "You need to be dependent," and "Stand on your own two feet."

Change for the Fear Racket Family

The pattern of the Rathorne family's interactions had become clear. We had recognized the two major games and some of the family rules; the parental commands had become apparent. However, we hadn't yet defined what the true injunctions were to Phil. These are, as I said, the messages from the parent's Child parts or what the actual child sees the parent's Child ego states doing with each other. This demonstration or command may be in agreement or in conflict with what the Parent ego states are saying, but either way, the message from the parent's Child will be far stronger than any from the parent's Parent. The child will always rely on the behavior that he or she sees the parent's Child doing.

It was becoming fairly clear to Phil that his parents were overly dependent on each other, and that in some general way he was getting a message from both of them to be fearful and to remain connected to the family. It was still therapeutically necessary to get that understanding into the concise form of real injunctions that we could all look at. Putting those injunctions into words and seeing where they had come from would provide the "clout" of insight that would strike Bert, his father, and Diane hard enough so that there would be some real change in the system.

After I had uncovered Diane's fear of her own anger toward Bert and we had labeled the fact that everyone in the family collected fear stamps, we didn't seem to be getting anywhere for a period of several weeks. We even said that the family's fear stamps were cashed in for rounds of clinging, but that realization still didn't have the impact we were looking for. So I began to go further back into the family's history, asking the couple to describe their history, the ways they had brought up Phil, and what they could remember about episodes in his childhood.

The family recalled and described various episodes and recollections back through the years until finally we seemed to be getting to the earliest fringes of Phil's memory. Phil described a scene that he thought was the earliest he could recall. It was his first day in nursery school, when he was about four years old, and he was eager to try out new toys. One by one, the mothers came with the rest of the children. They said their good-byes, and left, as it was a staffed program. Some children cried for a minute or two, but all of them were soon involved in play. Mrs. Rathorne alone remained, and Phil kept going back to her to clutch at her dress. He was feeling "a little afraid" as he recalled, and his mother ratified that fear, giving him the message that it was dangerous to separate from her. Finally, one of the teachers firmly led her to the door and insisted that she leave.

"Aha," I thought to myself as I asked everyone what message they thought Phil had gotten from his mother and what ego state it had come from. We finally agreed on the answer diagrammed in Figure 17.

Undoubtedly, there were other similar episodes in Phil's early childhood, but this one seemed to stick in his mind and in his mother's and thus served to be, in Transactional Analysis terms, the script scene—one vivid instance in which we could see the basic script messages from the mother's Child to Phil's Child. The thera-

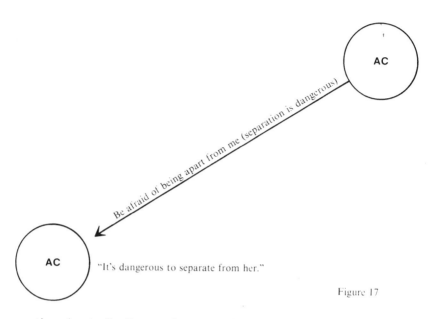

Figure 17

peutic value to finding such a scene is that it's simple, and is easily remembered as a concrete representation of the dynamics we talk about.

Once we had identified these basic Child injunctions and had explored the because part, we felt we'd spotlighted the force that was really keeping Phil at home, affecting both his ability to leave and his mother's deeper level desires to keep him. Just drawing this picture of the injunctions his mother had received from her mother (Phil's grandmother): Grandmother had a strong insight-impact (see Figure 18). Shortly thereafter, Diane was able to further clarify her dependency feelings toward her husband, finally saying from her Child, "I'd never want to live after my husband died."

In the subsequent weeks, Phil seemed more and more confident. Although both parents were still giving very mixed messages, and many of our findings about the family script hadn't yet penetrated very far into their Child feelings, I felt that Phil was ready to get a permission from me to get on with his life and get out of his home. I delivered it in a form I've found useful in emancipation problem cases like Phil's. I first used a challenge from my Critical Parent

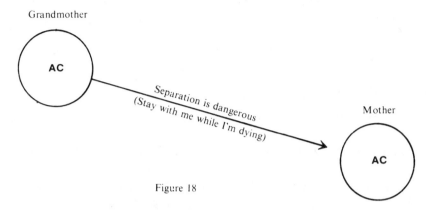

Figure 18

like this, "You'd be crazy to move out, you've got a car, you get your laundry done, you can come and go anytime you want, you never have to worry about shopping or getting meals...." Phil's response was, "I've got to get out of that family." Phil was really coming to see how static his parent's situation was. His Adapted Child was more confident, and he recognized the script pattern, which being younger and with a more easily hooked Adult, he appreciated more quickly and more fully than did his parents. He could see that his mother was bribing him to stay connected with the family. This challenge exposed the bribe and Phil's Child's part of the mutual holding on. It was a spur to the natural tendency for a young person to individuate, or differentiate, from his or her parents.

Phil moved out, and the mother became angry at me and persuaded her husband (it didn't take much) to quit the therapy. I couldn't, therefore, go further with working out the details of the family script, as it involved all three of them; nor was it as appropriate in their case. My initial assignment had been Phil and his fears, and he continued to work with me in individual sessions. His mother objected to these individual sessions, and, in one long and angry phone call, she berated me roundly for "taking her boy away." This case clearly shows the accuracy of the basic assumptions in family therapy that the family is indeed a system and that the parents often don't want to change the balance in the relationship. In Transactional Analysis terms, they don't want the script to be interfered with.

THE JOHNSONS, AN ANGER RACKET FAMILY

Morality and Rebellion

Families hooked hard on the anger racket have often given me a somewhat more exciting time in therapy than those in the guilt and fear rackets because there's usually a zesty conflict simmering between family members. Also family members used to responding to any challenge with anger are likely to get angry at me when I start to explore their relationships. Both of these factors were abundantly present in the first several months I worked with the Johnson's and their daughter Alza.

Alza was fifteen when her mother first contacted me and we began therapy sessions. There were no questions in the minds of both parents that *she* was the problem. In brief, her mother said, they wanted her cured of her "lying and stealing," which had become an increasing problem both at home and at school.

I began to get a feeling for the family when the father and mother arrived for the first interview ready to fill me in on how bad Alza was getting to be. "We just don't know what to do with her," Sally Johnson began. "We can't trust her around the house. She's supposed to be on a diet to lose some weight, but she raids the ice box when we're not there and then denies it when we find half the ice cream gone."

Ralph Johnson put in his oar, "Her grades are going down in school, and the teachers really are getting fed up with her, and I can understand that, because about all she gives anyone these days is a real surly response. That's what it is, just surly and mean. There's really something bad going on in her head, just bad, and it's gone far enough!"

As I was listening to these descriptions, which were amplified in a number of directions, I was sizing up both Mrs. and Mr. Johnson.

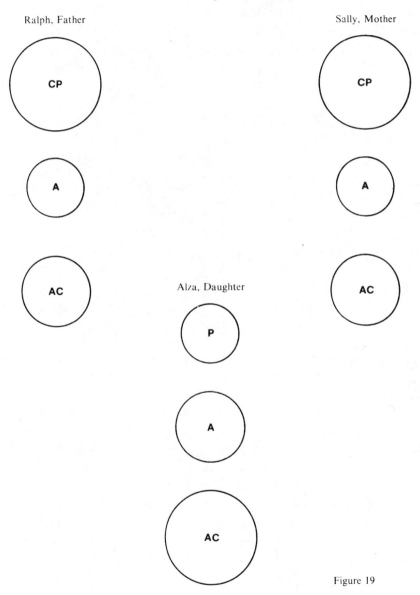

The Johnsons, an Anger Racket Family

Ralph, Father

Sally, Mother

Alza, Daughter

Figure 19

He obviously had been strongly taught that men were to have the power in families and that this power was to be exercised almost wholly through a huge and tyrannical Critical Parent. His wife's tone was more complaining, and while she sounded just as convinced as Mr. Johnson that Alza's lying and stealing were terrible and had to be stopped, it was clear that he would come down on Alza the Hardest when "things had gone far enough," as he put it. I noted too, that both parents were overweight, and that neither seemed inclined to look at me directly in the eye. When they were talking about Alza, their attention seemed focused on an image of her, somewhere just to the right or left of me. When they answered questions about themselves, they shifted their gaze around and often dropped it to the floor. That kind of nondirectness often indicates Child parts which are leery of being "found out," and so I decided to check on ways truth was handled in this family. After all, I'd been told that Alza's problems were lying and stealing. How had Sally explained her absence to Alza this afternoon, for instance? "Oh, I told her I was going shopping," she said. There was something of a sly twinkle in the eye that I caught just briefly. The principal pattern of transactions between the spouses, at least as I could generalize about it after the first few interviews, is hypothesized in Figure 20.

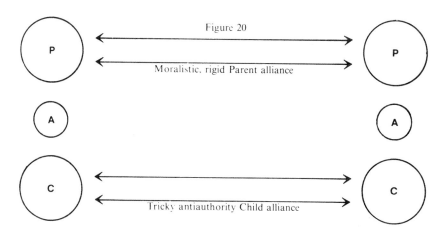

Figure 20

Moralistic, rigid Parent alliance

Tricky antiauthority Child alliance

Not OK Child ego states of individuals with an anger racket are less likely to be downcast and deenergized than those of persons with the guilt and fear rackets. Instead, these anger racket Child states are likely to be aggressively engaged in a cycle of games dominated by Kick Me and NIGYYSOB. This situation was certainly the case in the Johnson family. The amount of energy devoted to conflict, or preparation for conflict, is symptomatic of the strong intrapsychic conflict between the Parent and Child ego states in the family. It's as if to keep the intrapsychic conflict from being recognized, to avoid perceiving the unsettling nature of this "Be Moral" or "I want to have fun and rebel" set of contradictory commands, a lot of energy is projected outward to generate conflict between the actual parent and child.

Alza came to the next interview, and, sure enough, the first thing I saw on her face was a resentful, surly sulk. I also noted that she, too, was overweight. The sulk was saying, from her child, "Just you wait, goddamit, I'll show you!" The immediate crisis, it appeared, was that her father had accused her of stealing a couple of dollars he thought were missing from his wallet, which he had left around the house in various places, and of using it to buy some candy. Alza denied taking the money; she said that he'd forgotten how much he had, like he usually did, and that she hadn't been buying candy. Ralph Johnson's reply was, "We don't care if you eat candy and gain some more weight, just don't lie about it and tell us you're not doing it when you know you are!"

It was a standoff. Alza bristled and remained surly but refused to be cowed. I asked her how she was feeling. "Mad," she replied, and she dug her heels a little more defiantly into my carpet. At that point I decided to introduce the family to Transactional Analysis and began by discussing rackets and suggesting that it seemed to me at that point the members of this family collected anger stamps and thus had an anger racket going. I then continued with my basic Transactional Analysis lecture.

In the next few sessions, we explored the various things that made the different family members angry. Ralph's boss, it turned out, was often on his back, criticizing his punctuality, his efficiency, or something else. Ralph would get pretty burned up after a few days, and at these times his criticism of Alza would also increase. I asked him what he'd do about it besides criticizing her. "Oh, I have a few beers after work," he said, "and we get even with him." "How?" I asked, since I'd gotten the diverted eyes and the sly smile on that one, and he told me how a little extra would be included on the expense account, some spare parts and supplies from the company's stock would "wander," and so on. Sally commented, "That company really screws people who work for them, their customers, everyone, they're rotten right up to the top" (an Ain't It Awful game).

By now, I could see that the ego states most active in this family were Critical Parent and Not OK Adapted Child. I also saw that there was a decided lack of Adult observation of the discrepancies between the rigid moralistic Critical Parent demand, and the tricky rebelliousness and rebellious anger-collecting Adapted Child states. The dominant pattern of transactions between the parents and Alza is diagrammed in Figure 21.

Alza was a past master at Kick Me, a game that, as noted, is a major one in many families. She knew an astounding number of ways to get both her mother and father to blow up at her (her

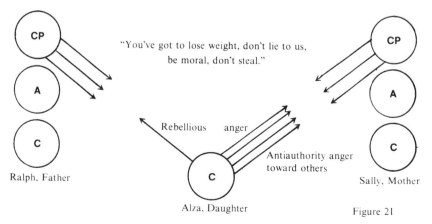

Figure 21

father's blowups were usually the most violent). Alza used the anger
stamps collected from these episodes to reinforce a strong Not OK
feeling and to justify another cycle of the game, as well as overeating. It is not accurate to talk about the "start" of a cycle of these
games, of course, because it was repeated continuously in this
family, and the ending of any stage was the beginning of the next.
Nonetheless, we can diagram an arbitarily chosen "first" stage of
the interactions, as shown in Figure 22. Then, whenever Alza felt in
need of some negative strokes and wanted reinforcement for her
perception of herself as Not OK she provoked either parent (see
Figure 23). Following, of course, is the Kick, which, with Alza's
father, was more of a NIGYYSOB attack (see Figure 24).

Alza responded to the kick by collecting a number of anger
stamps. Since her father's Critical Parent was so strong that she
could not fight back at it very much, many of these stamps served to
justify her overeating, which was the only way that the Child could

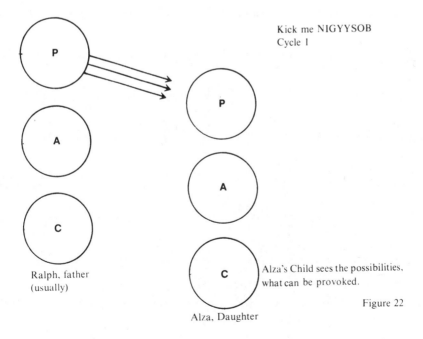

Kick me NIGYYSOB
Cycle 1

P

A

C

Ralph, father
(usually)

P

A

C

Alza, Daughter

Alza's Child sees the possibilities,
what can be provoked.

Figure 22

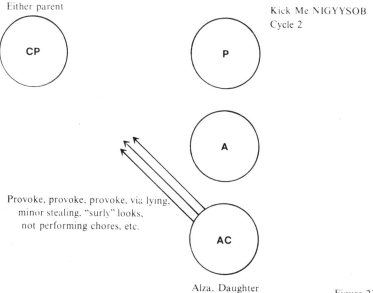

Either parent

Kick Me NIGYYSOB
Cycle 2

Provoke, provoke, provoke, via lying,
minor stealing, "surly" looks,
not performing chores, etc.

Alza, Daughter

Figure 23

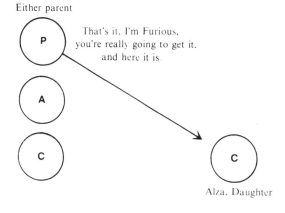

Either parent

That's it, I'm Furious,
you're really going to get it,
and here it is.

Alza, Daughter

Figure 24

get any gratification and show rebelliousness toward others (see Figure 25).

Finally, with enough of these reactions, Alza's father was justified in carrying his NIGYYSOB to the level of rejection and fairly outright condemnation of Alza's basic worth (see Figure 26).

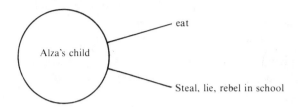

Figure 25

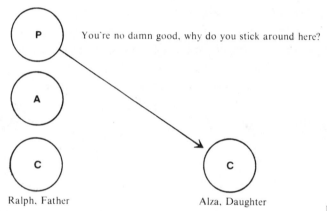

Figure 26

TA-Structural Analysis of the Johnsons

The fact that the NIGYYSOB game went to such lengths in the Johnson family soon led me to apply some other perspectives as well, including the structural views of Minuchin and others. I had begun to wonder how Alza's mother fitted into the rejection pattern and whether she participated somehow in the NIGYYSOB sequence, and if so, why. It became apparent that she went along with Ralph's general reactions to Alza and with the Kick Me—NIGYYSOB game cycle, but from a somewhat more Adult and Nurturing Parent stance. That is, she made numerous "helpful" suggestions to Alza about losing weight, managing her relationships at school, and so on, playing I'm Only Trying to Help. When her aid was apparently ignored or rebuffed, she also could get into the "you're no good" posture from her Critical Parent.

The parents clearly had a coalition with each other and were excluding Alza from the family boundaries. The nature of this pattern became more evident to me when I reconsidered the ego state similarities and transactional pattern between the parents, which showed two strong Critical Parent states in agreement about the world and two tricky Child states in agreement about overeating, rebelling, sneaking in extra on the expense account, and other ways of getting "out from under" the Critical Parent states. Implied in that pattern was a fairly strong intrapsychic barrier between the Critical Parent states and the Adapted Child states, as we've suggested before in discussing the reasons for the violence of the angry conflict in this family. The stages of this exclusion-scapegoating process, as I finally worked them out in Transactional Analysis terms, are diagramed in Figure 27.

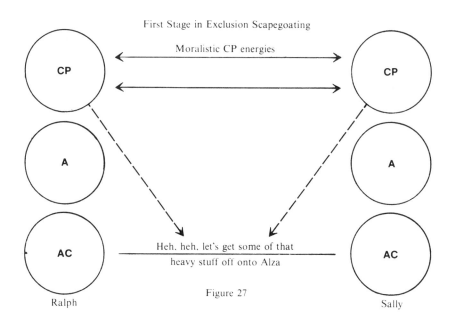

First Stage in Exclusion Scapegoating

Moralistic CP energies

CP   A   AC   Ralph

Heh, heh, let's get some of that heavy stuff off onto Alza

Figure 27

CP   A   AC   Sally

Although it appeared that the alliance was between the Parent ego states (and a non-TA therapist would have to say it was just between the parents and in some way difficult to define), the operant alliance was really between the Adapted Child parts of both Ralph and Sally, which were conspiring to maintain their own freedom to rebel, steal, and so forth, by diverting the energies of the Critical Parent states (see Figure 28). Alza's resultant anger was particularly deep and hurtful because the Adapted Child of one or both parents is usually very interdependent with the Adapted Child of the child, and the Child of the child feels reinforcement and support from the Child parts of the parents. In Alza's case, she was getting almost entirely rejection, a "don't be" injunction from those Child parts. In fact, the mother later admitted in couple therapy, "I can't wait until she gets out of the house." The father said, "I know I shouldn't feel that way, but I feel that way, too."

The unstable element in this situation was, of course, the possibility that Alza might actually "get lost" and leave her parents' Child

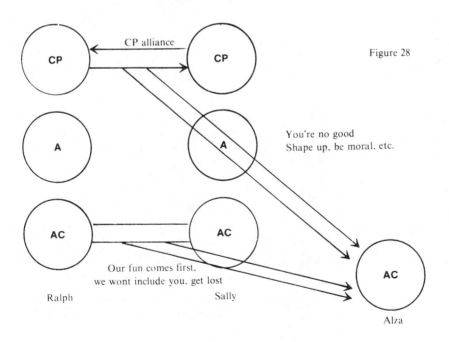

Figure 28

parts alone with their own Critical Parent parts again, but the fact that there were younger children (so far not mentioned nor brought into therapy) meant that probably once Alza got old enough to act on the rejection messages and leave, another child would be set up in the same position. When I suggested this possibility to the parents and got further into their own relationship, they began to take seriously the possibility of change and work toward it.

Exposing the Anger Family's Script and other Actions for Change

I have found that anger families are hard to work with for several reasons, not the least of which is the fact that they're likely to get angry at the therapist over and over again. In cases where there's a lot of fear of the anger underlying the anger itself, there's often an attempt to get the therapist scared as well. Naming the attempt to scare me has usually snapped such patients out of that pattern. That fear of anger didn't exist in Alza's family. Adult states in anger racket families are virtually frozen out of the action when it comes to family situations. The kind and rigidity of Parent messages that usually produce that Child frustration expressed as anger have usually been passed on for a number of generations in that family's history. It's difficult, then, to get the Adult observing either the family processes or the inherent conflict between the Parent and Child states.

In the case of the Johnsons, Ralph seemed to be the strongest initial obstacle to change. At first he resisted applying PAC at all, wouldn't budge from believing that Alza was the family's problem, and maintained his moralistic Critical Parent posture. Then, I began to find out some more about that Parent. It had originated in part when, at the age of twelve, Mr. Johnson's father had died, and his mother had emphasized that, "He had to be the father now, be a big man." Twelve-year-old Ralph Johnson took seriously the job of helping out his mother. Thus, in addition to its moralistic, critical side, his Parent now often operated toward Sally in the rescue games of Why Don't You, and I'm Only Trying to Help. We dia gramed this couple interaction together one week (see Figure 29), and I asked Sally how her Child responded to it. She finally identified the feelings shown coming from her Child and, after some sympathetic probing, was able to say that she really dreaded Ralph's homecoming when he was in a high dudgeon, moralizing and making everybody in the family feel bad. He seemed to perceive something from his wife's statement, and I saw him use just a little more Adult as he responded to the transactions in the family. At about the same time, we began to get into their Parent to Child interactions, though we were also getting more deeply into the nature of their relationship to Alza and the different messages and injunctions they were sending her.

We began to get at the reality of the family's scripting when, for what seemed to me to be the tenth or fifteenth time, we identified a cycle of the Kick Me-NIGYYSOB games between Ralph and Alza, and it suddenly seemed clear to Sally that a conflict of Ralph's at work fell into exactly the same pattern. I saw a shock of recognition start to spread over his face, and I decided to ask, "Are you

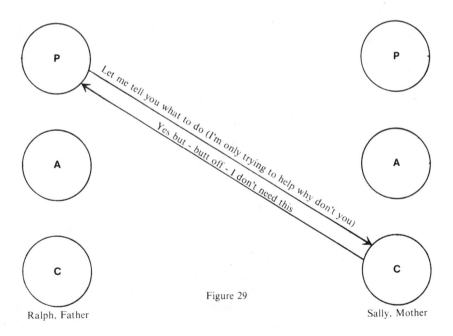

Figure 29

Ralph, Father   Sally, Mother interested in an idea why her Child is so much like your Child?" He couldn't very well answer no, and so I drew Alza's script matrix in general terms, as in Figure 30.

We's already identified the Parent messages that Alza was getting—messages which had been more than usually negative—and I could imagine Ralph thinking, "Oh, that's just the same old thing," until we got to the vector transaction from his Child to Alza's Child. "What should we put here?" I asked, "What words would get at it?" He said nothing, so I went on, "The thing that's important here is the kind of world your Child tells Alza's Child it is, and how to handle it." I think your Child says, "They don't like me and everybody rejects you." They pondered this for a few moments and Sally put in, "You have to fight and it's awful." Ralph mulled over that and mumbled that there might be something to it, but since he seemed quite tense I shifted the attention back to the drawing, essentially playing a short transitional game of Psychiatry to give him time to absorb a quite threatening idea.

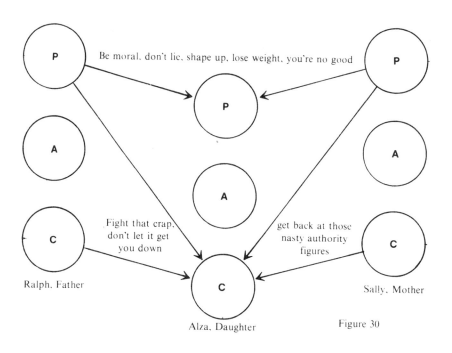

Figure 30

"So your behavior is telling Alza how to handle that kind of world," I continued, "and the reason that you get so frustrated by her behavior is that you know, at least to some degree, that you're showing her the same thing."

From then on, for a number of weeks, we talked about Ralph's and Sally's parents and how similar scripting had taken place for them. I kept trying to hook both their Adults by saying, everytime we discussed a family episode or there was a fresh conflict, "What do you think you're doing?" (to Alza and their other children). I've found this one of the most reliable ways to get an anger racketeer's Adult into the action, and when I make very sure that my tone of voice is quiet, the question is taken as Adult by the patient or family member about ninety-five percent of the time. Those times it isn't, I just keep trying; or I wait until they ask a question, meaning that they'll listen.

We began to conclude together that the same conflict that existed between both parents' Parent and Child states was being passed along to Alza and was probably the reason for a lot of the distress and internal conflict which she felt in her own life, totally apart from her interactions with the family. Both parents were struck forcefully by the script diagram, and we talked about it for several weeks. Sally's reaction was initially the deepest. She kept saying, "I never realized what was happening, that's just terrible, and we've got to stop it." Ralph's response was a bit slower, but he began to take a new attitude when, after one particularly strong lapse into his tyrannical Critical Parent, I asked Sally how she felt and specifically how long she thought the marriage was going to last if Ralph kept his Parent in action that way. He butted in, "Forever, we really are a good team...." Sally paused thoughtfully and said, "I doubt if it will last two more years. I've just gotten so sick of what is happening to the kids, and the more I think about it, the more upset I get."

I could see that Ralph was getting very anxious. He'd never heard his wife say anything like that before, and she said it very, very convincingly in a level Adult tone. I said to him, "Aren't you relieved?" "You're always so critical of the family. If your wife wanted out you could go somewhere else, and yet you seem anxious and angry. The fighting Child of yours isn't so sure you want to face the world alone."

Ralph admitted the truth of what I had said, and from then on the change was wondrous to behold. He swung what we soon found to be a very good Adult into action, observing his own behavior and sorting it out very methodically using PAC. It also helped that we drew *his* script matrix and talked more about the real feelings of his Adapted Child. He'd gotten double messages from his mother after his father's death. She wanted him to be the big man, but she couldn't, of course, really allow him to measure up to his real father. Consequently, she'd given him a lot of deprecatory Critical Parent messages, and he'd built up an angry Not OK Child, which could cover up its unsureness with the belligerent fight-back behavior he was now demonstrating to Alza (see Figure 31).

About this time, fully realizing the scripting they had been giving Alza, Ralph and Sally Johnson accepted responsibility for doing something about their own relationship in order that the other chil-

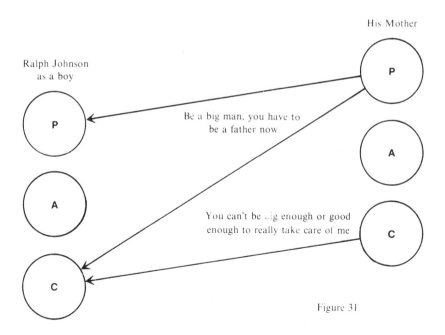

Figure 31

dren in the family wouldn't develop the same problems Alza had. We broke off the family sessions, and I began seeing them as a couple.

A Cure for the Anger Racket Trio

The Johnsons continued in couple therapy for about a year with the express purpose of knocking that anger and rebellion script for good. I was especially impressed by Ralph's progress. After I'd "gotten this attention" by asking his wife how long their marriage might last under present conditions, his commitment to using the PAC sorting system to analyze and plan behavior was one of the strongest and most consistent I've seen. In any stress situation, he would sit down and plan his communication, and generally he could stick to it. Alza was still extremely provocative toward his Critical Parent (if the parents needed any reminder of how important their enterprise was, her behavior reminded them quite often), and he could keep from getting hooked about ninety-five percent of the time—a significant accomplishment.

The growth of Ralph's Nurturing Parent was another impressive sign. Earlier, his wife had turned off to him sexually almost all the time because her own mother had been quite like his tyrannical, "I'm only trying to help your Critical Parent," and she had decided that her masochism in the face of that type of Critical Parent only would go so far. Ralph needed to be in the passive position, and she could then tell him more of what her Natural Child wanted in terms of play and sex.

Sally spent quite a lot of therapy time getting a handle on her mother's and her own Critical Parent, which were deprecatory (given to put-downs). Her mother refused to treat her as an equal even in adult life. One of her mother's favorite points for criticism was the cleanliness of the house, and since her mother visited fairly frequently, we could see the destructiveness of that Critical Parent. Finally, with Nurturing Parent permission from Ralph and from me, Sally finally told her mother, in effect, to "butt out" and never to bother to criticize her housecleaning again. Sally's mother didn't change, but that one confrontation between her and her daughter, we found, was a script release for Sally; Sally's tendency to criticise Alza sharply diminished, since she finally felt free of her script injunction to make herself available to be criticized by her own mother.

Overall, the couple told me that they were happier with each other. Sally said her husband was more considerate in the relationship, and she felt free to relate sexually. Ralph was rightly proud of his accomplishments and his social control and said that he felt much less like he had to be the big macho husband. Perhaps the best indicator was their final message to Alza when she moved out to go to college, "We feel better about ourselves, now, and we're happy to help you if you want us to pay for some individual therapy for yourself." In short, they had allowed her to begin to individuate and separate from the family; they also realized that she could use some remedial help to compensate for the family history and were glad to give it. She took their help with, as far as I know, very positive results. Oh, and lest I forget, all of them lost a great deal of weight.

THE WALLACES, A HURT RACKET FAMILY

As I've already said, one of the things I find most attractive about the Transactional Analysis school of therapy is the many different and often overlapping ways of seeing and saying things simply and the fact that many of them can be diagramed. A picture is often therapeutically worth at least ten thousand words. In one family, we may spend much of our time emphasizing games; in another, we may focus more on the scripting that is taking place; in another, we may look at the OK Corral and its life positions.

Although I've found different people in families with guilt, fear, or anger rackets playing the roles of Persecutor, Rescuer and Victim (Karpman 1968), the triangle doesn't seem to stand out in those families; and when I've mentioned it in passing, no sparks seem to light. Hurt racket families are another matter, and one of the points of the case study we're about to explore is the crucial role

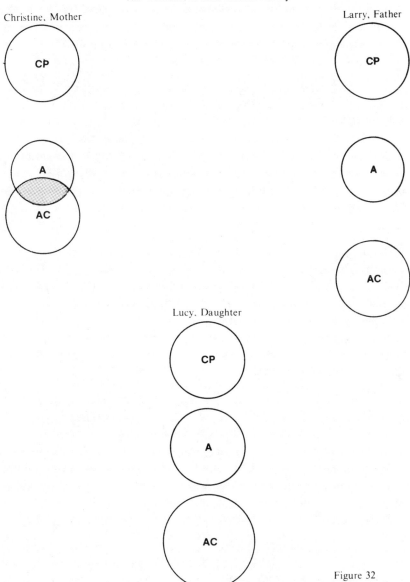

The Wallaces. A Hurt Racket Family

Figure 32

the drama triangle played in the family and the way that exposing it led to significant family changes. For me, the concept of the triangle first proved useful therapeutically as I worked with the Wallace family. Since then, it has seemed that if I sense a strong drama triangle, I usually also find a hurt racket, and vice versa.

There wasn't much doubt about the racket diagnosis with the Wallace family. Hurt was sticking out all over the place as I began with them. We met initially in intensive family sessions in the hospital. Christine Wallace, the mother, had been briefly committed when she claimed that mystical spirits were lifting her around and causing her to run into various objects around the house; that is, these spirits were persecuting her, harming her. With her Adult contaminated by her Child quite severely (the structural reason for the delusion), she could only say, "They're persecuting me (the family), they put me in the hospital to hurt me, and you're going to give me some drugs and they will hurt me." In the initial interviews, I found out that the oldest child living at home—Lucy, age sixteen—had a persistent hurt in her stomach. The mother spent a lot of her time attacking the father, and he felt hurt by that and solaced his Child with some drinking.

Most therapists will agree, I think, that families with a paranoid schizophrenic like Christine constitute one of their more impressive challenges, and sometimes I marvel a little that we really do stand a good chance of helping someone this unhappily disturbed, as well as the others around her. It's no easy job to change the pattern of hurts and projection, which is diagrammed, in TA terms, in Figures 33 and 34.

Of course, it wasn't any great challenge to get each of the Wallace family members to say how they were being hurt by someone else; they could have gone on regaling me and accusing each other for hours. Such is the typical enjoyment that distinguishes a good full-swinging hurt racket. The problem was in getting the Adult ego states in the family to observe the remainder of that hurting system, so that they would begin to think of the rest of the system everytime they began to feel a hurt.

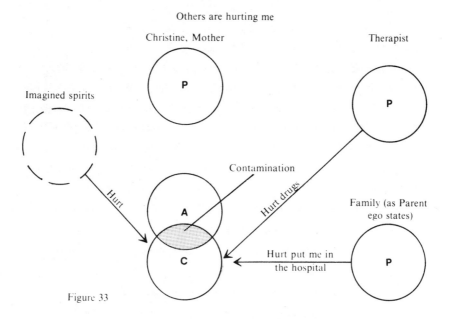

Figure 33

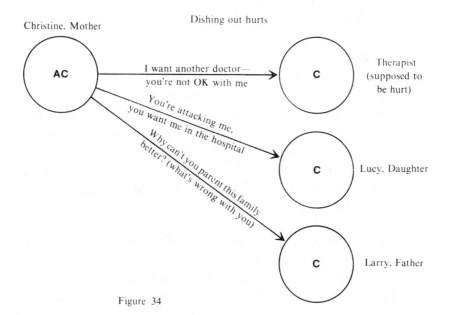

Figure 34

I began to get through to Lucy, the daughter, rather quickly, by following up on a long tirade of her mother's one day near the end of her hospital stay. Christine had lapsed into a strong "I'm OK, They're Not OK, the problem is all in the family" line and was blaming each of the other family members in turn for sending her to the hospital. Lucy got most of it because Christine suspected she'd put her usually passive father up to the temporary commitment. I took a piece of paper and drew this diagram (Figure 35).

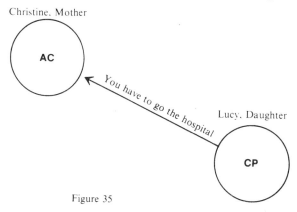

Figure 35

I then said, "Lucy, your mother's saying that you're hurting her. How do you feel about that?" "Well, when she's in the hospital, she doesn't spend all of her time telling other people how fat I am," Lucy said. She continued, "You should hear her whenever she's at home and talking to one of her friends. She's sure to say, 'Poor Lucy, how awkward she must feel, being so overweight. She can't get into her clothes, I'm only concerned for her good.'" "So she hurt you at home, with the overweight thing?" I said. "Do you feel like you're getting back at her if she gets bad enough to have to go to the hospital?" I asked. "Well, maybe—just a little," Lucy admitted grudgingly. "But we'll get you out of the hospital just as soon as we can," Larry Wallace, the father, chimed in, changing the direction of the conversation back toward Christine. I pointed out that the things diagramed in Figure 36 had just happened.

"In lots of families," I explained, "we've found that people get into these roles a lot of the time and that they switch from role to

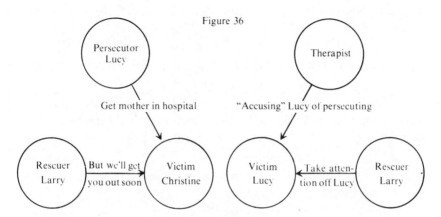

Figure 36

role very quickly sometimes. Let's go back to your mother hurting you, Lucy. You're the victim in that little episode—Who rescues you?" We discussed those repeated times when Christine attacked Lucy, indirectly, by commenting to one person or another about her eating and overweight. George, Lucy's older brother, said, "Oh, I just tell her that the way to get along with mother is not to be hurt, just to ignore that kind of stuff." We drew the particular rescue shown in Figure 37.

At that point, Christine chimed in, "You're all against me a lot of the time. Just the other day there was that phone call, and...."

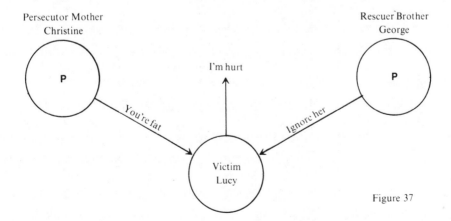

Figure 37

As everyone contributed to the story, it turned out that once again Christine had given a persecuting stroke to Lucy, but this time, Lucy had escaped to a friend's house. There she had her friend telephone home to let her father know where she was. Christine had answered, and asked, "Who is this?" Lucy's friend replied, "I can't tell you. I have to talk to Mr. Wallace."

Christine was hurt that Lucy wouldn't communicate with her, though she'd begun the cutoff in communication with her initial persecuting move. In this case, we decided, Larry and Lucy had formed an alliance and had dished out a persecution to Christine, one they knew at least subconsciously would fit right in with her paranoid perceptions. I thought we probably had an example of detouring here, too; that is, Larry had somehow encouraged Lucy to respond in this particular way, in effect attacking Christine through his daughter. I've seen many other examples of a weak or ineffective spouse fighting in alliance with a child or children, in a relatively passive way, against the other spouse; it's a coalition. In this case, Larry was carrying most of the parenting, but was still a relatively passive, ineffective person (see Figure 38). In particular, neither his Child nor his Parent could stand up to the demanding, constantly criticizing Critical Parent that Christine had.

Although it was difficult to get Christine to see her own roles in the game at this point because of her still severely contaminated Adult, I could get the rest of the family to see, in Transactional Analysis terms, just what her Parent messages were. They then could begin to work on Adult ways of coping with them, and get somewhat more comfortable while we worked together on decontaminating Christine's Adult. The major messages are diagramed in Figures 39 and 40.

In the context of the Wallace family system, as already partly noted, most of the rescuing from these largely persecutory messages was going back and forth between Larry, George, Lucy, and the younger children. Both George and Lucy, making up in part for their father's on-and-off parenting and escapes into booze, were what might be called Busy Parental Siblings in that they had become a surrogate parent for the younger sibs. George, before he

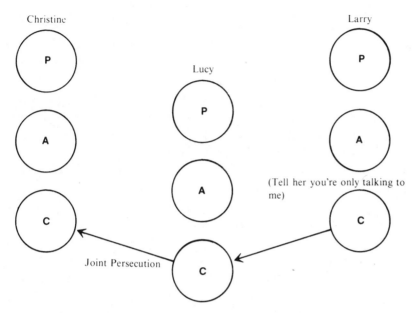

Christine

Lucy

Larry

(Tell her you're only talking to me)

Joint Persecution

Figure 38

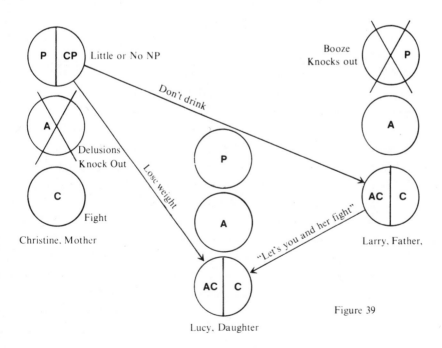

Little or No NP

Booze
Knocks out

Don't drink

Delusions
Knock Out

Lose weight

Fight

"Let's you and her fight"

Christine. Mother

Larry, Father,

Lucy, Daughter

Figure 39

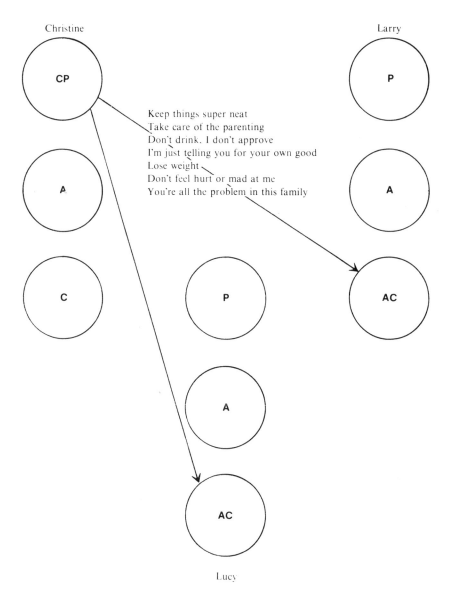

Figure 40

went off to college (getting out of the family system, as he saw it), had parented Lucy, and now Lucy was parenting the younger children. She used her Nurturing Parent to cook for them, telling them in turn "not to pay any attention to mother," and so on. Characteristically, Christine's Parent disapproved of this role of Lucy's, claiming instead that Larry ought to be able to keep the whole family in order. However, her Child example, abdicating the role of parenting, encouraged Lucy to take over. There is always some abdication of the parental role, inconsistency, or even rejection by the Parents involved when one sees a Busy Parental Sibling.

The Hurt Racket Family's Games

When Lucy and George, in particular, saw how the Persecutor-Rescuer-Victim triangle described many of the transactions in the family, they became more interested in Transactional Analysis. We then moved into identifying the games that each person played to get into a Persecuter-Rescuer-Victim interaction with the others. This process, in turn, showed specifically what each person was getting into the interaction *for*—that is, what particular view of themselves they were reinforcing.

It became apparent that Larry's game was Look How Hard I'm Trying, a continual passive "getting along" with his wife's problems; but he was collecting purple hurt stamps with the ultimate goal of justifying his escape from her demanding Parent, the marriage, and his own fairly sizable Critical Parent. Whenever he satisfied his Critical Parent that he had tried very hard during a particular difficult family episode, he could trade in some of his stamps for a few beers, escaping the burdens and not feeling guilty about it. His Child, at this point, would say "poor little me" and his Parent would give him a temporary "out," because he really "had tried."

Christine's game was an escalating Kick Me, with a strong and particularly resistant Why Does This Always Happen To Me? She would persecute the rest of the family mercilessly with that demanding Critical Parent and then cry "foul, foul" when anyone began to fight back. Her stamps were saved up to justify an abusive tirade, which of course would lead others to cry foul again, fight back harder, and provoke another round of Why Does This Always Happen to Me? Such a cycle with paranoids is particularly difficult to break.

Lucy's Major game was I Want Out of Here. She moved to a foster home.

It was at this point of persecuting by Christine that the concept of life positions really came to have meaning for this family. They could see that Larry's was "You're OK, I'm Not OK" and that as long as he clung to that position he, at least, was protected against doing anything risky to get the family's problems toward resolution. George had picked up a little of his mother's "I'm OK, You're Not OK" to defend himself against his mother and to be able to dish out those messages to the other siblings by saying, "Don't pay any attention to her." He had gotten rid of his mother and her problems by moving out, or at least he thought he had. Lucy, also, was in the "You're OK, I'm Not OK" position with her father. Christine's paranoid position was, as Transactional Analysis theory defined it, "I'm OK, You're Not OK." Her frequent reiteration that the problems were in the rest of the family fitted with that neatly. But in all cases, the major stamp in everyone's collection was the purple hurt—"I'm wounded"—variety. "How do we stop collecting them?" Lucy, George, and, to some extent, Larry began to ask.

As they were getting more sensitive to the feeling of having their Adult plugged in, rather than responding to other family members with Parents or Child, I suggested that they start consciously using the strategy shown in Figure 41. Of course, they had to watch very closely for the hooked feeling indicating that their Child was about to collect a hurt stamp from a particular transaction, paste it in the stamp book, and sulk over it a little. Instead, they had to make a decision to turn their Adults on with very specific questions to the person who they felt had just dished out the hurt.

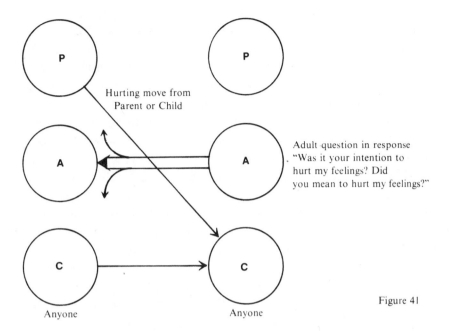

Hurting move from
Parent or Child

Adult question in response
"Was it your intention to
hurt my feelings? Did
you mean to hurt my feelings?"

Figure 41

Anyone   Anyone

And A Double-Bind, or Corner, Game Comes Up

At about that time, the family went to visit one of the grand-mothers over a holiday. The reactions when they returned gave me a further important characteristic of this family system. The first thing I heard on their return was that the children were very upset that they had been required to visit and to say "such an awful long time," as Lucy said her younger brother had complained. The immediate reaction from Christine was "I'm hurt that they feel that way. They shouldn't feel that way."

This episode was my first hint that there really was a Corner game going on in the family. This Parental transactional pattern toward the children in the family basically involves the message, "You shouldn't feel the way you feel." This surface level Parent message indicates that a more fundamental double message is coming from both of those ego states. (We'll see a little later what the fundamental double message was from Christine Wallace.)

If comment is absolutely forbidden (as in "You don't think or feel the way you do—You don't think what you're thinking"), severe thought disorders result, and the only way to reconcile the events taking place is to become crazy. "You don't think" constitutes nonvalidation of the emerging Adult ego state. The result is that the child cannot separate ego states and does not know who he or she is, or what the real self is like. Some parents issue a deprecatory double message that constitutes another form of "You aren't thinking/feeling the way you do," to wit, "What's wrong with you, are you really sick, are you really bad, are you really stupid?"

Christine was giving moderately confusing Parent messages, I decided, when she hurt Lucy by telling friends that she was overweight. The message to Lucy was, "I'm hurting you for your own good." She would hurt other family members and say in various forms, "You shouldn't feel hurt," and to her husband, the messages were "Take care of everything but are you *really* OK?"

Fortunately, Larry's Parent was rational enough to keep his Child from being driven crazy by these messages and he had passed on enough of his rational Parent to Lucy and the other children to give them some protection as well. In fact, Lucy's first definition of what she wanted from the family therapy was quite a rational one, "some more tools for handling mother." However, this situation also meant that the mother was quite isolated within the family and that neither parent was getting any nurturing from the other, making the family system quite impoverished in the interactions needed for real happiness and growth.

Getting at the Family Scripting

After about fifteen sessions with the Wallace Family (Christine, Larry, the parents; and Lucy, George, the two older children), we had formed a good idea of the Parent messages coming down in the family and we had hypothesized that a Corner game was being played by Christine, involving in one way or another all of the other family members as respondents. Those first fifteen sessions were hard ones and particularly so for me because I find I can't use humor easily or frequently in a family with a Corner game and paranoia. The individual labeled "paranoid" particularly is very suspicious, and there is a tension in the family produced by the ever-present Corner transactions, which makes everyone else edgy. Consequently, the main thrust is a persistent and serious "dragging out of the Adult."

Nonetheless, I survived that first segment of the therapy and I had loosened up Lucy, Larry, and George considerably. They had a good idea of what their Adults were and how they could function if they paid strict attention, and they could even laugh on occasion. Even Christine was a little less suspicious, although she was getting progressively more edgy and upsettable as the other family members increasingly failed to react as they previously had to her persecutions and Corner moves.

A Family in the Bathroom

The upsetting of Christine's equilibrium brought us to some crucial insights about the family system and the scripting dynamics on which it was based. During this period, Christine had greatly intensified her insistence on cleanliness. I was struck by this when I made a home visit (something I try to do with every family at least once, although scheduling difficulties often make it possible). As I walked in the door, she was still fussing around with the vacuum cleaner. I began to think about dirt and about cleanliness and finally about the bathroom as a likely site for this family's basic concerns. The bathroom was my Child fantasy, at least, as I mulled over the cleanliness worry.

What about the bathroom?" I began to ask the people in the family, and soon I hit pay dirt. Lucy said that her mother *still* was nagging at her about whether she'd had a bowel movement and that Christine had done this ever since she could remember. Christine hadn't mentioned it before, but now she let loose and went into a long fuss about how worried she was (I pointed out this was her Child) and how much she had had to nag (her Parent) to get everyone in the family to do that very important thing *every day*. She had been brought up in what we call a "colonic irrigation" family, one that bought the once fairly widespread view that fecal material was disease-dirt, and that if you didn't get it out of you regularly, you'd get sick or die. We explored this subject and the other feelings the family could begin to identify once the matter was open.

Lucy said, "Mother seemed so awful worried about it, really scared. She gave us the idea that we'd *die* if we didn't do it every day." "Oh, it's very important," said Christine. "I learned that when I was growing up. When I didn't go, my mother took me to a doctor to find out what was wrong."

Lucy said, "Mother seemed so awful worried, about it, really scared. She gave us the idea that we'd *die* if we didn't do it every day." "Oh, it's very important," said Christine. "I learned that when I was growing up. When I didn't go, my mother took me to a doctor to find out what was wrong."

I told the whole family, first, that it doesn't make any difference at all how often a person moves his or her bowels. I also told them that I thought we were starting to get at some basic script messages, and I introduced the idea and diagram of the script matrix. After we'd all worked on filling in the messages and injunctions, it looked like the diagram in Figure 42.

Christine's mother used to call her selfish and Christine felt she couldn't ask for what she wanted until I gave her the permission (see Figure 43).

Lucy remembered another hurt in conjunction with the bathroom business: Her mother was so concerned about moving bowels that she wouldn't leave the bathroom, costing Lucy her privacy and sending the message, "You can't keep from being hurt—you can't cope by yourself." But Lucy said there was some other feeling connected with the whole thing that she couldn't quite pin down, and it seemed important to her. I mulled it over and thought to myself that we were getting to a touchy area. I began to feel very much like the "You're going to be hurt, you're going to die if you don't do what I say" was a projection of Christine's rejection or death wish toward her children, a frequent characteristic of paranoids. Lucy was getting sensitive to that, and Christine was becoming increas-

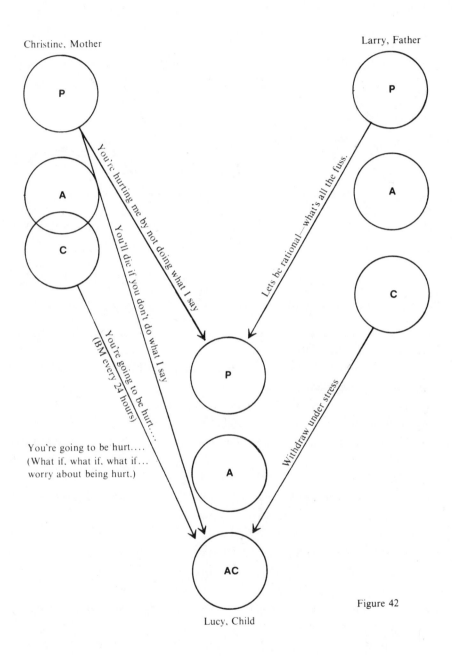

Christine, Mother

Larry, Father

P

A

C

P

A

C

You're hurting me by not doing what I say

You'll die if you don't do what I say

Lets be rational—what's all the fuss.

You're going to be hurt....
(BM every 24 hours)

Withdraw under stress

P

A

You're going to be hurt....
(What if, what if, what if...
worry about being hurt.)

AC

Figure 42

Lucy, Child

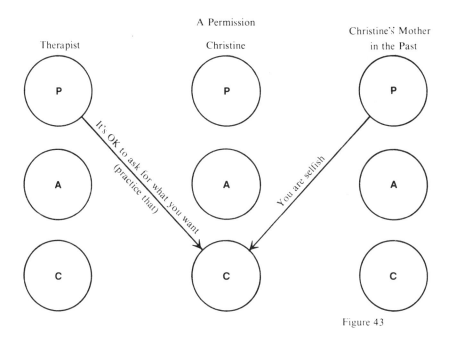

Figure 43

ingly frightened as we got closer to it. So I scheduled an individual session with Christine and one for the family without her and explored these areas.

The basic double-bind, or Corner, game was because Christine's own mother had felt quite rejecting toward her, I suspected. Christine would have picked this up just as Lucy was doing but would not have been able to feel it. It is too dangerous to feel hostility toward someone as critical to you as a parent. So the hostility was projected outward (that was the paranoia) and the double-bind message going to Lucy was as shown in Figure 44.

Now, it should be noted, we had a much more specific focus on the Corner game. It has just to do with "You shouldn't feel the way you feel," but we identified the feeling and it was a life-threatening one closely tied to the family's racket and the Persecutor-Rescuer-Victim drama triangle (hostility, hurting, persecuting, victimizing). Or, in the terms of Bateson et al. (1956), it could be said that we had discovered a basic family rule, or rather a system of two, in conflict—"feel hostility" and "don't feel hostility." We also had

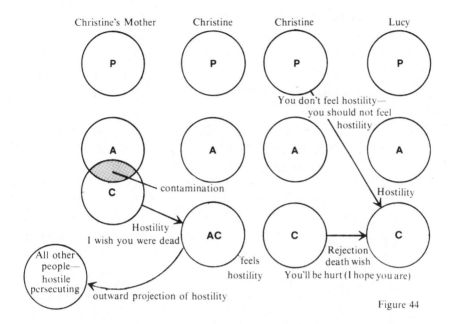

Figure 44

something close to a classic situation in schizophrenia: the grandmother on the ceiling running the life script of the grandchild. In
this case, Lucy was being saved from outright schizophrenia by the
fact that the Corner game was not too severe (as we've already
noted) and by the fact that her father's Parent and Adult weren't
inclined to play Corner.

With these understandings beginning to hit her, Christine finally
began to change. The Parent in her head was still cornering her
Child with "You aren't suppose to feel," but her Child showed
something was getting through, in the form that she reported one
session: She told us that she'd dreamed about giving her daughter
enemas, too. At first she just wanted to think that the dream meant
she was concerned about the daily bowel movement syndrome, but
then I asked her about her feeling about enemas, and if she could
remember any in her own childhood. "Oh, I hated them," she said,
at the same time saying that her mother (as we'd expected) had
used this device frequently. "Did they hurt?" I asked. "Oh I
thought they did, yes," Christine said. "So what were you doing

hurting Lucy in your dream?" I asked. "I thought everyone else was out to hurt you, and here you are hurting her."

At first Christine denied that interpretation of her dreams, but I responded that she was afraid of seeing herself that way. After all, it was very frightening to admit to the capacity to hurt another person, or the actuality of it, if you'd been hurt and if you'd begun to recognize the extent of your hostility toward your own mother. This realization finally cleared the way to giving Christine permission to take transactions from other people in ways other than as hurts, and, at long last, I could get her to report she'd tried the same tactic of "Were you trying to hurt my feelings?" that the other family members had been using with her for some time. To have offered this permission earlier would have been pointless because I gave it in a strong Nurturing Parent way; if it had been given before she would have been unable to separate the feelings in her Child from the other parts of her personality, and she would have taken it as one more persecution. Now, however, we'd named the curse of the double-bind, and we'd revealed the curse of that hostility. There had been something of an "Aha," a therapeutic bull's-eye, striking her Parent, Adult, and Child simultaneously, and she was prepared.

Toward a Cure for the Hurt Racket Family

It took some time for my direction "not to take nearly everything from others as a hurt to affect Christine," but the major step had been taken toward getting the whole family out of the bathroom. A redecision by parents to change the family system either produces relief or strain in the offspring. In this case, the sense of relief was predominant. Lucy felt more comfortable in the family. She and her mother began to practice saying, "Were you meaning to hurt my feelings?" quite regularly. We could occasionally joke in therapy, making an absurdity about something that would have been a "terrible, awful hurt" some time before. Larry was less inclined to withdraw and drink or to suffer in silence when his needs were being overshadowed by Christine.

Christine came to the conclusion that she need people and that this was OK. She could then ask with her Adult for what she wanted. Before this therapy experience, she thought such asking was selfish and therefore Not OK. After her Child part was given permission by my Parent to need and want people, the hurting stopped. Gratification in the family (gold stamps) was the result of their transactions.

THE HOUSTONS, A MULTIRACKET FAMILY

Eric Berne once said that example of good research is to try to disprove a hypothesis. The hypothesis I chose for dysfunctional families is that they have predominantly one racket. However, the Houstons demonstrate multiple rackets, and this family is being presented for that reason.

Over the years, I've worked with many families and I've found that those who continued in therapy beyond crisis intervention, those that I really got to know, all operated with one dominant racket per family. All, that is, except the Houstons. The Houstons employed all the rackets I've identified and they played them through a screen of alcohol and drugs. My work with them was a little like playing tennis in a tightly walled court: As the ball in such a game might ricochet off any wall toward the player, so the Houstons might come at me from any angle.

The first bounce with this family came from the angle of concerned parents with a teenage son on drugs. Jonathan Houston, the father, called me at my office. "We've got to see you, Doctor, our group therapy leader recommended you. Our son Tom has been suspended from Mills High School for coming to class under the influence of drugs." The calm, well-modulated voice betrayed no emotion as he related this request and information.

I checked my calendar and scheduled a family session the following day. This session, I told him, would be for the purpose of evaluating the situation and would be most helpful if both parents and son were present.

"Oh, Sally and I will be there, Doctor. I'll tell Tom we're coming and invite him to join us, but I'm sure he won't come. He can't talk." He went on to describe to me the effect that twenty or more Seconal pills each day was having on the boy. Apparently, his speech was very slurred, and he walked with an uncertain shuffle.

When they came in, we talked for a while about the drug Seconal and its effects. Tom had drifted into the losers' crowd at Mills as a freshman and had had no trouble keeping himself supplied with pills. His father also told me that he made sure there was plenty of beer in the refrigerator. In addition to the Seconal, Tom usually drank two six-packs of beer in the evening. Both parents described their son as depressed.

They went on to tell me that they had begun group therapy in TA because they felt that they were drinking too much and fighting a lot of the time. A year or two earlier, they had moved temporarily to Canada to take part in an experiment with LSD, but as they had found that this venture was not helping their marriage, they abandoned the project and returned.

When the initial hour was over, we agreed to meet the following week, and they told me they'd do their best to get Tom in to see me. In the weeks that followed, I did see Tom several times with one or both parents and several times alone. When I saw the name Houston on my appointment list I never knew who would walk in the door. Sometimes Sally came alone, a few times Jonathan came by himself, Tom seemed to prefer to be alone, and they did come in combination, too.

On one occasion when both Sally and Tom were in my office, she turned to Tom and said, "You're sick!" Whereupon Tom, who was usually silent and passive, erupted with an openly hostile retort.

The erratic pattern of attendance at therapy sessions forced me to gather my data about them in bits and snatches, but gradually I was able to piece together a picture of the parent couple. Jonathan kept himself under very tight control. He did not allow himself to expose any feelings to me. His aging mother, who was dying from breast cancer, made her home with them. His father who had already died, was described as "a real crab." Jon worked as a low-level manager for a local·company and had been with this same concern, except for the brief interlude in Canada, since his graduation from college. He had no outside interests and spent nonworking hours drinking vodka and water. When he was drunk, he was hostile and fought with Sally. Since childhood, he had suffered from asthma, but he never complained to me about this. He only mentioned the name of the drug he took daily to minimize its effects.

Sally had completed her training as an R.N. and had worked for several years prior to their marriage. She no longer worked outside the home. In addition to Tom, who was then sixteen, she told me they had an eleven-year-old son, Fred, and an eighteen-year-old daughter, Joyce. She said that when she woke up each morning she was so anxious that she had to have a drink just to get breakfast on the table for the others. The thought of doing the accumulated chores of housekeeping sent her off for another drink and by late afternoon she was usually drunk. When drunk, she also was very hostile and fought with Jon and the children.

One afternoon, I arranged to make a house visit and found them very much as they described themselves. Sally was drunk, and Jon was drinking. When it was time for me to leave, Jon took out his wallet and said, "Before you go, I want to pay you, Doctor." "Aw, put your money away, he wasn't worth it!" shouted Sally, her tongue slurring the words garrulously.

Tom contributed to this family picture when he described to me a scene in which he came in to find Sally sitting in the kitchen table, naked. As she started to hurl incoherent jibes at the boy, she lost control of her bladder and urinated all over the chair.

At our next office session, I went over some of the principles of TA with them and drew the diagrams of their ego sates shown in Figure 45. As we discussed how these transactions seemed to work, I reminded them that it was okay to let their Natural Child parts out more. In their conversations with me, they both appeared to be operating from their Adults. We exchanged information for the most part; only rarely did any feeling response come into our

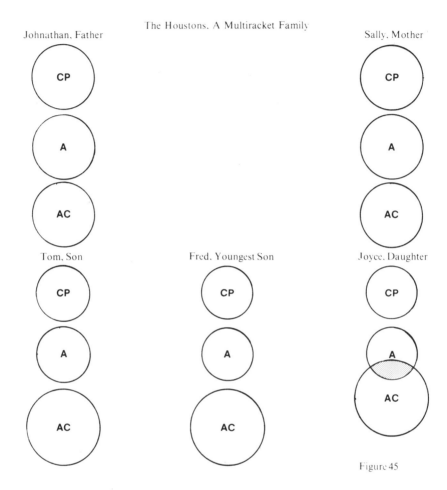

The Houstons, A Multiracket Family

Johnathan, Father

CP

A

AC

Sally, Mother

CP

A

AC

Tom, Son

CP

A

AC

Fred, Youngest Son

CP

A

AC

Joyce, Daughter

CP

A

AC

Figure 45

sessions. At this same time, Tom appeared to have a huge Critical Parent with some Nurturing Parent, an average Adult, a large Adapted Child and a very small Natural Child. As they prepared to leave at the end of that session, I told them they would have to stop drinking at the end of that session, I told them they would have to stop drinking at least on therapy days, or I would not continue to work with them. They readily agreed to try.

My contacts with this family continued with no predictable pattern as to who might show up, but with an increasing assurance that whoever it was would be sober. Those scheduled visits were not my only contacts with them. Every few weeks I would, in addition, receive a middle-of-the-night phone call. On then first of these, I spoke to Jon, he was calling from the emergency room of our major hospital, and again I was struck by the calm of his voice. "Tom's taken an overdose, Doctor. He looked pretty bad so I called the ambulance and they brought him straight here to emergency."

After ascertaining that Tom would probably pull through, I asked the father, "How about you? How're you feeling?" "Feeling? Me? I'm fine, Doc," he replied. Later I talked with the doctor who had been on duty when they brought Tom in, and he remarked that he'd never seen a parent remain so completely calm and appear so unaffected in any similar situation.

I asked Jon how he could remain so completely unemotional in the fact of a life-or-death crisis like that one had been. He thought for a minute and said, "Well, I thought that's the way I should respond. My father often said I must never complain or tell anybody about my feelings. It was okay for me to say 'I'm fine' but nothing else. I'm a nice guy. But, Doctor, I don't always feel like a nice guy."

Tom recovered from the experience and returned to school. It had been a scary ordeal, and he began to consider the possibility of getting off drugs.

My next frantic call was from the boy. In barely intelligible words he told me that he'd almost killed his mother. When he was calm enough to elaborate I found out that Sally had again set up an argument with him and he felt he couldn't handle it any longer. It seemed that Sally habitually behaved in a provocative, seductive manner toward Tom. At this time he felt that in order to avoid incest with his mother he had to kill her. We hardly had time to discuss this, however, before he called again. This time, his voice was more controlled and he said, "I'm calling to cancel our appointment for today. My mother's dead."

After Sally was duly buried, the father and son came again to see me. Sally had been making some real progress in the weeks preceding her death. She was able to stay sober more of the time, felt less anxious, and even mentioned the possibility of returning to nursing. The attending physician reported that she had thrown off a blood clot and it lodged in a vital artery causing death. In the moments before she expired, she looked at Tom and said, "I'm going to die." I can't help but wonder if perhaps she didn't hhoose to die rather than change her lifestyle and break up her Never script.

One of the last things I remember Jonathan saying to me at the close of my last therapy session with him and his wife was, "Well, Sal, Horewitz hasn't cracked you yet!" But, I did come dangerously close. Sally had been able to talk about her feelings on several occasions when I saw her alone. She's usually begin with a game of Harried, ank she'd tell me she was depressed or anxious. When I pressed her to tell me exactly what it was she was feeling, however, she became more specific and we were able to talk more intimately. She revealed to me that her mother had been very competitive and had generally not wanted her to exist. Her father seemed to have been a good, reliable man, but he was unable or unwilling to protect his child Sally from her destructive mother. As one would expect, Sally grew up with unmet dependency needs and probably decided to be a nurse to show her mother that she could take better care of people—a response to the competition. It seemed that she was given a Never script, and she married Jon because he seemed to be a "nice guy" who would *never* make her do anything.

Sex didn't seem to play a very important or very active role in their marriage. Sally told me that she really didn't like having cunnilingus done to her, and she probably never had orgasms. However, she didn't mind doing fellatio and seemed to be seeking some more intimacy with Jon than he was able to share.

In the weeks immediately following Sally's death, I felt a need to consolidate what I'd learned about her life in order to go on with the still living members of the family. Jon, on the other hand, really don't want to pursue this process. His expressions at this time were of bitterness rather than grief. He commented that the older children had often asked why they didn't divorce, since they fought all the time. He told me that he felt saddled first with his mother, then with Sally, and now with the kids. If it hadn't been for Tom, Joyce, and Fred, Jon would certainly have walked out the door with a one-way ticket. As we talked, I speculated about Jon's life script. Was it After? "After Mother dies, I can....After Sally dies, I can...." Perhaps, but that conclusion didn't fit my current observations very well. Jonathan was living in very much the same way he'd lived before Sally's death—working, drinking, taking asthma pills. About a month later, his mother died, and again there was no real change in his life patterns.

One afternoon Jon settled back in his chair and said, "You know, Doctor, I'm a nice guy. My Dad always expected me to be a nice guy, a Little Lord Fauntleroy." We talked on for a few more moments about his dad and about other things he'd said to the boy Jon, and a pattern began to emerge. It looked like Never, again: Never feel anything, never do much of anything, never take a stand, never be. It even extended into his sex life, as he told me he could never get an erection anymore.

With this basis of two Never scripts I was able to bring some of this chaotic, oscillating behavior into a clearer focus. We talked about scrips; that is, Jonathan, Tom, and I did.

Then the focus came back on the younger generation—Fred and Joyce. Joyce I only saw a few times. She was eighteen when the family first came in, and I told them that I thought she would soon get pregnant. She did, had an abortion, and maintained her residence outside the family home. I was quite sure that she would become pregnant because I quickly sensed that the mother and father had never settled the oedipal question for either of their older children; that is, the children had never had the assurance that mother was enough woman for father and vice versa. Therefore, when Joyce reached maturity her father would behave in a provocative way toward her, frightening her with the possibility on incest. They played Uproar to prevent this actually taking place, and Joyce had to become involved sexually with another man in order to break away from home.

Tom had faced a similar problem with Sally, of course. He had tried to have sex with two different girls in his class, but he failed each time. At about the time of his mother's death and shortly after, he was very troubled by homosexual feelings. One day he saw me alone and confided that he was only able to masturbate when he thought of other men's genitals, and he found this very disquieting. We discussed the general cultural aspects of sexual orientation, and I gave him therapeutic permission to explore his feelings. I assured him that it was really OK with me. However, the real turning point for Tom came when he was able to share this concern with his dad. On that occasion, Jon drew on his deepest Nurturing Parent strengths and responded that it was okay with him if he was homosexual, and he'd love him in just the same way he always had.

At the same time Tom was wrestling with his sexual feelings, he was also experimenting with heroin. When this fact came to light, I didn't mince any words but came on straight Parent and told him, and also Joyce, to knock it off right now before they got hooked. Both of them quit.

Alcohol still clouded their lives, however. One night Tom staggered home very drunk and fell, ripping open his right kneecap. After surgical repair and several weeks on crutches, he was able to walk again. However, the damage was severe enough so that he would probably never to able to walk any distance, stand for long periods of time, or be completely mobile. At this point I was able to get him to go to the Rehab Center for vocational counseling. He found some responsive people there and became involved in a training program. The accident with his knee sobered Tom up. He became a much more moderate drinker and drinking stopped being a problem to him.

Drinking stopped being a problem for Jon, too, as the direct result of a physical crisis. Following Sally's death, he continued downing at least half a fifth of vodka with water each evening. I imagine that he'd been drinking at about that same rate since he became an adult, or for better than twenty years. His liver rebelled, and I had him hospitalized for tests. There was no doubt: Jon had to knock off the booze. The experience scared him enough that he stopped drinking completely and has remained dry ever since.

Fighting was not as amenable to change, as the fighting in this family system had very deep roots and served too many functions.

As I thought bout the families both Jon and Sally grew up in, I saw mothers who failed to meet the dependency needs of their young. Again, in the current family I saw Tom and Joyce, both of whom had ulcers by the time they were eight years old, again with unmet dependency needs. The anger engendered in the child from unmet needs smoldered in all of them, erupting whenever the individual was drunk. Thus, the fighting was a product of this unresolved hostility. It also served all of them as Uproar to avoid incest and intimacy. Tom, when I first met him, played Kick Me, and Sally responded with NIGYYSOB—more fighting.

Fighting sometimes was reflected in the Persecutor's role of Karpman's triangle (1968). Tom often appeared to be Victim, with Sally Persecutor and Jon Rescuer. However, they could and did switch these roles at will. As these recognizable games were identified and the family agreed to avoid them, Tom commented to me that he could just keep still and say nothing or he could get real mad, but he never did anything in between! No one in that household was able to state a point of view clearly and decisively.

For homework, I directed Tom to practice stating clearly what he felt. This assignment was made following a session in which he'd told me that his dad had brought home a woman who was cooking and cleaning for them. She had been there for several weeks and had started helping herself to an occasional can of beer from Tom's own supply. He'd tried not saying anything, but found himself getting madder and madder. Finally he blew his top and had a big fight with her—fighting again. I told him it was okay to tell her simply not to drink the beer he bought.

It was interesting that I learned of this new woman in the household from Tom. Jonathan had never mentioned her at all. He regularly came in to see me and ticked off the news of every other member of the family, completely omitting any real report of himself. He seemed to be obsessional. When I asked him about her, he admitted that she was there but added that he still was unable to have sex. I reminded him that when he decided to let his feelings out, freeing up his Natural Child, he would be able to have sex again. So far, he didn't express any interest in exploring that possibility.

He did, however, include in his news report the item that Tom was engaged! Again, Tom had said nothing about having a girl friend. Apparently, she was someone he had met at the Rehab Center. She was beautiful and confined to a wheelchair.

As Tom and I later talked about her, he asked me if I thought he'd be able to have sex. I gave him permission to tell her about his earlier experiences with failure to have an erection and also pointed out some things they might try to enhance the possibilities if they decided to go ahead. When I saw him again, he assured me that everything had worked fine and he was looking forward to finding a job that would enable them to establish a place of their own.

Tom, the original identified patient, was now out of the blame frame. He went off drugs, was not dependent on alcohol, was learning to express himself clearly so that he didn't have to fight, appeared to have stabilized his sexuality in a comfortable way, and became generally game-free.

My work went on with Jonathan and the youngest son, Fred. Jonathan recognized his Never script but remained locked into it. When Jon and I were reviewing his situation, he observed that it had been nearly two years since he'd quit his job in the wake of his health crisis. Now, after two years of sobriety, his physical health was again stable, and it appeared to me that he certainly would be able to return to work. I knew that he was puttering around the house, doing little fix-up jobs from time to time, but was mostly feeling depressed. He sat a great zeal of the time in a large over-stuffed chair and stared at the TV.

"I think you are able to work again. Why not try?" I asked him. He shrugged his shoulders dispiritedly and said nothing. Jon was able to observe his son learning to express himself; he could see that it worked well, yet he was still unwilling to give it a try. He was still clinging to the pattern of absolute passivity or violent angry outbursts. Jonathan seemed to have decided that he would never get well.

As Fred now enters his teen years, I will be available to him and will hope that as he sees Tom living a generally more satisfying life, he too will strike out for a new script. Certainly Fred will need help in the future.

This family with their "shoulds" and "oughts" often seemed to be operating a guilt racket. Their constant fighting or preparing to fight certainly fit the pattern of an anger racket. The consequences of their drinking and fighting left them all in the hurt racket. And the parents living with their own horrible hostility left them operating in the fear racket. There werenlargely unresolved questions of sexuality for all of them. There were unmet dependench needs and inability to practice intimacy. All of this enabled Jonathan and Sally to live out the injunctions of their Never scripts—"never feel," for him and "never be," for her. Indeed, this was a family whose life plan required all the rackets in the book.

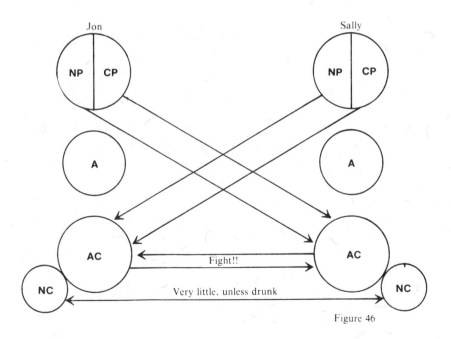

Figure 46

CHAPTER 6

Working
with
Couples in Therapy

Work with a couple is, in a sense, work with the basic foundation unit of the family. In each of the family case histories presented in chapter 5, there were from two or three to a dozen sessions during which I met with the husband and wife alone. Of course, in the normal pattern of clinical practice, a therapist also meets couples who do not yet have children, as well as couples whose children have grown up and have moved away from home.

A couple may be listed on my appointment pad as Mr. and Mrs. Smith, Jean Jones and Sam Smith, Tom Jackson and Sam Smith, or Sally Peters and Joan Adams. Couples—be they traditionally married, seriously cohabiting, heterosexual, or homosexual—all seem to exhibit similar patterns and have similar relationship problems. The cases in this chapter all happen to be heterosexual couples as are most of the couples in my case load. However, when I do encounter nonheterosexual couples, I find that they have the same kinds of problems.

It is often a stormy crisis, an impending separation, or the apparent "problem" of one spouse that brings a couple into therapy without their children. For couples involved in family therapy these husband-wife sessions usually start when we begin to discuss strictly sexual matters to talk about script injunctions that predate the children. In both cases, the basic area of concern is, "What brought you two together in the first place, and how does that relate to your current situation?"

When a couple is conversant with the fundamentals of TA and has talked briefly about the current "problem," I usually ask, "What brought you two together in the first place?" It's a natural question, one you might ask of a new acquaintance in casual conversation. Certainly, it is a part of any case history. Yet common and ordinary though it may appear, this question has profound implications in couple therapy. The couples are usually obsessive, depressed or schizophrenic.

LIKE LOCK AND KEY

Over the years therapists working with couples have observed that their neuroses fit together like a lock and key. As we begin to try and understand a particular lock and key, it's helpful to start with their own courtship experiences and listen to each partner's explanation of why they chose each other.

As a couple tells me about the events leading up to their marriage, or commitment, I stop and with their help, diagram what was happening in each individual's ego states. One thing we try to discover is what it was that the Adapted Child in each person was searching for. This Adapted Child will be *Not OK* in TA terms, for it is the Not OK Adapted Child that promotes the distress that brings couples into therapy. The Not OK Adapted Child usually searches for a particular Parent response in the spouse (see Figure 1).

Sometimes during courtship or early marriage, the spouse is able to give this response freely, but with the pressures of parenthood,

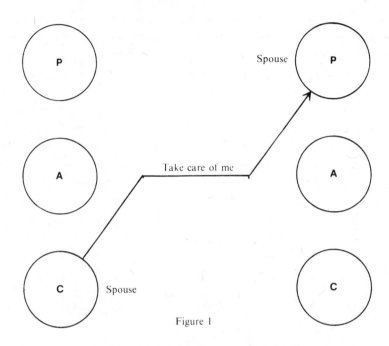

Figure 1

job changes, or other life events, becomes unable or unwilling to continue responding. The Adapted Child is then thrown into a panic, and some crisis will ensue.

There are at least three identifiable Not OK Adapted Child needs as diagrammed in Figures 2, 3, and 4. These three possible Adapted Child personalities can be termed *obsessive, depressive,* or *schizophrenic.* It is interesting to note that when one spouse has a readily identified kind of Adapted Child, that same kind is usually echoed in the spouse. Perhaps the behavior of one is more obvious. The distress may be greater in one than in the other, but a very similar ego state will nevertheless usually exist in both. It also follows that both spouses will have similar Nurturing or Critical Parents.

Since both spouses tend to feel and need the same responses, there is the potential for a quick understanding of what is going on with couples who also have good functioning Adults. And if they choose to use their Adults and exercise the options (Karpman

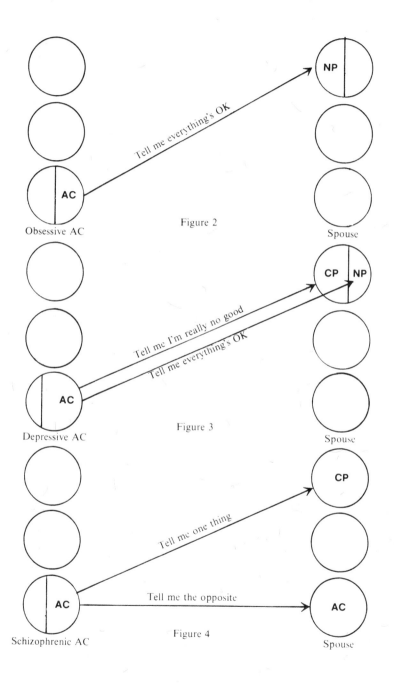

Figure 2

Obsessive AC

Spouse

Figure 3

Depressive AC

Spouse

Figure 4

Schizophrenic AC

Spouse

1971), they may be on the way toward a more intimate relationship in weeks rather than months or years.

The Broken Record

One of the three Adapted Childs might be diagnosed as an *obsessive* personality. He or she focuses their life energies, but not willfully, on one notion and plays this notion over and over in their heads like the old record player needle stuck in a cracked record. The notion, or notions, may be of different sorts, of course, but it's obvious as one listens to him or her that a single idea keeps recurring in the conversation. The energy consumed by this endless repeating of a single idea leaves the obsessive individual drained and usually quite passive. He or she is willing to let others take the lead and make the important decisions; in some cases they may also be very controlling.

Sam was just such a person. He came with his wife Shirley at her insistence. Seeing me was a last-ditch effort to stave off a separation. They came into the clinic as part of a family therapy group, but I quickly determined that their difficulties lay between the parents and were in the sexual area. When I feel that this is the case, I prefer to see the couple alone at least for a few sessions, rather than meeting with both parents and children together.

One afternoon as I met with Sam, we began to talk about his listlessness and his inactive feelings about life. Finally, he said, "Okay Doctor, how do I get over my passivity?" (this is a passive question). I thought a moment and said, "Maybe you ought to see a psychiatrist." His reply was, "Fine, I'll try it. Do you know any?"

As we talked, I observed that Sam was obsessed with a need to have constant reassurance from a woman. He needed to hear that "everything will be okay." In fact, Sam needed this message so desperately that one woman giving it wasn't enough. He had to have two (see Figure 5).

Shirley and Sam had been married for several years and had two children. They got married three months after Shirley became

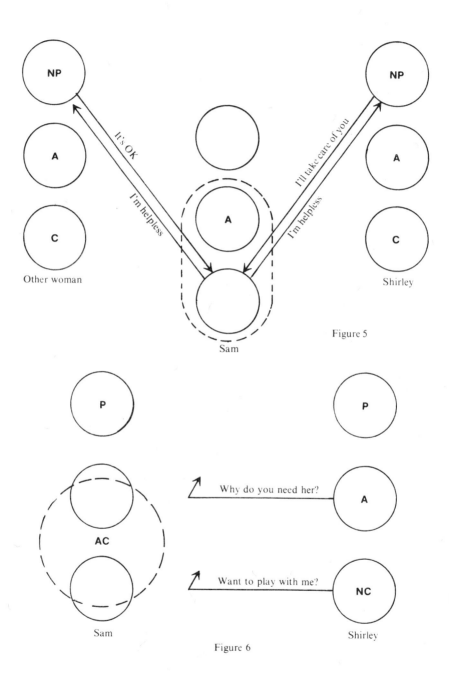

Figure 5

Figure 6

pregnant. Apparently Sam used this conception to escape from a potentially oedipal situation in his own family.

Shirley had been programmed to wait on men and take care of them. Sam's Adapted Child recognized this as the response needed and promoted their getting together in the first place. Shirley's programming was somewhat obsessional, too, but to a less crippling degree. This condition became embarassingly apparent to me when Sam withdrew from therapy and Shirley continued to see me alone. She transferred her need to wait on men to me! For example, she brought gifts.

Sam was not able to bring his Adult into use to try any options, and instead he chose to stop therapy when Shirley announced that she was filing for a divorce. She did have a functioning Adult, and she saw that there was a great deal more to living than just serving whatever guy happened to be around (see Figure 6). Eventually, she reprogrammed herself to seek other, more satisfying roles with men.

The obsessive Adapted Child searches for a strong Nurturing Parent response. When I talked with Sam, I used my Nurturing Parent to suggest some ways he could diminish his obsessive pattern and make their marriage a more mutually satisfying operation. When there is an obsessive need on the part of an Adapted Child to the spouse's Nurturing Parent, the therapist can suggest that he or she ask, using the Adult in a nonexploitative way, "Can you tell me everything will be OK? My Child needs to be reassured."

Then, as the partner understands what is going on, he or she may simply respond with a hug and the words of reassurance. By asking with the Adult, the obsessive person refuses any response the spouse might consider making from the Critical Parent. It is the Critical Parent response that produces or reinforces the "Not OK" anxiety in the Adapted Child. This anxiety triggered the confrontation between Sam and Shirley.

Of course, the spouse may not honestly choose to give the reassurance for the seventeen hundredth time. He or she may be tired of the transaction. If so, he or she can say so with the Adult again. This change will probably be painful initially, but it does open up the possibility for candid dialogue and offers the potential for a move into a closer relationship.

If Sam had continued in therapy alone, I might have suggested that he brings his own Nurturing Parent into the act. His own Nurturing Parent could send messages to his Adapted Child, messages of reassurance. These messages would be grounded in the information his own Adult processed about the world, as it really is, and would thus be valid; that is, his Adult could program his Nurturing Parent to give these messages.

Sometimes the Adapted Child chooses a spouse because he or she senses that person's Nurturing Parent will supply the response it needs. But other times, the Adapted Child is looking instead for a strong Critical Parent.

The Popped Balloon

The second of the three Not OK Adapted Childs may be called a *depressive* personality. From time to time, this person's life energies are as immobilized as those of a limp balloon. He or she will not respond readily to those around them and will feel unable to begin even the simplest tasks. An air of grief may be observed in such an individual's face, though the known events in their lives are not necessarily tragic.

Usually one spouse is suffering depressive distress and comes into therapy alone. When this happens, I ask the other spouse to join in our sessions as quickly as possible. It is almost certain that this person, too, will be somewhat depressive. However, since the bouts of depressive distress are interspersed with relatively stable periods, these people are often able to reprogram themselves and relieve much of their suffering.

Such people need to marry someone who has a strong Critical Parent to replace the real critical parent of their childhood. There seems to be a need to have the familiar pattern of depression reinforced. I think that the depressed person repeats the relationship (script) that initiated the depression in the hope that by repeating it the dilemma may be solved.

When a patient appears suffering depression and is joined by his or her spouse, the therapist can expect to see two strong Critical Parents and two depressive Adapted Childs. This pattern is indeed what I found as I got to know Jack and Jenny.

Jenny came to me following a three-week hospitalization for "depression." Jack accompanied her, loudly voicing his feelings of helplessness in the face of her condition. "Well, I've told her a hundred times to snap out of it!" he said as we began our session.

Jenny had been working as a librarian when she met Jack. He was then selling playground equipment. After their marriage, he decided that selling wasn't really for him and he enrolled in our local university to study agriculture. Jenny continued with her job and became the breadwinner in the household.

As we talked, I sensed that Jack feared that he would lose his autonomy as a result of his becoming a student. He had also become dependent economically on Jenny. Jenny was very supportive of his return to school, and they both seemed to feel very positive toward each other and their marriage. Jack's strong Critical Parent became more vocal as his own anxious Child grew more afraid of losing autonomy in the new situation. When Jack's Critical Parent got pushy and angry, Jenny responded by becoming anxious and depressed.

Together we diagramed what was happening in PAC terms in their relationship and began to consider some of their options (see Figures 7 and 8). I used my own Parent to give Jack permission to make a joke out of some of his angers, so that Jenny would not be intimidated. He agreed to try this strategy, and it worked well.

We continued to meet in weekly sessions, and they gradually told me more about their life together. Jenny not only worked and earned enough money to pay for their basic needs, but she also maintained a pleasant apartment and enjoyed preparing the foods Jack particularly liked. Although Jack never complained about Jenny's homemaking, he never complimented her either.

I asked him if his real parents had ever said, "You take things for granted." He told me they did; in fact, they complained that he always took everything for granted. I pointed out that his father

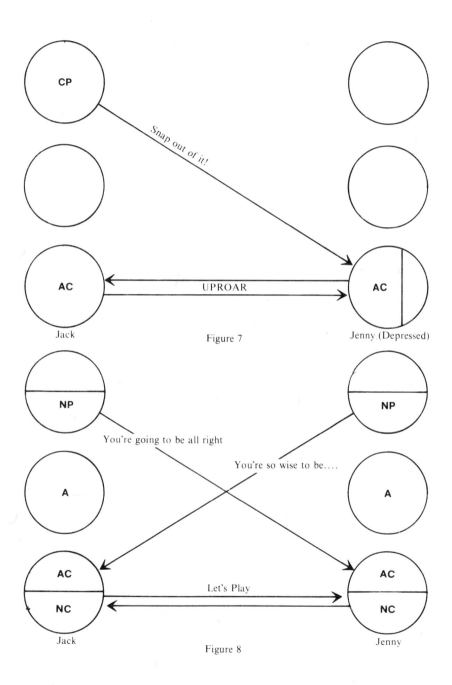

Figure 7

Jack

Jenny (Depressed)

Figure 8

Jack

Jenny

probably never stroked his mother either. He thought a moment, and he began to smile as he shook his head slowly in the affirmative. Then, I again used my Parent to give him permission to stroke Jenny positively for doing the things that especially added to his comfort. They reported later that this stroking had also helped.

When Jenny's Child became frightened, they fought with each other and Uproar ensued. I told them that when they got into the next Uproar game, either or both might use their Adults and say, "You hurt my feelings. Was that your intention?" Nearly always, the responded no, and the Uproar ended. Jack and Jenny didn't destroy each other's self-esteem as many couples do, but they did collect anger stamps.

Jenny was terribly afraid of losing stroking. As I talked more with her, I found that she had had a serious operation as a preschooler and throughout her convalescense was cared for by a nanny, although her mother was present in the house. She felt that she must be Not OK or her own mother would have nursed her during this critical time. Children often feel this way if they are cared for by another person in the presence of the parent. This fear of losing stroking let Jenny to respond to Jack's anger in an intensely frightened way. These fears of dependency and loss of stroking were reflected in a mutual fear of intimacy. Their game of Uproar, of course, successfully thwarted any potential closeness.

In the years since Jenny had left home, she talked at least once a day with her mother over the phone. After she hung up the phone, Jenny reported that she always felt upset. Finally, one day when she mentioned the phone conversations in therapy, I asked, "What are you getting out of this relationship with your mother?" Jenny thought a minute and replied, "Nothing but upsets." I responded, "So, why don't you cut off the relationship?" I used my Parent to give Jenny permission to terminate her mother-child relationship with her mother. Once I did that I also had to give her some protection, so I said, "When you have the urge to call your mother, call me instead."

The following week I asked her how it was going and said, "Was it hard to give your mother up?" Jenny had called several times saying how hard it was to resist the urge to pick up the phone when it rang and she thought it might be her mother. She would stand there as it rang, tears smarting in her eyes, for the first time or two. When the ringing stopped, she called me. It takes the protection of a therapist along with the potency that he or she has built up in the relationship to overcome negative injunctions from the real parent.

When Jenny dropped the phone conversations with her mother, she stopped hearing her real critical parent, and Jenny's Adapted Child was depressed less of the time. We talked in therapy about her bringing in her own Adult to conteract the Critical Parent in Jenny's head and Jack agreed to muzzle his Critical Parent, too. But Jenny's Adapted Child was very accustomed to feeling depressed, and it grew anxious without the Critical Parent attention. It resisted any change in feeling.

Later, as their relationship improved, Jenny would invite reassurance from Jack's Nurturing Parent and he would respond, "Yes, sure, you are going to be all right and I do love you." Then, Jenny often replied, "Well, I don't believe it." In saying this she discounted his reassurance.

When a couple comes in for therapy with depressed Adapted Childs and Critical Parents, it is often possible to make suggestions and give permissions as I did with Jack and Jenny. There are positive things each can do with his or her Adult to improve the relationship. They also can learn to exercise their nurturing of the husband or wife's Nurturing Parent. Finally, they can restrain their Critical Parent responses. As their Adapted Childs grow accustomed to receiving more positive stroking, depression will become less and less of a problem.

Occasionally, I see only one half of the couple, the individual who is depressed. My first act is to try to get the spouse in, too. However, if the spouse is unreachable, unwilling, or unavailable, there are still some options open. Again, I begin by diagraming the transaction that triggers the depressive response in the patient's Adapted Child and we talk about why that Adapted Child selected the current spouse in the first place.

As we talk, I identify the phrases or injunctions that the patient's Critical Parent is fond of using. Once the patient can recognize these key phrases as they occur or are heard inside the head, then the Adult is able to intervene with an option. The Adult can tell the Nurturing Parent to lay on some positive strokes or it can tickle the Natural Child into making a joke out of the Critical Parent's Diatribe or it can program the Natural Child to coax the Adapted Child.

In therapy, we talk about the episodes that ended with a new depressed, immobile feeling, and as we repeat this process, the patient becomes more and more adept at spotting the Critical Parent. Once identified, it can be dealt with. As we talk, I continue to stroke positively whenever it seems appropriate, as the person with the depressive Adapted Child needs to learn to accept positive stroking if he or she is to attain a more stable functioning mood.

The Ripped Rag

Is it good because now you have two? Or is it bad because you no longer have the whole? The third Adapted Child, the *schizophrenic* personality, is never quite sure. This Child's reality testing may be accurate enough so that she or he functions in most life situations but not quite accurate enough to be truly reliable. This person may have been diagnosed as a borderline schizophrenic. We are learning that schizophrenics are the product of families in which the adults give the children conflicting messages. Thus, the schizophrenic Adapted Child is looking for a partner who will continue to give and receive these double messages.

One husband I knew often told his wife, who had a schizophrenic Adapted Child, "I like to see you talking with the other women when we go to parties. Babies and pie baking, that's what you're best at." This same man often came home with very sexy cocktail dressed for his wife to wear when they went to social gatherings— dresses in which she could not help but look extremely provocative.

The spouse, then, provides the same sort of split-meaning communication that the original parents did. The person with the identified schizophrenic Adapted Child may flutter around a lot but is unable to use his or her life energies in a fully functional way because he or she never quite knows what is going on. Schizophrenic Adapted Childs may think they do, however. Such a person commonly projects his or her own feelings onto the spouse all the time. This same wife told me, "Jason is so mad at me!" when, in fact, it was she who was angry with him.

Both the practice of projection and the split-meaning communication practically guarantee that these couples will spend a lot of their time together fighting. Such was the case with Lillie and John (see Figure 9).

Lillie and John fought all the time. They came into couple therapy after a particularly disastrous fight that threatened to send them off in separate directions. "No wife of mine is going to kiss another man in my house! That's too much!" "Well, John," I said using my Adult, "If that's too much, how much would be about right?"

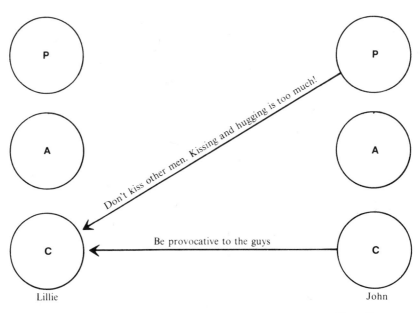

Figure 9

Lillie might have been diagnosed as a borderline patient. She did function, but her sense of reality was distorted. As we continued to meet, I observed that she never listened to what anyone else said. She was always sure that she knew what they were thinking or feeling in her own head, and she projected these notions on the speaker instead of receiving the spoken communication. John also had a disturbed Adapted Child, and he needed to receive both Nurturing and Critical Parent messages from Lillie, too.

We talked about this situation at great length, and they both entered into these discussions in a friendly fashion until about five minutes before the end of our hour. Then, all hell broke loose as they played out another round of Uproar. They both feared intimacy so very much that they dared not leave my office as friends. It might have been this facility to engage in Uproar that brought Lillie and John together, as well as their complementary Adapted Child needs; as games chosen by the Adapted Child to thwart intimacy often become the basis for a marital relationship.

When their Uproar-on-leaving pattern became a regular occurrence, I arranged to change the appointment time of my next patient, who had been the last one of the day. Thus, I could continue working with Lillie and John into the evening if need be. When a couple or family engages in Uproar in my office, I do everything I can to keep them in the therapy situation until they are able to work it through to some resolution.

The following week, true to their earlier performances, Lillie and John began their verbal battle just as their usual hour was ending. As they shouted at each other, I noticed that they also glanced toward my wall clock. Both seemed poised ready to dart through the door when the hand signaled the hour. At this point, I calmly announced that my next patient wasn't coming that day and suggested that we see this "problem" through.

"What's right, or what seems true to you about what John's saying?" I asked Lillie, trying to hook her Adult. "Well," she faltered for a moment, and I thought maybe her Adult would reappear, but in a flash she was back into the angry exchange again. I persisted in trying to appeal to their Adult ego states and finally did get them to diagram with me what was happening. All three of us were weary when they finally left the clinic that night. They had, temporarily at least, resolved the Uproar, but the truce was an uneasy one.

Later that week, I was not at all surprised to find a phone message from Lillie, "We've decided to stop the therapy. John doesn't feel that you are helping us." And I never heard from either of them again.

EVERYBODY LOSES

Sometimes it is quite obvious as a couple describes their life together that one of these Adapted Child needs was a key factor in bringing them together. Other times, these needs may be present, but they are not so clearly evident at first. Early in treatment, it may be the general patterns of behavior that absorb most of the attention. When a particular game dominates the life of a couple, the therapist will be looking for the forces that motivate that game. In the theory of TA, games are played to advance the life script, and the script is determined by injunctions about how to live that had been received from the real parents of long ago.

The emerging adult, embued with those script injunctions and emotionally clutching that life script, searches out a mate who is willing to join in the games which further that particular script. This choice is not left to whim or fancy; rather, it is quite certainly dictated by the givers of the script.

Thus, when a particular game is overwhelmingly evident in the life of a couple, they can be sure each chose the other because of an apparent willingness to engage in a marital relationship involving the game. Apparent willingness is an important consideration here because we often find that a couple seeks help when one party is no longer willing to continue with the original game.

One of the games I see as a therapist often is *Alcoholic*. Steiner (1971) provides a thorough discussion of all the elements of this game. The individual who needs to play the Alcoholic game, of course, chooses just the right person to play with. In my experience,

TA has a strong chance to help the alcoholic reprogram his or her behavior, so that he or she may become a functioning family member and, if he or she chooses, a social drinker.

Richard came to see me after a drinking bout during which he beat his wife quite badly. She had retreated to a motel with the children and was refusing to see him. After our initial interview, I called her and invited her to meet with me. I explained to her that people usually came to me because they wanted something, but this time I was going to do the asking. I asked her to come to therapy with Richard, and I convinced her that only with her input was there the possibility of ending Richard's abusive drinking. I was certain that it was a function of the relationship game they were playing that sent him off on his sprees.

As I pieced together their story of the previous weekend, it seemed that Richard had called home around 7:00 on Friday night, saying he would be home in an hour. Then, he went to a bar near his office and began to drink. He did this nearly every Friday night. Finally, he staggered home around midnight. Eileen was furious, and the fight was on.

I showed them how this whole transaction was simply a game of Kick Me. Each time Richard played it, he picked up another anger stamp. In addition, since he was very drunk, he did not risk having a sexual encounter with Eileen. They both seemed to have a positive attitude toward each other, and they showed some interest in finding out more about how these games worked. Richard spent most of the time in my office being ingratiatingly charming and operating for the most part from his Child.

I asked Richard, "Why don't you call Eileen and tell her when you really will be home?" Again his response came straight from his Child. "I've worked so hard all week, I just can't think of anything but having a little relaxed fun." This was his Child saying, "Look how hard I'm trying." Eileen often spoke to him in, "Why don't you..." terms, which he always "yes, butted." So, this time the structuring game appeared to be part of their everyday dialogue.

The fact that they returned to my office several weeks in a row reinforced my initial impression that they both really wanted to get themselves into a new place in their relationship. And so, as homework, I instructed Richard, using my own Critical Parent to work on not getting Eileen mad. As we continued to talk, Richard was able to tell us more about why he wanted to have Eileen angry. If she was mad and he was drunk, there was, first of all, no question of having sex. He was thus relieved of the need to worry about his own adequacy to meet Eileen's sexual needs. It seemed that Richard's self-doubts came from his mother's Critical Parent messages. She had been confined to a wheelchair with a crippling arthritis condition during most of his childhood, leaving Richard thwarted and unable to voice his disagreement or anger directly because any upset intensified her pain. Richard's responsibilities or duties surrounding her care filled much of his out-of-school time when he was a child; and as he completed his education, her care threatened to take over his entire life. His escape was his work and his wife. He had hoped that Eileen would take over most of her care, but Eileen had other plans.

For Richard, then, being drunk and mad freed him from sexual activity and allowed him to vent some of his rage. This rage could not, dared not, be vented directly at his aging invalid mother. In addition, he released the rage toward Eileen when he was drunk, as he was unable to discharge it when he was sober. The latter rage stemmed from her refusal to rescue him from his mother.

Eileen also promoted the general hostilities. She used her Child to provoke him, taunting him into thinking that she was having an affair with another man, a "real man" who could meet her sexual needs. Although she wasn't really having an affair, she perceived that creating this illusion was the way to "get" was her own father, also an alcoholic. Eileen carried with her a great load of unresolved anger toward her real father, which she now tried to release on Richard, the "father" in her own family. Their relationship could be diagramed as shown in Figure 10.

As they progressed at this stage in their treatment, Richard began using his Adult more to tell Eileen exactly when he was coming home, and then he did arrive at that hour. In return, she agreed not to be angry if that hour was later than she really liked. I

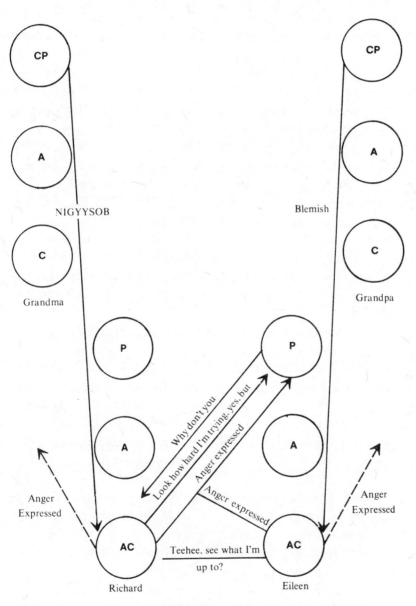

Figure 10

also suggested that they both agree not to be deliberately provocative toward each other. Eileen, by this time, had read quite a lot about TA and games. She decided on her own to knock off all her own games, and, in particular, not to play her role in the Alcoholic game.

The tension in their home seemed to ease for a while, and Richard gradually stopped drinking on Friday nights. Then, it was Eileen who exhibited distress. She came to me asking for sleeping pills, complaining that night after night she couldn't sleep. As we talked, they both realized that one of the effects of Richard's drinking had been to eliminate their sex life. Now that he was sober and around more, there were more obvious opportunities for sexual intimacy, which caused Eileen to panic. Her Child became very frightened, and Richard went on his first drunk in weeks.

This shift often happens with couples who are making new decisions about their transactions. One spouse progresses into a new set of transactions, frightening the Child of the other spouse. As usually happens, this change discloses their mutual fear—the fear of intimacy.

Richard and Eileen stuck with their therapy through this painful period. Richard moved out of the house into a halfway house for alcoholics. Eileen restored calm to the household and soothed the children back into a more normal life-style. Eventually, they did work through their feelings about intimacy, and this family began living together in a game-free, quite comfortable relationship.

By playing the game of Alcoholic, couples can successfully avoid intimacy forever. A fear of intimacy is also behind the ongoing Uproar games practiced by many couples. Both of these games are rather generalized in their effect; that is, both Alcoholic and Uproar successfully prevent not only sexual intimacy between the marriage partners but also the candid conversations that might be called intellectual intimacy. Both games prevent intimate relations with the children and close family friends as well.

There are several other life-dominating games, however, that are more specifically sexual in their orientation. To be sure, they also inhibit to some extent intellectual intimacy, but that is not where the action is. These games are usually initiated by the young, inexperienced person who feels inadequate sexually. Later in life, he or she may have acquired some confidence in his or her ability as a lover and may have decided not to engage in this game. That point is often the time to initiate therapy.

One of these potentially destructive sexual games played by couples is Rapo. The lead player in this game feels inadequate sexually but behaves in a very sexy, provocative manner. It is a role that could be played by either a man or a woman, but I've observed it more often among the women I meet in therapy.

Charlotte Vorcheck had probably spent twelve to thirteen years playing Rapo when she came with her husband Ken to the clinic for family therapy. At first, we met together with their children, Pam and Sean. As the family seemed rather hostile and contentious, I wasn't particularly surprised when Charlotte called and announced that she was not coming to therapy again.

Several weeks later, I got a call from Ken, and arranged to see them the following day. At this point, I wanted to see Charlotte and Ken without the children to see if we could find out what was making Charlotte so very angry. When they arrived, Ken explained that they were now separated, but he was visiting with the children each Sunday afternoon.

"Last Sunday when I arrived at our house she was curled up by the fireplace wearing a negligee I got her last Christmas. It's one of those kind of filmy ones, you know, and she looked so—well, you know. So I thought, maybe she misses me. Maybe she'd like to get together again. I took the kids to the zoo, but I kept thinking about her all afternoon, and when I brought them home, I asked her if she'd like to come over alone to my place that night." Ken paused and looked over at Charlotte. She sat, unusually quiet, tightlipped. "When I said that, she flew into a rage at me, like it was wrong for me to suggest such a terrible thing. Well, I couldn't take it anymore and I picked up a beer bottle and pitched it right at her head—only I missed and it went through the front window."

Charlotte added, "He wasn't just a little mad, Doctor, he was really mad, and I got scared. I said something like, "You get out of here' and he did. But, he came back after I'd given the kids their supper. When he walked in I thought, 'look out, he's going to beat me up or kill me or something.' He never touched me, just got out some tools and fastened a board over the broken window."

As we talked further, it became clear that her only reason for accompanying him to my office had been the hope that they might be reconciled, but purely for economic reasons. The brief separation had shown her what living as a single parent on a limited allowance was like, and she didn't like it. However, she refused to see why wearing a filmy outfit and then turning down his invitation to sex made Ken angry. Apparently, this had been her pattern of behavior with him right from the beginning of their relationship.

I asked her what she thought had happened when she appeared partly so scantily clothed, and she replied, "Nothing, nothing at all. Why should what I wear make any difference?" I continued, "Well, I don't know why it should, but evidence seems to suggest that it does. Ken, at least, becomes excited when he sees you partly clothed and angry when you refuse to have sex with him." Trying to make contact with her reasoning Adult, I asked, "Doesn't that indicate to you that something happened following your appearance in the negligee Saturday?"

"No, it doesn't," Charlotte answered. "Ken is just unreasonable. All you men are alike. You think women are dying to have sex any old time, and when we turn you down you get mad. What a woman wears or does not has nothing to do with it. I was just trying to get the kids ready for Ken's visit." Charlotte's response came from her Adapted Child, her Adult was not accessible at all. The major transaction taking place between Ken and Charlotte might be diagramed as shown in Figure 11.

Charlotte never returned to therapy, but Ken continued to see me alone for several months. The companion game for Rapo is Kick Me, and the payoff is usually anger stamps. Ken than began to understand his role in this pattern as his Adult recognized his own game of Kick Me. As a younger man, Ken had been scared of girls. His own inexperience in the area of sex and an underlying fear of intimacy led him to choose a wife who acted sexy but who rarely

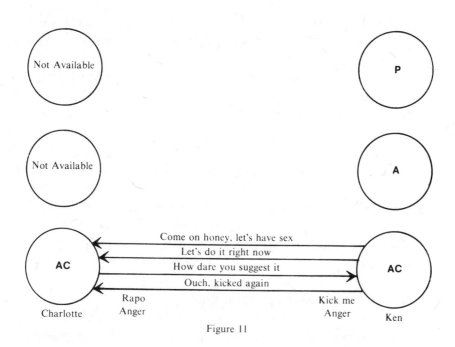

Figure 11

called on him to perform. He had a wife who was also afraid of intimacy.

Now, as an older more experienced man, Ken was no longer satisfied with the opportunity for extremely infrequent limited sexual expression. As he continued in therapy, he gained some new perspectives on intimacy and his fears subsided. I saw him perhaps half a dozen times following their divorce, and he subsequently discontinued therapy. At that time, I felt that when he again formed a lasting relationship with a woman, she would not be a Rapo player.

Another basically sexual game that stems from feelings of inadequacy in that area and influences the choice of a mate is *Who Needs You?* Again, in this game one partner feels more inadequate and frightened of sex, meaning that he or she turns the other partner down when sex is offered. The rejected partner then has sex with someone else and says, "Who needs you?" to the spouse.

The Huntingtons were playing this game, and it seemed as if a divorce were inevitable when they decided to give Transactional

Analysis therapy a try "for the sake of the children." Don Huntington had become an alcoholic and regularly came home drunk. As Alice refused to have sex with him when he'd been drinking, he began to visit the local prostitutes. When he returned home aftereach of these outings, he told Alice all about it in explicit detail. His closing line after describing each episode was, "So who needs you?"

Fortunately, Don and Alice each had good functioning Adults and they quickly picked up the basic theory of Transactional Analysis. As we talked, it became apparent that both Huntingtons were picking up hurt stamps. Don got them whenever Alice refused to have sex with him, and she got them following his description of sex with a prostitute. As often happens with hurt stamp collectors, they both got some satisfaction just from feeling hurt, but they also experienced some anger. The anger bubbled out in a general hostility between them much of the time.

Alice, in her refusal to have sex, played the classic "frigid woman." When they were dating and first married, this posture relieved Don of the pressure to perform sexually. As a younger, inexperienced man he'd been rather ambivalent about the whole thing. Thus, they chose each other partly because their apparent interest in sex seemed to be about the same. As the years passed, however, Alice became more frigid, and Don less ambivalent.

Frigidity for Alice was mostly a matter of feeling very inadequate and inexperienced in sexual matters. She didn't know what she wanted or how to find it out. As this couple began to understand with their Adults how this game pattern operated, I gave Don the homework of sharing what he'd learned about sex with Alice. In doing this, I was giving both of their Child parts permission to play.

After two or three tries, their Child parts began to relax and were much less fearful. Alice proved an apt pupil. Gradually, she discovered what she did enjoy most, and she learned how to ask for it in a way that assured her of getting it. Both of them used their Nurturing Parents, too, to reassure and encourage their frightened Child parts. As they moved into a more game-free, more candid relationship, they felt much better about themselves and each other. The need to collect hurts faded, and Don's drinking problem diminished. What happened with the Huntingtons can be shown by the diagrams in Figure 12.

As you may have noticed, a general concern over one's ability to be an adequate sex partner underlies sexual games. Problem drinking is also often associated with them, as is physical violence of some sort. One game that involves physical violence rather heavily is *Make Someone Suffer*. Although this game takes many forms, I've most often seen it played in the Make Mother Suffer version.

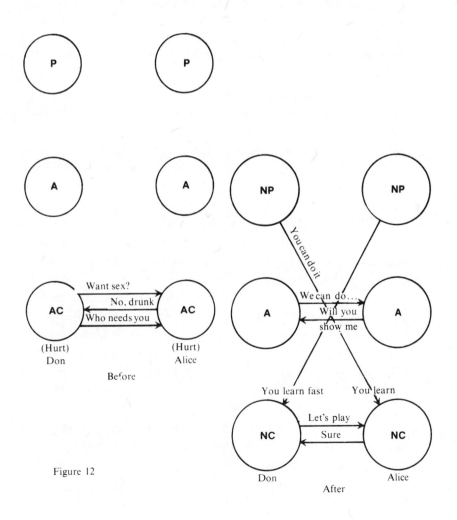

Figure 12

Dwight Hoffer was hell-bent on making mother suffer each time he flailed his fists against his wife's body in a drunken rage. Maureen called me one morning from the Women's Refuge to which she and the children fled the night before. I agreed to meet with her later that afternoon, and she assured me that Dwight would be there too. She seemed confident that once sober again he would be tractable enough to come.

The nurse practitioner at the Refuge had stitched up the split skin above his right eye and had bandaged it, but several other exposed bruises on her cheeks and jaw were puffy and purplish. She walked with some difficulty as she entered my office, but apparently there had been no broken bones. From her movements, I could imagine that the bruises I saw on her face were repeated on her body as well. Maureen Hoffer was a full-time wife and mother and probably a rather neat, pleasant-appearing one under normal circumstances. As she appeared that first afternoon with her husband, however, *battered* was the first word that came to mind.

Both were subdued and tense, so I began the hour by taking their case history. As they told me about their earlier life, I caught a glimpse of Dwight's mother, a critical harsh woman who do that day harassed him at every opportunity. When Dwight had met Maureen, she was working in a small manufacturing plant as an administrative assistant to the president. He saw in her a capable, organized, and perhaps even powerful woman. He wanted a woman who would protect him from his mother.

They married, and it became apparent that Maureen was not going to be effective in ridding Dwight of his mother. About the same time their first baby came along, Maureen suddenly became Dwight's "Mother." As we noted, with marriage and particularly with the advent of children, the spouse takes on the attributes of the real parent of that sex. Thus, when Maureen became a mother, she took on for Dwight the attributes of his real mother. He also took on the attributes of her real father. As a result, when Dwight vented his drunken anger by beating up Maureen, he was angry not only because she failed to protect him from his critical mother, but also because he was in this way able to beat up Mother through Maureen.

During the first hour, they relaxed just a little, and I was able to introduce some of the concepts of Transactional Analysis. I think the only thing they really took away was the notion that they did have some options or choices. They did not have to continue living as they had in the past.

The bruises had faded when the Hoffers came in for their second interview, and they both seemed genuinely hopeful that somehow things would work out. I continued to see this couple, for the most part alone but from time to time with their children, for about nine months. We unraveled their script matrix and its injunctions. Progress was jerky, but they did move into a more comfortable functioning relationship.

About six months ago Dwight called to tell me that he'd spent the afternoon with his mother, now in a nursing home. He'd asked her to tell him about her own parents, his grandparents, who had been dead for many years. The story she told was not a happy one; her parents had been harsh and demanding. He commented to me that knowing this and considering her in this light, along with the reality of her advancing age and loss of vitality, somehow diminished his own feeling of being harassed. I asked him if she still was as critical of his life and w "Oh, she says the same things, Doctor, that she always said, but somehow it doesn't matter so much anymore."

And Dwight's response is the one I wait for patients to be able to make. It comes from the Child, where the real change must take place. It doesn't depend on Adult reasoning, although there may be valid reasons involved. It's a feeling response that doesn't need an explanation; it is enough that it's there.

Game playing is not always as physically violent or destructive as the Alcoholic game. Sometimes, it is the identified difficulty in a marriage because one or both partners begin to recognize their patterns as ones they've seen before. People play the same games they learned from their own parents, and after a marriage is well underway, a couple may find that they are becoming a replay of the scenario that ran at home twenty or thirty years ago. At this point, one or both may cry, "Bring down the curtain! Stop the show!" If only one spouse recognizes the rerun, the other partner may be left holding the racket.

Jason was left in this bind. He worked at the local lumber mill, and each evening for the past twenty years he had slammed the back door, banged his lunch box on the kitchen table, and yelled, "Hi Honey, I gotta tell you what happened to me today...." It was always the same: Someone discounted him; someone made his job harder. Martha ritually replied, "Yeah, Honey, ain't it awful."

One day, Martha went to her Friday ladies club and heard a speaker talking about TA. She spotted their ritual game as a classic *Ain't It Awful,* and after the meeting she bought a book describing the games people get involved in. "Aha," she thought as she read, "so that's why we never really talk to each other!" That night, instead of giving her usual response she said, "You're really feeling that things went badly today at work." This was the kind of response that according to her reading she thought might break up the game.

The game initiator, however, is always scared to death of any change. He or she becomes agitated and tries to escalate the game. "You don't really give a damn how my day went, you never have!" he snapped.

I saw them a week or so later in therapy, and after they told me what had happened I diagramed the transaction (see Figure 13) and pointed out the potential for intimacy if the game is phased out. As Jason and Martha began to recognize the games they played and followed my suggestions for breaking up these transactions, they asked, "Why did we get into that habit anyway?"

THE SHOW MUST GO ON

There is a third way that couples may come together, and sometimes this factor is the one most quickly recognized in the course of therapy. In our discussion of life scripts we noted that usually that plan is quite specific in describing the supporting cast. If a person

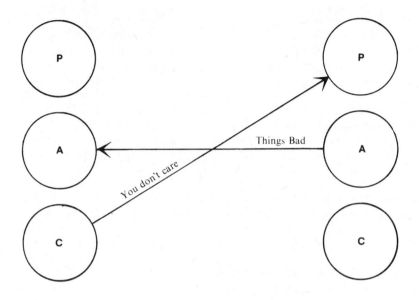

Figure 13

is scripted to marry or have relationships with the opposite sex, we can be quite certain that the script will call for a particular kind of player. When patients are able to reconstruct their life scripts, they also are able to look at those casting directions as well.

We've already observed the Critical Parent-Adapted Child relations in the case of Jenny and Jack. Jenny as she continued to provide for Jack's comfort never clearly demonstrated a need or expectation for appreciation. In fact, she sometimes used his lack of appreciation to collect a few blue depression stamps. Although Jack's script injunction did contribute to the relationship problems he and Jenny were facing, it didn't extend into his relationship with others away from home.

Phil Rathorne (chapter 5) on the other hand, found his script injunction so strong that it colored almost all of his behavior at home, at work, everywhere he went. He heard the mother in his head saying, "You've got to be afraid of them, they're out to get you!" The script scene for Phil came when his mother refused to leave him the first day in nursery school. Although we had talked about this and other early childhood episodes when he saw me with his parents, it wasn't until he began working with me as an individual and later with his girl friend that he absorbed the full import of it.

In my office, Phil confessed that he was scared to death of cars, buses, trains, and planes. He always arranged his work so that he could travel on foot from his apartment to his employment. He was at this time about twenty-five years old and was leaving home for the first time. Shortly after he made this break, he became interested in a young woman. Up until this time, he had avoided any real contact with women his age. He met Inga at his job, and when she returned his interest, he found himself feeling much worse rather than better.

By this time, Phil had talked enough TA with me that he knew his reaction of feeling worse was significant, and he persuaded Inga to come with him for several therapy sessions. I met them several times, and as we talked I learned that Inga, a fiercely political woman of Chinese heritage, had declared early in their friendship that they might never have sexual intercourse until Phil vowed his total commitment to her political persuasion. Now, Phillip was a strikingly apolitical young man. He had never before been particularly interested in government systems and was even less so as his fascination with Inga grew.

Phil and Inga were not fully cohabiting, but they did spend three or four nights a week together. She always came to bed in bra and panties and lay provocatively in his arms until they fell asleep, but she denied him any penetration or relief. She was clearly fulfilling his script injunction, "They (Inga) are out to get (frustrate, hurt) you."

At this time in our discussions, Phil knew what his script injunction was, and as we analyzed what was happening in their relationship he recognized the playing out of his all too familiar script. Inga did have some positive feelings toward him, and they then consummated their sexual roles several times before drifting apart.

In the weeks that followed, Phil continued to see me alone, now determined to kick his script. To do this he needed to use his

Adapted Child very deliberately to unscript himself. I told him to imagine himself being four years old again, to visualize the room in which his nursery school was held and to feel how he felt that day more than twenty years ago. He let himself enter fully into this experience and began describing everything he could remember—the pet turtle, his new "big-boy" boots, and so on. Then I asked, "Can you decide not to feel that way now?" Luring the Adapted Child into making this kind of redecision sounds quite simple, but for many of my patients it proves to be an elusive thing.

In therapy we may return to this exercise of imagining the past several times before the Adapted Child can make the new decision. An understanding of scripts and script injunctions in the Adult can help smooth the way, and, of course, an appeal to the Nurturing Parent for support and encouragement in the new decision helps too. But it is the Adapted Child who plays the key role.

During these weeks, I used my Parent to give Phil permission to recognize first his injunction and then to alter it. As with other major changes, this altering is usually frightening to the individual, and again I assured Phil that he could call me any time and talk, that I would protect him as he moved into his new significantly less fearful life.

Phil did become acquainted with several other young women, and when I saw him last, he had just given up his apartment and was moving in with one of them. He grinned and said, "You know, I'm about fifteen miles from my job now. I take a bus to BART and then the MUNI right to the door!"

As couples open up their thinking and begin talking about their life scripts, they usually become more consciously aware of the needs of their Natural Childs, too. When the games are knocked off and the crisis subsides, couples begin to acknowledge the vague stirrings of this ego state.

It is the Natural Child who beckons, "Come on, let's laugh, let's have some fun, let's make love!" But couples whose Natural Child parts are free to make, accept, and act on this invitation are usually playful, functioning couples, and I may meet them in life situations but not in therapy.

The actively functioning Not OK Adapted Childs choose partners to meet their needs, play their games, and so advance their script injunctions and fend off that much feared intimacy. These couples are the ones I meet in my office. There is something inherently dysfunctional and pathological about this whole phenomenon.

CHAPTER 7

A Time
to Play

CAN THE KIDS COME OUT?

Remember how important the response to the question, "Can the kids come out?" was when you were five or six years old? Play was your major daytime activity then, and play usually meant finding someone to play with—a playmate. A quick yes to that question often signaled the beginning of a play-filled day.

How much more vital is the response to that question today as we consider the plight of families and couples in therapy. Although play is usually not the major daytime activity of adults in our culture, it is nonetheless that quality of "playfulness" that accompanies creative work, adds the dimension of joy to our relationships, and satisfies the longings of the Natural Child. It still is a question that must be answered with a resounding yes if these families and couples are to grow beyond the current crisis and become fully alive.

Whatever the identified "cause" that brings a family into therapy, we can be sure that these are people who are not coming out to play or at least not to play with each other. They are a little like the toddlers who, when left in a room full of toys, only hit at each other and cry.

Through effective therapy, a family can become aware of the specific things they do or say that interfere with their play, and perhaps they will decide to alter these patterns of behavior. In TA the terms will knock off their games and make new decisions about their life scripts. As they do these things, they will become more candid in their conversations and more playful in their behavior with each other. It is this playing that leads to intimacy, and intimacy is what families are all about.

TELL ME TRUE

If a family is to move into a more intimate relationship and begin to play with each other, it seems to me that they must learn to listen well and communicate clearly. They must first learn to listen well and communicate clearly. They must first learn to listen to their own Natural Childs. All too often the voice of the Natural Child has been suppressed or disregarded for so many years that the individual hardly knows what it sounds like. When asked, such people really don't know what their own Natural Childs might like. They really don't know *how* they would like to play.

To get acquainted with a couple's Natural Child the therapist must listen with his or her own Child. As this listening goes on, the therapist will begin to discern what it is that the Natural Childs in the couple might really want. Of course, the therapist can also go off on a fantasy trip of his or her own, too. To avoid the latter, I usually check out my Child's idea with the couple using my own Adult.

Several years ago I worked with a couple who were both on the staff of our local junior college. They came into therapy with their son Jamie, but I saw them for the most part as a couple because their difficulties with him seemed to stem from their basic couple relationship.

Kevin complained, "Martha just can't let herself go. We never do anything just for fun, and our sex life is practically nonexistent!" For her part Martha seemed to be constantly scared. As we talked she told us that her father had been explosive in his anger toward her, and her earliest memories were her fears that he would yell at her or punish her again. She was living out her adult life now with a very strong set of have to directions, the strongest of which was "have to produce"; she had quickly risen to the number-two spot in her department at the college.

It seemed to me, as I looked at her, that her own Critical Parent was probably saying, "You have to shampoo and curl your hair every morning...have to keep your eyebrows tweezered neatly... have to be sure your outfit is just right or people will find you unattractive." Actually, most of the time when I saw her, she was more attractive than many of the women her age whom I had noticed in our town. What might her Child then really want? I guessed that Martha might want to hear that she was attractive to Kevin and hear it both when she had taken pains to appear so and at other times when she hadn't. I checked this out with her, and she replied, "Why yes, I'd really like that. How did you know?" Then of course, it was Kevin's homework to tell her warmly, affectionately, and *often* just how appealing she looked to him.

But what of Kevin's Child, what did it really want? When I asked him, he looked intently at the floor, then at me, and shrugged his shoulders, "I don't know...." He frowned and moved his shoulders again, hunching into a new positive in the chair. I said, "I'll bet you'd like a really good massage starting at the back of your neck and working down to the base of your spine, aye?" Kevin responded, "That sure would feel good. Yeah, it really would. My Dad used to give me back rubs when I was a kid, but nobody's done it for a long time now."

Martha bought a book on massage and a bottle of body oil that very night. Apparently, she studied it well and practiced it several times because when I next saw them Martha was a little less fearful and Kevin was smiling and said, "That was fun."

For Kevin and Martha, this was a way to *begin* to play. They each experienced listening to the voice of their own Natural Child and acknowledging it. They also heard each other's Natural Child desires. It was a start. As we went on with our meetings, they practiced telling each other what they heard from their Natural Child, and as time went on they grew more and more comfortable about doing this.

The role of the therapist in this process is, of course, first to help individuals hear the desires of the internal Natural Child ego state; but once heard, these desires also need to be communicated and acted upon. Here, the therapist gives permission to overcome any past parental injunctions that may be standing in the way of play.

The giving of permission often takes the form of prescribing homework activities. Sometimes I simply prescribe that a time each day must be set aside for play. The playtime homework may be started rather early in the therapy sessions; it need not wait for the unraveling of the script or an explanation of the theory of play. As soon as I sense they are ready to take some positive action, I usually prescribe some homework play activities with couples in which one or both partners are in the habit of putting down the OK feelings in the other person's Child. Play can be practiced, and the players will soon forget that they are doing homework. I have them using their Natural Childs to play with each other.

For example, one spouse may really want to be hugged and kissed more during foreplay. That person then might tell his or her partner, "I want to be hugged and kissed all over!" For one couple I saw in therapy, simply learning to do this was all they needed to unblock their sex life and get them started playing. In this case, the husband always waited for his wife to initiate the sex play. He spent a great deal of time worrying, "Will she?" "Won't she?" When he learned to assert himself and say, "I'd like to have sex with you tonight," the problem vanished.

As each partner begins to assert him or herself and declare their needs, the therapist can give them permission to describe these needs regardless of how outrageous this may seem to either of them. The couple can then take time to listen to each other's fantasies.

Albert Ellis (1971) in his rational emotive therapy takes on the question by saying, "What if you did ask for something like fellatio and your partner refused? Would it be so terrible?" Partners need not act out all their fantasies or needs in order to play. Often, simply taking them out and responding verbally in a warm understanding way is enough. Again, I caution patients to beware of the Adapted Child. The Adapted Child may try to take over, declaring what it wants and then making an Ain't It Awful game if the spouse turns this wish down.

Asking a spouse for what you want seems simple, yet in life it often is surprisingly hard. I met one day with a very successful trial lawyer in our town. I had known him for several years by his newspaper reputation. He had successfully defended a notorious syndicate figure and was front-page copy for weeks during the trial. I was surprised to hear this eloquent man call and make an appointment to bring his wife and meet with me to talk about their problem, which he described as an inability to have sex during the past five years.

When they came to the office I asked what difficulty had prevented them from having sex for all these years. The attorney replied, "My wife won't do what I want." Then I asked, "And what is it you want?" He replied, "I would like my wife to do fellatio on me." His wife's face brightened and she exclaimed, "Oh, I don't mind doing that!" And, that was the end of their therapy with me.

The setting of my office and the mystique of "therapy" was all it took for this normally very persuasive talker to speak assertively about sex to his wife. Fortunately, she responded positively. Their transaction might be diagrammed as shown in Figure 1.

Several years later, I met with another couple who had a similar problem but one that required more treatment time to work through. The husband in this case came on basically Adult and told us that he wanted more sex than he was getting. When he said this his wife exclaimed, "Why? I let you have it once every month!" "Once a month isn't enough!" he shouted.

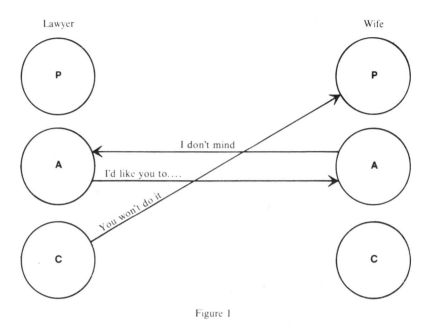

Figure 1

The frequency with which a couple experiences sex together is a major concern of many couples seeking therapy. It is important here to remind them that the need for sexual expression does not build up like a reservoir. Unfulfilled, an individual will not break apart like a ruptured dam. Normal people can and do go without sex for prolonged periods of time for a variety of reasons and suffer no harm. Of course, in a functioning marriage, there will be sex. It has been said many times that if sex is good in a marriage, the mountains become molehills; but if it's not good the molehills become mountains.

When people complain that they don't have sex often enough, they may also be thinking that when they do make love it isn't all that great an experience. Sex can be merely a ritual or a pastime as is fully discussed in *Games People Play* (Berne 1964). However, when a couple approaches their problems in this area from the position of *play*, they usually find that they have sex more frequently and the experience is more generally satisfying. For is sex is approached in this way—that is, playful—loving sex can be a very special form of intimacy.

When couples learn to listen to their own Natural Child voices and actually communicate to each other the ways they particularly want to play, a general playfulness will begin to flow through their relationship and will be visible in many ways. One of the quickest and easiest ways to observe this happening is in the behavior of the real children in the family.

When Joe and Joanne Moulenarie (chapter 5) first came into therapy, their daughters Betty and Jill did not play with each other in my office. Apparently, they didn't play at home either. Betty spent most of the therapy time looking miserable, and Jil kept herself occupied with the Lincoln Logs. After their parents began to play with each other, these two girls suddenly began to make log houses in my office. Their parents reported that they also played happily with each other and with other friends at home.

If parents are unable to let their own Natural Childs play, we can be quite certain that the real children in the family won't be playing either. This was the case with Tim.

Tim's teachers remarked that he seemed to have his own bubble around him at school and he rarely played or mingled with the other children. On the occasions when he did choose to interact with the kids, it seemed to be with the intent of picking a fight. At home, Tim kept pretty much to his room, playing alone or watching TV. His contact with his parents was generally limited to setting up "lets you and him fight" sessions. Play was not a part of this child's everyday life.

As the parents in the family grew less fearful and practiced playing with each other, Tim began to be able to play, too. He joined the Cub Scouts and found a buddy for the first time in his life. Significantly, too, his teacher was pleased with his progress in school. When a family gets better, the children usually do better in school.

In families such as the Johnsons (chapter 5) where the children are teenagers, we can expect to see a change in friends and activities. Alza dropped out of the losers' crowd when her parents' relationship was improved. In some schools this crowd is the drug group, in others it may be those who just never are in on the mainstream action. Often, as friendships shift, the newly well teenager will develop an interest in a team sport, become proficient in tennis, or accept the responsibility of chairing a school project. They will begin to get in on the fun and usually their grades will also improve.

WHO'S AFRAID?

Again and again, in describing the course of treatment with families and couples, there is the notion "he did thus and such because of a fear of intimacy," or "she acted in this way to avoid the possibility of intimacy." Almost without exception the people I meet in therapy are afraid. They may at times be afraid of dependency or afraid of submission. They are frequently afraid of intimacy, perhaps because they fear that in intimacy they will surely lose self. Yet one grows very lonely in this world without intimacy. Intimacy, as we have said, is what families are all about.

Why is a fear of intimacy so common among our patients? This fear seems to originate in childhood in families where mother and dad fought and discounted each other or withdrew and discredited each other. Observing such parents, the young child is left to visualize the primal scene as something to be afraid of. If the everyday mealtime intercourse between parents is hurtful, damaging, or dangerous, the child can only support that intimate or sexual intercourse is also a hurting thing, a thing to be feared. Hence, that child grows to adulthood with a fear of intimacy.

In families where mother and dad are playful and affectionate with each other over the breakfast table, children grow up assuming that intimacy and sex are also playful, tender, happy experiences. They do not grow up afraid of intimacy.

Dispelling these fears, then, goes right along with the process of learning to play. In fact, these two aspects are so interwoven that it is difficult to divide them at all when dealing with real people in life situations. It is only here in theory that we can pull them apart and examine them. Fear stands in the way of play, but loving play is the antidote for fear.

I have described how couples do this in preparation for sex, but the same mode of interacting is in no way limited to sexual activities. Play is a way of communicating that works in all the conversations of the day, and it is by employing this clear candid style of communicating day in and day out, in the thousands of mundane matters a husband and wife must deal with, that it functions to build the OK-ness of self and dissipate fear.

For example, we might imagine a couple faced with the need to buy a new car. Catherine might say, "I really like that new green color and I need the space of a station wagon." Then, Chris says, "I understand that green's your favorite for a car color and I know you need lots of room. What I want is a car that gets good mileage and is feasible for me to maintain." He's accepted her view and also expressed his own. Now it's her turn to accept his priorities. They will still need to do more talking and probably gather more information before they make a choice. But they are beginning with the basic premise that each one has a right to have an opinion in this matter, that each of them has the right to be, to exist.

This premise seems so simple, and yet when the right to be, to hold one's own opinion, and to own a self is denied or threatened in those mundane conversations between family members, we find people who feel Not OK and who fear intimacy.

Thus, it is very important that partners practice recognizing the other's right to be in all their conversations with each other. Such recognition continually shows an ongoing respect for the autonomous self of the other person, assuring him or her that the self is not in jeopardy in the relationship. Each partner does have the right to own an intact self, to be, to exist without threat of engulfment.

Beyond describing the experience of candid conversation, we can simply observe that loving play drives out fear and opens the way for warm intimate relationships between mates, their children, and perhaps a selected few others. Full intimacy is not a state into which one invites the whole world; rather, it is wisely reserved for a chosen few. However, once intimacy within this smaller circle is attained, the individual finds it possible to enter freely into open, warm relationships with more casual acquaintances as well.

When the self is comforted and its right to exist is firmly established, the Adapted Child moves into a stronger feeling of OK-ness; the old Not OK with its fears will vanish like the fog at noontime.

As mom and dad feel OK themselves, they will be playful with each other and, at times, with their children. There will be time for building sand castles, for walking barefoot in the mud, for marveling at the rhythm of the surf. There will be seeing, doing, feeling, sharing whatever life offers to the fullest. As mom and dad take the lead in this joyous playing with life, the children will see "Life is good. Live!" They will grow up in the fulness of this experience, and they will know that they need never fear intimacy. And, who knows? If this awakening sweeps the land, in the next generation there may be no need for us, no role for therapists, no reason to learn TA.

CHAPTER   8

Where to
Get Training

Dr. Edward W. Beal (1976) describes current trends in the training of family therapists and subdivides the training into different orientations by teaching members. The classification of family therapy theory has to do with a scale he sets up with different types of therapists from an A to Z. The A is an experiential orientation. Centers that fall at the A end of the theoretical scale include the following:

Menninger School of Psychiatry—Topeka, Kansas
Family Institute of Chicago—Chicago, Illinois
University of Wisconsin Medical School—Madison, Wisconsin
University of Colorado Medical School—Denver, Colorado
University of Minnesota Medical School—Minneapolis-St.
  Paul, Minnesota.

Midwest Family Therapy Institute—Minneapolis-St. Paul, Minnesota
Amherst H. Wilder Child Guidance Clinic—Minneapolis-St. Paul, Minnesota

The assumption of therapists at the A end of the scale is that relationships are significantly influenced by the expression of inhibition of affect or emotional tension. Direct expression of this tension or affect is, therefore, appropriate and indicated for the maintenance of healthy relationships in a family. Therapists at the A end of the scale use group psychotherapy theory and techniques. TA is at the A end of the scale. The modality for emotional growth is considered by these therapists to be the therapeutic relationship between the therapist and the patient. They emphasize the subjective experience of therapy and the subjective awareness and intuition of the therapist to guide the therapy. Some of these therapists conceptualize family therapy as a technique to facilitate individual psychotherapy. The A therapists also consider indications and contradictions for family therapy.

The process that is primarily studied by therapists at the A end of the scale is the one that exists among members of the family group in therapy and between each of them and the therapist. A variety of techniques is used within the framework, including family sculpting, psychodrama, Gestalt therapy, behavior modification, encounter group techniques, interpretation of unconscious conflicts, and group process techniques.

Centers that fall at the Z end of the theoretical scale include the following:

Philadelphia Child Guidance Clinic—Philadelphia, Pennsylvania
Georgetown University Postgraduate Program in Family and Systems Theory—Washington, D.C.
Groome Child Guidance Center—Washington, D.C.

The assumption of therapists at the Z end of the scale is that emotional tension leads to a process that manifests itself in the structure of family relationships. They believe that this tension is maintained or resolved by the nature of the communication pathways or the relationship system through which it is transmitted. Some Z therapists believe that changing communication pathways and feedback systems is the appropriate method of intervention in a dysfunctional family. Others believe that a family relationship system can be modified by changing the part an individual plays in the relationship system.

The following institutes fall at the M position on the theoretical scale:

Boston Family Institute—Boston, Massachusetts
Center of Family Learning—New Rochelle, New York
Bronx Psychiatric Center, Albert Einstein College of Medicine
　—New York, New York
Nathan W. Ackerman Family Institute—New York, New York
Family Institute of Philadelphia—Philadelphia, Pennsylvania

The type of family therapy practiced by the faculty at the M centers has characteristics of both the A and Z ends of the spectrum.

As of now we have no good diagnostic classification for family therapy. I suggest, in a preliminary way, that families can be classified by rackets. This area needs further research.

To get Transactional Analysis training call or write:

International Transactional Analysis Association
1722 Vallejo Street
San Francisco, California 94123
Phone: (415) 885-5992

CHAPTER 9

Training
Troubles

The following chapter is a tape of one session of a study group with two psychiatric social workers led by me, held weekly for an hour and fifteen minutes. Permission to tape was received from these therapist. They were told that the taping was to be used in a book.

Kathy: I see your tape recorder going and I realize that I am about to sabotage your book. I'm thinking that at least between now and the end of October that I don't want to come anymore and em—

Jim: How come?

Kathy: And that's just for a couple of reasons. One is that my schedule is really crazy what with going to Brussels and getting married and all that. The other is that I got a message from Sandra [a social worker who had been in the group] on my machine and I didn't call her back, but she said that she is not going to be here. And, my problem Jim, is that I had hoped there would be a big crowd here so that we could gather a lot of energy from a lot of people, but with just the three of us, it's not enough input for me. I'd like to continue to come. It it's going to continue to be just the three of us, it's not enough. So—

Jim: I'll see and will let you know.

Kim: And I'm going to do the same. I feel the same way and I don't want to come alone. I wanted a group to share. What do you think? How do you feel?

Jim: I offered it as an opportunity for a group to get together and discuss difficult problems. I know that we see people individually, but the original intent of this was to be a study group, and a group is not just one person.

Kim: Have you been disappointed that more people didn't come?

Jim: No, actually I felt that when JoAnn [another social worker who came intermittently] was coming here there were four, and I felt that that was about right. Because—

Kathy: Yes, that was really good. Four to five provides enough energy and that would be fine with me.

Jim: Also, I was thinking that if there were more than five people, some would tend to get left out and not get a chance to participate. I don't know how you feel about that, but usually with five people, an hour and fifteen minutes would let everyone get a little something. I feel that to devote an hour and fifteen minutes to one person is not really practical. Usually, fifteen to twenty minutes lets people bring out all they want to say about something that is difficult. I think four or five would be well suited to this. Apparently, Sandra would like to be in the group. However, by vociferously wishing me good on my vacation, then canceling the next time, coming late the next meeting, then backing out altogether. I got the impression that hse had another consultant who she felt was duplicating what was going on here. Also, the other reason she gave was that she wasn't talking about private practice in general. I said this was not true, that she could discuss features of private practice, but she had carte blanche to bring up anything she wished. She said that running into Berkeley [where the group met] was not what she wanted to do at this point, and I told her I would be available if she changed her mind. If you know some people or have some people that want to get in on the study group, fine.

Kim: Yeah, I'm sorry that she decided to drop. I guess the other reason I was thinking of and I'm dissatisfied about is as follows. If we continue with this group after November 1, one thing I want from you is more help on "how tos." Sometimes you will say some really good things with regard to what's going on with a person, and it's helpful, but I end up not knowing what to do.

Jim: That's one thing that I'm sure could be improved upon by stating what to say.

Kim: Actually, I had seen this more as training than as a study group. I think I got some really beneficial stuff, and what I feel I need is some more really psychoanalytical techniques of exploring. It helped me tremendously. Also you know I didn't feel like coming because I had the flu, and while that's well and good, is there anything else that came up for you in my not coming? I've had some patients respond to that. As long as you can say yes that was the reason, but did you have any other thoughts about it? And, yeah, I didn't want to come and was glad that I had the flu. So that's been very helpful. Something I'd like if we reconvene in November is that you get a firm commitment say from three other people. There will always be a dropout, but I feel we could handle five.

Kathy: I agree with you that more than five might get a little unwieldy.

Kim: I'd like training from you in the form of feedback on how I'm handling it and perhaps a little less psyching out my client. Possibly an abbreviated version of what you have been doing to psych out a client would be helpful. Including it in meandering guides eludes interest, and I lose sight of how this effects the treatment of my client. You really don't need to psych out your client as much as you need to learn how to be in treatment. As you should know, I don't want to do away with psyching out the client. I'd like you to think or say, "How are you treating her or what's going on?" This would help me to get some feedback on how I'm working as a therapist. How does that strike you?

Jim: Generally, I avoid that unless people ask for it because I don't believe that consultation is treatment. When I was a resident my consultants would force me to be treated and try to trap me into therapy, then tell you what you should talk about in your own analysis. I think that is wrong.

Kathy: I really have appreciated that you haven't done that. And that's a different point of view. I would like to have an agreement with you that if I wanted that as part of my consulting you would check some things out with me.

Kim: I see where you're coming from. I wouldn't like the kind of thing that you got, but what I would like is my problems pointed out that interfere with my treating clients. I think that my own personality and issues do effect the treatment. I don't mean by working on my issues, but working on how I am as a therapist working with a client, which is different from something else. So you haven't resolved things with your mother, that's why [laugh], you know. What about resolving this with your mother? Instead of saying you know. Is she looking into something about her mother or it looks like, you know, both good and bad like you have both strokes and criticism?

Kathy: I guess there is a delicate balance of that. I had a similar experience in graduate school of getting supervision and was very reluctant to bring up problems simply because I always ended up getting them turned on me and what was the matter with me.

Jim: I wound up seeing one consultant when I was in analysis, and the analyst was telling me how to treat children. My consultant was interpreting things to me and I said to the consultant that I got some useful consultation from my analyst. "Since you're doing his job anyway, I'll get the consultation from him." His jaw just dropped.

Kathy: Yeah, that sounds like it would be very difficult.

Kim: Yeah, very difficult to work that problem out. You're really at their mercy. Anything that you say that's confronting, they can say, "See your analyst." You better work that out.

Jim: I was sent to one consultant once that was silent. I had obviously concluded my clinical vignette, so I said to him. "Well, we're not here to explore my reactions to your silence so I think I'll leave."

Kathy: They can't take that. That's hostile.

Jim: Couple of things I've noticed in technique is that you seem to particularly want to gratify your patients. That is, your patient wants nurturing and you nurture. I think usually if you're discussing what the patient wants, and feeling that you don't have to do something about it is worthwhile because you know, you can say to a patient, "You want to mistreat and hurt me," without saying I'm not going to put up with it. I think that the patient will respond considerately. You hook the Adult seriously to think about it. Similarly, if you come on Adult, then you hook their Adult and you say, "Can you hear yourself?" Their Adult is a co-therapist. I think that's one way to stop patients who have receptivity problems. That is, they listen only partially. In some way you can say Yes But from your Child, but not hear the words, and there is no emotional impact. That is, it won't alter anything, so that what you're doing is bouncing off even though the patient can say the words back to you.

Sometimes it's the submission issue. They will Yes But just about everything you say to them, including your interpretation of how they are fighting you off. In your Yes But game, I think it is really a fighting off, and the issue is that "I'm not going to submit to you." Because no Parent can tell me anything is a payoff, but what it really means is, "I'm not going to submit to you." They say this with their Child. There is a point where they will almost get ridiculous about it. "You mean I have to submit to your interpretation that I'm afraid to submit." That's very common. It sounds funny but it happens a lot. And if you, under difficult circumstances like that, where you are bouncing off. You can either accept or okay, but don't bang your head against the wall. The person is so afraid of disintegrating that they simply can't receive anything unless they control it.

For example, from a patient I've been talking with for a long time now, how about you for some feedback? They will let you enter their mind at that point if they control it. But sometimes if the patient has a question, you make an interpretation that they wouldn't have been receptive to otherwise. I think the only other alternative, if they are not considerate with their Adult about how they are fighting off, is to have it out with them. "You know I just said something to you and you didn't listen. Why is that?" That's agressive, but it's not hostile. Or, "Can you hear yourself?" You're asking for them to think about themselves.

Some times a patient who "yes buts" if they start thinking about themselves will come up with their own interpretation to themselves. I think this is good because you are trying to set up a therapy so that they can leave you and be able to understand themselves when they get into emotional difficulties. They can then do it themselves.

A lot of people handle questions in a way that isn't really beneficial. You can all answer questions, but the reason that you don't answer questions is that there is something going on between you and the patient that the patient doesn't see. Like, I'm not making any sense. Does that make any sense? Or do you know what I mean? Or, all those questions have something in there that they are not telling you, so that if you say, "Why do you ask?" the patient will say, "Oh, I was wondering what your thoughts were. I was just curious, 'cause I've been talking and you haven't said anything." I have a patient that is constantly saying, "Do you know what I mean?" I asked him about it and said "Does that mean that you want reassurance that you are understood? when you keep saying,'You know what I mean?' " He said, "Yeah, I guess so, do you know what I mean?"

I know something you are doing that is incorrect. When a patient gets you feeling uncomfortable and frustrated you will let the patient know. I think you told us one woman, when you were frustrated, was afraid to attach herself to you. I wouldn't say that to a patient. I would say, "I think you want me to feel frustrated and eager to hold on to you" or something like that, rather than "I feel frustrated." Berne use to tell us that you don't say you are bored because there are all sorts of things about being bored with a patient. One is why are they boring you? That can be an interesting question. And, also, of central significance, Why are you being bored? I would use your own feelings to help in understanding your patient. You can use Parent, Adult, and Child in response to the patient. What is your Parent saying? For example, I had a family that was always quitting. I interpreted their fear of dependency on each other as well as on me for the reason they were always quitting.

Kathy: You are saying you can use your own feelings to interpret.

Jim: Right. So with my Critical Parent, I had to say, "Oh, let them quit." I looked at that with my Adult and I thought, they are obnoxious. They're always walking out; they're always quitting. So I thought to myself, are they trying to get me to a point where I kick them out because they are always walking out? They are always negative and they are producing a negative response in me. Maybe that's why they are having so many problems in their family. Everything is negative; nothing is ever nice. They are always saying negative things about each other, and the positive things do not get expressed. I was using my Critical Parent which was saying, "Oh, let them quit, "Gee, what a relief not to have to be seeing them." So you can see that both my Parent and Child were in accord about letting them go, so I used that to try and understand why they were doing that to provide a rational interpretation. Then I thought they are really afraid to commit themselves and they want me to let them go. So what I finally ended up saying to them was, "I think you want me to say, go ahead and leave, and then I'd be depreciating the therapy like you do."

The whole family—they're all here and they're all creating a dependency on each other. They had separate bank accounts after being married for ten years and, therefore, little trust or commitment to each other. When I saw them alone, one had individually been projecting all over the spouse, and I couldn't tell it until I got the spouse in. It turned out that they lost opposite-sex parents at the same age, and that trauma lead them to being fearful of dependency on anybody.

I'd like to give you an example about their receptivity. I said to this woman, who had seen me a couple of times, "I think you're afraid of the dependency upon me and you want to get out of this." She said, "Do you think so?" And I knew that she had not listened to what I'd said. Her Child was responding with, "Do you think so?"—not really taking it in. So I said, "What do you think?" She said, "Oh I don't know" and "Whatever makes it right?" I said, "That's even better than maybe." "What do you think?" She said, "I sure as hell do not want you running my life, I know that." I said, "How do you see me as running your life?" "You might tell me whether I should stay with my husband or not, and I couldn't see that happening." I said, "That part of the dependency would be that I'm trying to tell you what to do all the time."

I saw her husband who was also quitting, and I asked him if he saw this [seeing me] as a threat to this independence. He said, "Yeah, but I'm going to quit anyway." Yes But, and this was a time at the end of the session, so he did quit.

The daughter would never ask the parents anything including their opinions. I think she was fifteen and she went out with her friends all the time, smoked marijuana, came home at three in the morning, and then got up at eight in the morning and went out. It was really a chaotic family. I used my reactions to understand that they wanted me to push them away because they were afraid of the dependency. I was talking to myself in my head. I had a Critical Parent to Adapted Child dialogue when the Parent was saying, "Oh let them quit." That was also my Child. I just worked on why they did eventually terminate. The therapy wasn't really complete then. I've been yakking now, let's see—I guess my point was, "Don't tell them how you feel until you're sure it would be useful.

Kathy: I really like that, I understand and I feel that was right. When I did say that to her and it did work, you know, a whole other thing; she would start all over. She really hadn't come to therapy to work out. It was that I was frustrated about it. It would have been more helpful to her for me to have pointed it out, then act as I did.

Kim: Yeah, I really like that. Just checking how I feel and then reflecting to the client, "I think you want to get me—you know—in such and such a position."

Jim: The only thing I would say about that is that if you are having problems with the Critical Parent—that is, if your Critical Parent is prejudiced against a paricular client—you may be having reactions that aren't a response to a point. But that's a matter of having your own head straight. You probably have heard of treating schizophrenics by talking honestly and telling them how you feel.

Both social workers: Yes.

Jim: I was exposed to that once, when I was a resident.

Kathy: Otherwise they are going to know.

Jim: No. To promote closeness—you tell them how you feel in order to maintain a relationship. The theory is that you tell them if you are angry. You tell them if you are scared. You tell them if you are guilty. I don't agree with that at this point because I feel that they have enough problems without knowing what you're frustrated with. As a matter of fact, when I was in analysis, this one consultant kept telling me, "You've got to tell a schizophrenic how you feel. You've got to be honest with them."

Kathy: It seems to me that by telling my client how I feel puts out an expectation that they take care of me.

Jim: Yeah, True. The patient may respond to that also. If you say that to really an obnoxious schizophrenic and it's only in your office and it's only in therapy, then it's all right for you to do this, to let him know that you are angry. I would not say when I'm pissed at you because you're putting everything down. I would say, "You want me to be angry so you could control me like a puppet," and in that way you'd be controlling us both. That's more help to the patient. I have a colleague who used to treat schizophrenics and he is now heavily into family work, but he used to tell this one patient that he had murdered somebody, "You know I'm scared shitless everytime I interview you." And I think that was wrong. The purpose of that was to say to the patient, "Don't hurt me," rather than saying, "You want me to be afraid." If I go on in the hospital and the patient is saying, "Well I really have a terrible temper and blow up at the slightest frustration and you know, I'm going to get the next person that crosses me," I would say to the patient, "You are intending to frighten me. And I think that you are afraid of being alone with me. So I won't see you unless there is an orderly around." That's much more helpful than saying, "I'm scared of you."

Kathy: Yeah. I can see that.

Jim: You see those gut-level things that go on in my Child like being scared. I want my Adult to look at those. What I find most difficult, I don't know how you feel, is the patient that can communicate only by questions. I've tried to find why they communicate so much by questions, but I really find that sometimes I can't work with this kind of paient.

Kathy: You mean they ask you questions?

Jim: Yeah!

Kathy: Or they need to be asked questions.

Jim: No, they ask questions. They communicate by asking questions.

Kathy: Oh!

Jim: Sometimes you can figure out why they are asking questions, but other than that, they continue asking lots of quesions.

Kathy: Uh huh!

Jim: I thought those were the kind of patients I'd have problems with—they don't show any initiative of their own, just ask questions. Did you read that *Games That Analysts Play?*

Kathy: No. Is it a TA book?

Kim: Is it on your recommended list?

Kathy: Or an analytic book?

Jim: It's done by a guy who is not an analyst, but has had some analytical training, and a woman who has written several volumes. It's really good about patients who ask you something and you say, "Why do you ask?" They charge that the analyst may be afraid of answering the question directly. He is obviously hostile to analyst and goes through certain games like, denial of hostility on the analyst and denial of tension on the analyst part. There are messages you can be real to in response. I feel that in general it is really unwise to be real to a client. I'm not talking about somebody who has a knife at your throat.

Kathy: Then that's really an unsettled question, in therapy—the family therapist. Many of them seem to go through stages when they start out. They say, "Oh, I'm getting a stomachache now," so I know that something is going on in the family, I mean, I know, I really advocate using, you know, looking at their own selves. And letting the family know and then saying this might be something that the family is making me feel. And I imagine that a lot of them go through stages and say that's a bunch of bullshit. Everybody that I know in therapy says, "I used to do this, but now I think it's terrible." And I know that Minuchin in his book says when we first started doing family therapy we had no idea what we were doing. We just tried out everything. And now as we are doing it, we find, you know, some techniques that work. So I think that it is still and may always be an open question, rather than whether the therapist should let his own feelings come through more.

Kim: I think it is more how you go about using the questions, and I like your suggestions about using the awareness of the Parent, Adult, and Child.

Jim: In a family, you're not so constrained, regardless of the kind of therapy, to be pure about it. I think what is important to understand is that in family therapy if you're not there as the leader, not directing the show, not really telling them what to talk about, you're not there as a leader. You may get pasted on the wall—that is to say, become a sibling. We want to encourage a dialogue.

I was interviewing a family at the hospital and the identified patient was a seventeen year old. He was depressed, suicidal and somehow the father was a competitive alcoholic, and if there were any problems in the family he would just walk out and down to the bar and that was that. He didn't say much and he didn't volunteer much; and the mother was really very overweight and diabetic and produced a few words, but not very much. And as I saw how really distant these people were from me, I became depressed. I got sucked into the system, and then I used the PAC again with what they are all saying. My Parent was saying get them working on themselves. My Adult was saying why are you getting depressed to my Child. My Child was saying I want out of this—which is essentially what my patient was saying, "I want out of this." He was too dependent to get out, but what I did with that was saying, "I think we can sort things out here, but I need your help." I didn't know what went on in that family but said, "we need to help Joe over there." Then the father was less competitive, and was not trying to argue and began initiating talk. He began to say to Joe, "Your mother gets anxious when the boys are fighting." Great big six-footers, they'd get into fights and break each others ribs. Anyway, you can get sucked into the system for the moment, but with your family you can see that too.

Kim: I'd like to talk a little bit about my groups. I'd like to talk about one member of the group. The last session I worked with one member who called me up and told me she was going to quit, because she thought that she could handle this and that on her own and it was just too much money and too much time. So I workez with her a little bit about this, and it looked like that when she got better she could go off and live by herself and then she would stay away Her script was, you know, do it alone. She really glommed on and it seemed to fit for her. So I worked a lot with her and there have been several other people who when they brought up the subject that they had been thinking of leaving and I said that this was something maybe it was time to discuss. But nobody wanted to discuss it. I don't know whether we worked it through or if they took care of it or if it went underground. And another woman worked— this is the woman who is always looking for a job. She was a doctor's wife. She came across a program she really liked and she didn't know if she was going to do it. She was scared to do it and I just said to her, "Do it! Take it! It's just what you want!" Everybody was a little startled.

Jim: You mean you don't pull your Parent.

Kim: No. I don't usually come on like that. [They laughed.] And there was another woman in my group, I guess. There was this other woman who was involved in this triangle relationship and has been very unhappy. She's in love with this man, the closest man in her life, and she really hasn't had other relationships that are satisfactory. He is married and always on the verge of leaving the wife, and in fact did leave the wife. They were together for a few weeks, and now he's gone back and she is very upset about this. So she has another boyfriend who is kinda trying to get her back, and she can't decide if she should go back with him. And I said at one point, you know she was meandering. I said, "You tried it with Richard and you know that you don't like living with him. Why are you thinking about, you know, getting back together with him, for?" And she just burst out laughing when I gave her such a direct comment. So I'm just not sure, so I've been playing this whole thing back in my head.

Jim: That sounds Adult, Kim.

Kim: Worrying about it. Whether that's okay to do that. I'd just like to get some feedback. Criticism, if that's what's there.

Jim: Was it your Child or Adult that was pressured?

Kim: No I thought it was kinda Child. It was an exclamation. Yeah, this is Parent. "Hey, come on, what are you getting at, you've tried this whole thing before?" That's Parent.

Jim: I think you can see you are confused about when I started using TA. You were saying "why don't you" to a patient; then, "why don't you" is a suggestion or is the patient going to take it as "why?"

Kathy: Then, "why don't you" is an invitation to tell people "why, why—to do it. Why don't you go to the store and get some coffee?"

Kim: Because I don't feel like it.

Kathy: If you really look at it semantically the real question is, "Tell me why you won't, why you don't do it?" Even though the intent is theoretically a suggestion. "Why don't you do that," semantically, it's, "Tell me why you're not going to."

Jim: I used to be confused in my analysis. My analyst was saving, Why don't you do this; and I thought he was making a suggestion. Later I found out that it was a question.

Kathy: Does that happen to you in doing therapy? Do you experience things like that as a therapist?

Kim: Sometimes, somehow you lose your cool—Sometimes I just think really, "What somebody is about to do is utterly ridiculous" and I say it and I do consider it having lost my cool. Now unless it is something very specifically dangerous it is okay to just say it's not okay to do it. Generally when I do that it will be a Parent thing. I don't like it. Sometimes, however, when someone has done something really super, I guess it goes into that rather gratifying thing like, I really do want to say to people, "Wow!" I want to stroke them a lot.

Jim: And nurture.

Kathy: Yeah!

Kim: One reason that I would take this job is that I had an experience and there is usually something behind it. I had an experience where I was in a group; it wasn't a therapy group. I had been offered a job which was exactly my specifications, but I was going on and on about how I didn't want it, etc. There were all these reasons that I could find why I didn't want it and I remember the leader saying to me, "Take it, it's just what you want." That really kind of pushed me over the edge. So I had that in mind when I said it to her. I have a feeling that I'll get some kind of playback on my behavior in the group next time. And I'm worried about that.

Jim: Berne used to say, remember, sometimes people need permission not to do things. For instance, you've got a patient who should take a job or at least try it out and your Parent thinks so and it makes sense to your Adult.

Then tell them, "Why don't you?" Nothing the matter is coming out in Parent if you know what you are doing in your Adult, and you have checked it out with your own Adult.

Kim: Uh-huh. I thought her Child wanted to do it. I thought her Adult wanted to do it. I thought all three wanted to do it, but there was the scared part of her. She needed a push to do it in spite of the fact that she was scared. That was my judgment of the situation. That she didn't need to not do it. She didn't need permission not to do it. Which I would probably tend to do more easily than the push to do it.

Jim: This one gal who is yelling, "I want to do it myself!" She probably did that in childhood. "I can do it myself." My daughter does that. When a few years ago I offered to tie her shoes for her, she said, "Dad, I can do it myself!" Most kids I think are like that, but I check that out when the patient would say things or do things like that. Otherwise you become arbitrary in what's Parent, Adult, and Child. Otherwise, it's just an arbitrary definition that you check out with history.

Kathy: I'm confused about what you're scared you did wrong.

Kim: I just lost my cool. Had I really been *cool* and friendly, I wouldn't have given such strong advice in helping them work it out.

Kathy: So what's going to happen?

Kim: They're going to quit!

Kathy: They're going to want more advice and then you'll have to give it.

Kim: Oh that's all right. I can do that. I can handle that. This one woman who is in this situation can continue because I'd like her to. She's a woman who has had, what I think, what you interpreted and what I agree with—that is, afraid to be too dependent. She wants to call me during the week, but she stops herself or something. Sometimes she does call me.

Jim: It's also a fear of attaching herself to you.

Kim: She called me and needed an extra session outside of group and she came in to ask me if she should go back with this guy. Some of the questions were really impossible for me to answer. I didn't have any advice about it. She just kind of worked on this thing and she just found out that she was very upset and miserable about it. She got reinforced from the group, in the sense, that, "Yes, it is upsetting and there is nothing really that we can tell you. You probably are in the situation that you are in love with this man and you can't handle it. That's life!" I said what can we do? Is there anything that we can do to help you? Is there anything that you can ask of us? And I asked her, "Is there anything you can get from the group that will be helpful to you?"

Jim: That's really good.

Kim: She thought about it for a long time. She said she'd like to think about that. She's still looking rather hangdog, so I guess my Nurturing Parent said, "I don't know. I think one thing that you might do, you might ask Pete. You may want to be able to call somebody," and she thought that was a possibility. She really did love him. I don't know if I gave her a little too much.

Jim: No, I think that's good for a group because a psychiatrist did a study back in the late fifties, that if the cohesion in a group is good, if they are calling each other and they are talking about problems, they are in a curative situation. They are attracted to each other and that is the most curative thing that we have found in the treatment of groups. Not that the patient is really cured from his problem, but dropouts occur because they can't really attach themselves to each other. No, that's good. That's pure Adult.

Kim: Yeah! I think they are all too fearful of becoming too dependent. You know, they see themselves as dependent upon the group.

Jim: What I usually find are the people who are really in the throes of whether they are going to stay in the group or not. At this time I see them individually.

Kathy: In addition—

Jim: Not in addition, but as a onetime thing, to discuss the issue of dropping out. I would do the same thing with somebody and not really want to bring that out in a family session. He will say, "I don't think that I can make it. It takes too much time or I can't afford it." I'd offer him an individual appointment and he will tell you something that can't be expressed in the whole group.

Kathy: Then you keep that a secret?

Jim: Yes. There are certain things in family therapy that you don't want to come out, and in individual therapy you want everything to come out. Incest and the whole kit and caboodle.

Kathy: Suppose she finds out about the affair and knows that you knew all along?

Jim: What do you do with that? You can still treat it confidentially. Just like in a group when you know something, you ask the patient for permission. I know something about you, is it all right if I bring it up? Most people, you see, are seen individually before you see them in group. There are certain things that you will talk about alone that you won't talk about in a group unless it is something that I feel you can talk about and handle quite well. Take the guy who grew up with twelve children. He's used to having his needs met in delayed ways, whereas somebody who has been an only child is used to having their needs met immediai ly, so he will have more trouble in a group. Now I've found that in   lot of group dropouts, if you say, "Come to the group and we'll disc.ss it," they'll drop out anyway. If you see them alone, depending upon if you really focus on what the issue is, you can save seventy percent of all the dropouts.

I had a guy who was fearful of dependency on me in the group and very fearful of any direction. He came late one time; then he called me up before the next group meeting and said that he was dropping out because he thought that he had been helped, so he thought he didn't need me anymore. I asked if he would be willing to discuss it with me alone and he said sure. Everytime I made an interpretation he "yes butted" me. I was trying to hook his Adult. I said, "Do you hear the but and his reply was "but what." I finally ended up telling him that he hadn't listened to anything we'd talked about and I think your mind is closed so either you continue or you don't. He said, "Why do you think my mind is closed?" I told him nothing we had talked about had affected him, that he hadn't let me come in and stimulate his thinking.

I remember when I was a resident I used to think up these beautiful formulations, telling them to the patient. The patient wasn't listening. Sometimes, instead of interpreting a hellovalot I'll ask the question, "Are you really becoming dependent on the group?" That's an Adult forcing hook.

Kathy: Under what circumstances, or often how long, might you decide to ask a question as a question interpretation?

Jim: Say somebody's Child is really pissed and they are saying many goddamns, and they are really threatening. I wouldn't want all that emotion at that time. That's why I really try to hook their

Adult. "Are you afraid of this?" If I don't think the patient will really listen with his or her Adult, I'm not going to make an interpretation that I don't think they will listen to.

Kathy: Does the interpretation end up being more heard than the question by the Adult?

Jim: They have to be straight with you, if you ask them *if* they are afraid of something.

Kathy: Okay.

Jim: I mean they could deny it, but it is more likely to get at what they really feel. That's why when somebody is really quitting the program, you have to ask questions. People are very fearful of dependency. I don't know if you have experienced this yourself, but it's a terrible fear. You feel you are told what to do and you are subject to criticism, humiliation, whatever the word actually means. You lose a father, a mother, or anything else at a certain age—makes you afraid of losing a therapist, so you can't really attach yourself. It's a terrible feeling. So ninety percent of quitting has something to do with that fear, and it's worth asking of anybody that is thinking of dropping out.

Kathy: Say, Jim, what's a good book on psychoanalytical techniques?

Jim: Greenson's *The Technique and Practice of Psychoanalysis,* published by International Universities Press.

Kim: I really like the combination of two, transactional and psychoanalytic.

Jim: You know, I think I told you I had this patient that said TA doesn't change people.

Kathy: I've heard that too.

Jim: She was worried about upsetting me because I was a person known in TA circles. She would use PAC like most obsessives do, to isolate feeling. With her I wouldn't use PAC. I would just say, "You're afraid of this or you're afraid of that." You can do this because you don't feel OK about yourself. But I think that you need something besides TA to deconfuse the Child, whether it's psychoanalysis or Gestalt, etc. The use of TA isn't enough, and if somebody is an acting out hysteric or is very histrionic or a manic acting out, then I'll use PAC to get more intellectual. Then, it's good not to use the same defenses as the patient. With obsessives you might want to supply the affect with "Wow! That really must have hurt your feelings." It's like with a kid, sometimes. With a kid you have to supply the affect, "Wow! That really must have hurt when your mom said that." Then the kid might say, "Well my mom said I was just no good."

Kathy: You know with TA one thing that I don't like. Well, I'm not sure, I have to work this all out; I'll tell you about it in ten years. But this thing that TA therapists will say, well, I told them we identified their games and they know their script and they know all their injunctions, and they know where they are on the drama triangle, and they know all their drivers. Somehow they're not better.

Kim: Well, then I'd say, "So what!"

Kathy: Then, I'm thinking, here's a therapist sitting with a client, giving them this whole astrological chart, but the client really hasn't had much of a chance to say anything. They think that all psychoanalytic technique does is really give the client a chance to say all the things that they are scared to say. I think this is a wonderful benefit for clients. Clients really seem to appreciate that, rather than have the whole thing set out for them from just a little bit of information. That's what scares me about TA.

Jim: I think that if somebody is in a highly emotional state now that somebody is really playing NIGYYSOB, you can say [cheerfully], "Got Me!" That'll have some meaning to them. Somebody who has a lot of intellectual defenses—i.e., isolates feeling—I think that you really have to strain to find the affect, and somehow you supply it just like you would do with a little kid.

Kim: I really deal with very few schizophrenics. Most of the people I see are really very well functioning neurotics if even neurotic. So I really don't think that it is really that helpful to me to know all that. It's interesting, but it's really not getting into what's going on.

Kathy: Sometimes some of that stuff I find is like having some information and not telling them. They're telling me of knowing some of the definitions of TA and they're telling me what their positions are as a useful place to get going with people, when people are really scared to start exploring to just have that framework.

Kathy: I use PAC a lot, and I find that tremendously helpful just as the framework.

Kim: Yes.

Kathy: Maybe more.

Kim: I sure agree with you that a straight session of TA doesn't do it.

Kathy: Well maybe it does it with a certain kind of client. I don't know.

Jim: I think that what Berne originally talked about was that you can, if they really understand the games and scripts, have social control. However, the Child may feel a little confused, scared.

Kathy: Miserable. Lack of self-confidence.

Jim: I'm thinking that it would really be hard to reduce anxiety without knowing what they are afraid of.

Both social workers: Yeah!

Bibliography

TRANSACTIONAL ANALYSIS

Babcock, D. E., and Keepers, T. D. (1976). *Raising Kids OK*. New York: Grove Press.

Berne, E. (1949). The nature of interaction. *Psychiatric Quarterly* 23: 203-226.

———— (1952). Concerning the nature of diagnosis. *International Record of Medicine* 165: 283-292.

———— (1953). Concerning the nature of communications. *Psychiatric Quarterly* 27: 185-198.

———— (1955). Intuition IV: primal images and primal judgement. *Psychiatric Quarterly* 29: 634-658.

———— (1957.) Intuition V: the ego image. *Psychiatric Quarterly* 31: 611-627.

———— (1961). *Transactional Analysis in Psychotherapy*. New York: Grove Press.

————— (1963). *The Structure and Dynamics of Organizations and Groups.* Philadelphia: J. B. Lippincott.

————— (1964). *Games People Play.* New York: Grove Press.

————— (1964). The intimacy experiment. *Transactional Analysis Bulletin* 3(9):113.

————— (1966). *Principles of Group Treatment.* New York: Oxford University Press.

————— (1970). *Sex In Human Lovng.* New York: Simon and Schuster.

————— (1971). *What Do You Say After You Say Hello?* New York: Grove Press.

Dusay, J. (1971). Eric Berne's studies of intuition, 1949-1962. *Transactional Analysis Journal* 1(1): 34-46.

————— (1972). Egograms and the "constancy hypothesis." *Transactional Analysis Journal* 2(3):37-44.

————— (1971). *Egograms.* New York: Harper and Row.

Edwards, M. (1968). The two parents. *Transactional Analysis Bulletin* 7(26): 37-38.

Ellis, A. (1971). Rational emotive therapy. In *Directive Psychotherapy,* ed. R. J. Juryevich. Miami: University of Miami Press.

English, F. (1972). Sleepy, spunky, and spooky. *Transactional Analysis Journal* 2(2): 64-67.

————— (1976). Racketeering. *Transactional Analysis Journal* 6(2): 78-81.

Erickson, E. (1950). *Childhood and Society.* New York: Norton.

————— (1959). *Identity and the Life Cycle.* New York: International Universities Press.

Ernst, F. H., Jr. (1971). The diagrammed parent: Eric Berne's most significant contribution. *Transactional Analysis Journal* 1(1): 49-58.

tional Analysis Journal 3(2): 19-23.

Federn, P. (1952). *Ego Psychology and the Psychoses.* New York: Basic Books.

Goulding, R. L. (1972). New directions in Transactional Analysis: creating an environment for redecision and change. In *Progress in Group and Family Therapy,* ed. C. J. Sager and H. S. Kaplan. New York: Brunner/Mazel.

Goulding, R. L., and Goulding, M. M. (1976). Injunctions, decisions, and redecisions. *Transactional Analysis Journal* 6(1): 28-31.

Harris, T. A. (1967). *I'm OK, You're OK.* New York: Harper and Row.

James, M. (1974). Self-reparenting: theory and process. *Transactional Analysis Journal* 4(3): 32-39.

James, M., and Joneward, D. (1971). *Born to Win: Transactional Analysis with Gestalt Experiments.* Reading, Massachusetts: Addison-Wesley.

Kupfer, D., and Haimowitz, M. (1971). Therapeutic interventions, rubber bands, now. *Transactional Analysis Journal* 1(2): 10-16.

McCormick, P. (1977). *Ego States.* Modesto, California: Transactional Publications.

McGahey, C. C., and Blair, M. (1976). *Transactional Analysis Research Index: An International Reference Book.* Tallahassee, Florida: Florida Institute for TA.

Rissman, A. H. (1975). Trilog. *Transactional Analysis Journal* 5(2): 170-177.

Schiff, J. L., and Schiff, (1976). Passivity. *Transactional Analysis Journal* 1(1): 71-78.

Schiff, J. L. et al. (1975). *Cathexis Reader.* New York: Harper and Row.

Steiner, C. (1971). *Games Alcoholics Play.* New York: Grove Press.

———— (1972). Scripts revisited. *Transactional Analysis Journal* 2(2): 83-86.

———— (1974). *Scripts People Live.* New York: Grove Press.

Stuntz, E. C. (1972). Second order structure of the Parent. *Transactional Analysis Journal* 2(2): 59-63.

Thomson, G. (1972). The identification of ego states. *Transactional Analysis Journal* 2(4): 46-61.

GENERAL FAMILY AND COUPLE
THERAPY BIBLIOGRAPHY

Ackerman, N. (1966). *Treating The Troubled Family.* New York: Basic Books.

Bateson, G. et al. (1956). Toward a theory of schizophrenia. *Behavioral Science* 1: 251-264.

———— (1963). A note of the double-bind—1962). *Family Process* 2: 154-161.

Bell, J. (1975). *Family Therapy.* New York: Jason Aronson.

Block, D., ed. (1973). *Techniques of Family Psychotherapy.* New York: Grune and Stratton.

Brodey, W. (1968). *Changing the Family.* New York: Clarkson N. Potter.

Fitzgerald, R. (1973). *Conjoint Marital Therapy.* New York: Jason Aronson.

Foley, V. (1974). *An Introduction to Family Therapy.* New York: Grune and Stratton.

Glick, I., and Haley, J. (1971). *Family Therapy and Research: An Annotated Bibliography.* New York: Grune and Stratton.

Glick, I., and Kessler, M. (1963). *Marital and Family Therapy.* New York: Grune and Stratton.

Haley, J. (1959). The family of the schizophrenic, a model system. *Journal of Nervous and Mental Disease* 129: 357-374.

———— (1962). Whither family therapy. *Family Process* 1: 69-100.

———— (1963). Marriage therapy. *Archives of General Psychiatry* 8: 213-234.

———— (1963). Observation of the family of the schizophrenic. *American Journal of Orthopsychiatry* 30: 460-467.

———— (1963). *Strategies of Psychotherapy.* New York: Grune and Stratton.

———— (1964). Research on family patterns: an instrument measurement. *Family Process* 3: 41-65.

———— (1967). Cross-cultural experimentation: an initial attempt. *Human Organizations* 3: 110-117.

Note: There are excellent bibliographies in most of these books.

———— (1967). Experiment with abnormal families. *Archives of General Psychiatry* 17: 53-63.

———— (1967). Speech sequences of normal and abnormal families with two children present. *Family Process* 6: 81-97.

———— (1960). Testing parental instructions to schizophrenic and normal children: a pilot study. *Journal of Abnormal Psychology* 73: 559-566.

———— (1970). Family therapy. *International Journal of Psychiatry* 9: 233-242.

———— (1971). Communication and therapy: blocking metaphors. *American Journal of Psychotherapy* 25: 214-227.

———— (1971). Family therapy: a radical change. In J. Haley, *Changing Families: A Family Therapy Reader.* New York: Grune and Stratton.

———— (1972). Critical overview of present status of family interaction research. In *Family Interaction: A Dialogue Between Family Researchers and Family Therapists,* ed. J. Framo, pp. 13-49. New York: Springer.

———— (1973). Strategic therapy when a child is presented as the problem. *Journal of the American Academy of Child Psychiatry* 12: 641-659.

———— (1973). *Uncommon Therapy.* New York: Norton.

———— (1975). Family therapy. In *Comprehensive Textbook of Psychiatry,* 2nd ed., ed. A. M. Freedman et al., pp. 1881-1886. Baltimore: Williams and Wilkins.

———— (1975). Why a mental health clinic should avoid family therapy? *Journal of Marriage and Family Counseling* 1: 3-13.

———— (1976). *Problem Solving Therapy.* San Francisco: Jossey-Bass.

Haley, J., ed. (1971). *Changing Families: A Family Therapy Reader.* New York: Grune and Stratton.

Haley, J., and Hoffman, L. (1967). *Techniques of Family Therapy.* New York: Basic Books.

Minuchin, S. (1974). *Family and Family Therapy.* Cambridge; Massachusetts, Harvard University Press.

Montalvo, B., and Haley, J. (1973). In defense of child therapy. *Family Process* 12: 227-244.

Sager, C. (1976). *Marriage Contracts and Couple Therapy*. New York: Brunner/Mazel.

Satir, V. (1967). *Conjoint Family Therapy*. Revised edition. Palo Alto: Science and Behavior Books.

Satir, V., Stachowiak, J., and Taschman, H. (1975). *Helping Families to Change*. New York: Jason Aronson.

Skynner, A. C. (1976). *The Adolescent in Group and Family Therapy*. New York: Brunner/Mazel.

Wynne, L. et al. (1958). Pseudomutuality in the family relations o the schizophrenics. *Psychiatry* 21: 205-220.

Yalom, I. D. (1970). *The Theory and Practice of Group Psychiatry*. New York: Basic Books.

Zuk, G. H. (1971). *Family Therapy: A Triadic-Based Approach*. New York: Behavioral Publications.

References

Bateson, G., et al. (1956). A theory of schizc renia. *Behavioral Science* 1:251-264.

———— (1963). A note on the double-bind—1962. *Family Process* 2:154-161.

Beal, E. W. (1976). Current trends in the tracking of family therapists. *American Journal of Psychiatry* 133:137-141.

Berne, E. (1961). *Transactional Analysis in Psychotherapy.* New York: Grove Press.

———— (1964). *Games People Play.* New York: Grove Press.

———— (1966). *Principles of Group Treatment.* New York: Oxford University Press.

———— (1970). *Sex In Human Loving.* New York: Simon and Schuster.

———— (1971). *What Do You Say After You Say Hello?* New York: Grove Press.

Bowen, M. (1960). A family concept of schizophrenia. In *The Etiology of Schizophrenia,* ed. D. D. Jackson, pp. 346-372. New York: Basic Books. Also in M. Bowen, *Family Theory in Clinical Practice.* New York: Jason Aronson, 1978.

Crossman, P. (1966). Permission and protection. *Transactional Analysis Bulletin* 5(19):152-153.

Dusay, J. (1971). Eric Berne's studies of intuition, 1949-1962. *Transactional Analysis Journal* 1(1):34-46.

——— (1972). Egograms and the constancy hypothesis. *Transactional Analysis Journal* 2(3).

Ellis, A. (1971). Rational emotive therapy. In *Directive Psychotherapy,* ed. R. J. Juryevich.. Miami: University of Miami Press.

Ernst, F. H., Jr. (1973). Psychological rackets in the OK corral. *Transactional Analysis Journal* 3(2): 19-23.

Goulding, R. (1972). Script redecisions. *In Progress in Group and Family Therapy,* ed. C. S. Sager and H. S. Kaplan, p. 105. New York: Brunner/Mazel.

Goulding, R. L., and Goulding, M. M. (1976). Injunctions, decisions, and redecisions. *Transactional Analysis Journal* 6(1): 28-31.

Greenson, R. (1967). *The Technique and Practice of Psychoanalysis.* New York: International Universities Press.

Haimowitz, M., and Kupfer, D. (1971). Rubberbands. *Transactional Analysis Journal* 1(2):10-16.

Karpman, S. (1968). Script drama analysis. *Transactional Analysis Bulletin* 7(26): 39-43.

——— (1971). Options. *Transactional Analysis Journal* 1(1):79-87.

Kernberg, O. F. (1976). *Borderline Conditions and Pathological Narcissism.* New York: Jason Aronson.

Minuchin, S. (1974). *Families and Family Therapy.* Cambridge: Harvard University Press.

Montalvo, B., and Haley, J. (1973). In defense of child therapy. *Family Process* 12: 227-244.

Satir, V. (1964). *Conjoint Family Therapy.* Palo Alto: Science And Behavior Books.

——— (1965). Personal communication.

——— (1967). *Conjoint Family Therapy.* Revised Edition. Palo Alto: Science And Behavior Books.

Steiner, C. (1971). *Games Alcoholics Play: The Analysis of Life Scripts.* New York: Grove Press.

Index